Don Quixote
in
CHINA

The Search for
Peach Blossom Spring

Also by Dean Barrett

Novels
Hangman's Point
Mistress of the East
Kingdom of Make-Believe
Memoirs of a Bangkok Warrior
Murder in China Red
Skytrain to Murder

Non-fiction
Thailand: Land of Beautiful Women
Don Quixote in China: The Search for Peach Blossom Spring

Children's book
The Boat Girl and the Magic Fish

Published in the United States by
Village East Books, Countryside, #520, 8775 20th Street,
Vero Beach, FL 32966

E-mail: VillageEast@hotmail.com
Web site: http://www.deanbarrettmystery.com

ISBN: 0-9661899-7-3

Printed in Thailand by Allied Printing

Cover Illustration and interior design by
Robert Stedman, Pte., Ltd. Singapore

Publisher's Cataloging-in-Publication Data
(*Prepared by The Donohue Group, Inc.*)

Barrett, Dean.
Don Quixote in China : the search for Peach Blossom
Spring / Dean Barrett.
    p. cm.
    Includes bibliographical references.
    ISBN: 0-9661899-7-3
    1. Barrett, Dean—Journeys—China—Hunan Sheng. 2.
Hunan Sheng (China)—Description and travel. 3. China—
Description and travel—1976- 4. Adventure and adventurers—
China. 5. Americans—China. 6. Utopias—China. I. Tao, Qian.
Poems. II. Title.

DS793.H7 .B377 2003
915.1'215046—dc21
                                    2003109113

This book is dedicated to two extraordinary men: Peter Tan, a scholar and freethinker living in Zhong Shan, Kuangtung Province; and to Guo Tongxiao, a farmer and visionary living in Longting Village, Yangxian County, Shensi Province.

"What is the meaning of this trip?" –Hunter Thompson
Fear and Loathing in Las Vegas

"Those who dream by day are cognizant of many things which escape those who dream only by night" –Edgar Allan Poe

"What a travel it is indeed that is recorded in this book, and what a man he is who experienced it" –Basho
The Narrow Road to the Deep North and Other Travel Sketches

Don Quixote
in
CHINA

The Search for
Peach Blossom Spring

VILLAGE EAST BOOKS
FLORIDA

With much appreciation to Hilda-Gill Bonanno and Walter Bonanno, and Tom and Romi Chapman, for putting me up, not to mention putting up with me, during my search for Peach Blossom Spring. And for their unwavering encouragement of my many quixotic adventures.

CONTENTS

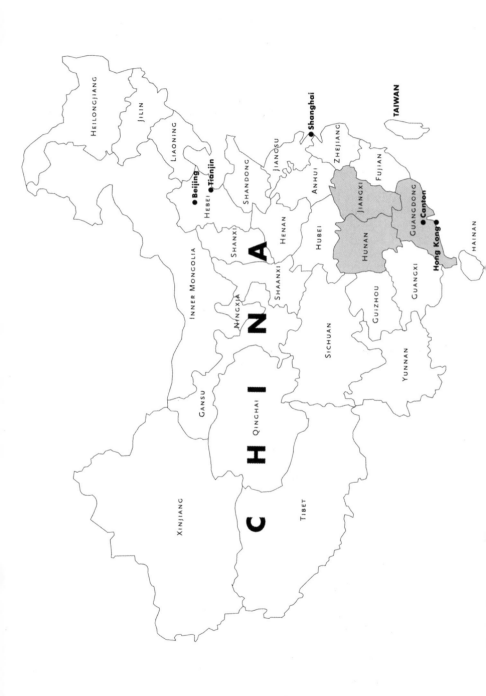

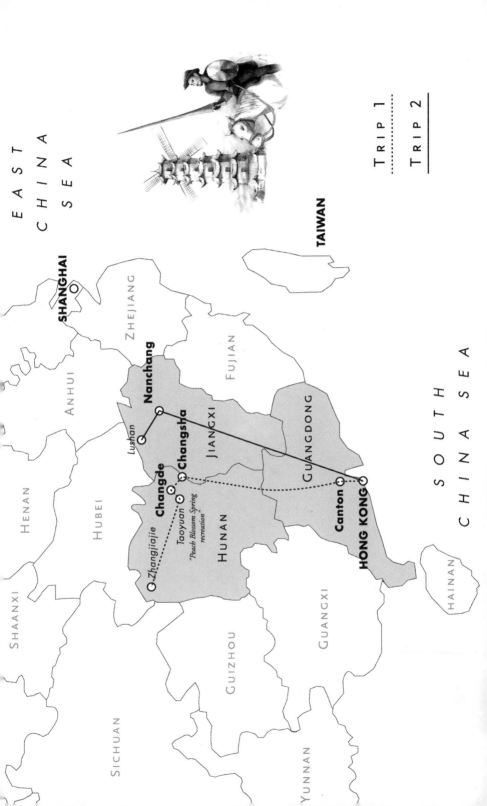

EAST CHINA SEA

SHANGHAI

ZHEJIANG

ANHUI

HENAN

HUBEI

SHAANXI

Lushan

Nanchang

Changsha

JIANGXI

FUJIAN

TAIWAN

Changde

Zhangjiajie

Taoyuan
"Peach Blossom Spring recreation"

HUNAN

GUANGDONG

GUANGXI

GUIZHOU

SICHUAN

YUNNAN

Canton

HONG KONG

HAINAN

SOUTH CHINA SEA

TRIP 1

TRIP 2

A Note on Romanization Systems

When I first began studying Chinese at Monterey's Defense Language Institute, I used the Yale System of romanization of Chinese characters, a modest, unpretentious, by-the-numbers sort of romanization. Later, at various universities, I began using the Wade-Giles system, you know, the one with the elegant apostrophes – genteel and aristocratic. There is also the communist pinyin system in use on the mainland since the mid-50's, which you can recognize by the plethora of godawful z's and x's – unbecoming, unsightly – dare one say – uncouth. There are also a few other systems lollygagging about including the one created by the late scholar Lin Yutang and his friends, not to mention the old postal spellings of place names. In this book, I may have in a few cases even merged one or two systems with my own ideas. If you are a China scholar you will easily tell how the Chinese words are pronounced; if not, you won't.

My advice is not to worry about it because most of the romanization systems in use seem to have been developed by people who have the same mindset as those who built the Great Wall – i.e., to keep foreigners out. However, one favor: please note that the "j" in "Beijing" is pronounced exactly as the "j" in "jack" or "jump." Dan Rather and other newsreaders who insist on pronouncing the "j" as if it were a French "j" (as in "je") seem to have been misled by the *pinyin's* "zh."

As for snatches of poems which have been translated by me or by others, please remember what a wise man once said: "translations are like mistresses; they can be beautiful or faithful, but not both." With few exceptions, that certainly applies to translations of Chinese poetry and to any English translation of literature of a tonal language. As the late scholar, H. A. Giles, wrote, "translations may be moonlight and water while the originals are sunlight and wine."

Introduction

To be perfectly honest – and for much of this book I will be exactly that – the truth is if I could have one wish it would be that I could write like Paul Theroux. His wonderful travel writing has a kind of dispassionate moroseness, a cerebral melancholy, an intellectual despondency running through it which, in itself, seems to lend credence to his opinions. A man not easily moved is a man whose opinions we value. A man not readily impressed is a man whose convictions we respect. Those difficult to excite seem to possess a great wisdom while travel reports from the pen of skittish, often irrational, frequently paranoid, creatures like myself seem certain to be met with outright suspicion if not destined to be entirely ignored. This is my fate and I have learned to accept it. I can only attempt to make up for what I lack in moroseness, melancholy and despondency in other ways.

As the reader travels with me on my search for Peach Blossom Spring, he or she may sense that I possess more than a tad of immaturity in my soul; to which I can only say in my own defense that it has long been my most tenaciously held belief that nothing is so deadening to the human spirit as emotional maturity. It has been my experience that people with emotional maturity tend to miss all that constitutes the human voyage: the absolute horror and the inexplicable beauty; the obvious tragedy and the inexpressible joy; the ever-present absurdity and the irrefutable logic. People with emotional maturity do not search for Peach Blossom Spring. People with emotional maturity do not search.

And what exactly *is* Peach Blossom Spring, known in Chinese as *T'ao Hua Yuan Chi*? It is the best known work of the Chinese poet, T'ao Yuan-ming (T'ao Ch'ien), a short description of a utopia which, despite its brevity, has had a tremendous impact on generations of Chinese poetry and fiction. T'ao, one of China's most beloved poets, lived during the tumultuous Six Dynasties period, specifically during the Eastern Chin dynasty (AD 317-420). Known as "the Gentleman of the Five Bamboos," "the prince of hermits," and as "poet of the garden and field," T'ao espoused Lao Tzu's attitude toward life: "The Way *(Tao)* never acts and yet nothing is left undone." He retired early from the life of an official and lived as a Taoist gentleman-farmer, working in his fields, writing poetry and drinking wine. His poems on nature have been compared to those of Robert Frost and his style was later admired and even imitated by the greatest poets of the T'ang and Sung.

In *Peach Blossom Spring*, T'ao describes how a fisherman sailing along an uncharted stream comes upon a radiantly beautiful peach orchard where "a myriad of scented petals floated gently downward, painting both sides of the river with their soft splendor." Entranced by the orchard's almost preternatural loveliness, the fisherman explores the orchard and, as he does so, notices an eerie radiance from within a narrow passage in a mountain cliff. He enters the passage and suddenly emerges into a land of beauty and mystery, a halcyon, idyllic agricultural community. In the China of the fisherman there is almost constant war and turbulence, and existence is at best precarious, yet here he is astounded to find "vast farmland and imposing farmhouses, fertile fields, beautiful lakes, mulberry trees and bamboo groves."

The villagers are surprised by his arrival but are pleased to converse with him. They tell him that their ancestors fled tyrants centuries before; and they have been hidden from the world of sanguinary wars, internecine feuds and constant suffering and know nothing of the outside world; nor do they wish to rejoin it.

The fisherman is treated by the farmers as an honored guest, and is feasted with all the fruits of their harvest and their finest wine. When the fisherman describes to them the violent and turbulent world he comes from, they shake their heads and sigh. For several days, the fisherman lives among them, spellbound by their good will and guileless ways. He watches in admiration as the people follow neither kings nor calendars but only the natural rhythm of nature. He senses a happiness and contentment in the villagers that does not exist in the China he knows.

Excited as he is by his discovery, the fisherman eventually requests permission to leave Peach Blossom Spring. The villagers allow him to leave, asking only that he not spread word of their existence ("let your knowledge of us go no further"). This the fisherman agrees to.

Despite his promise, however, he carefully marks his route and reports what he saw to officials. The officials report this to the prefect of the district who sends out an expedition in hopes of finding the utopia but to the fisherman's amazement his markings have mysteriously disappeared and the mission ends in failure. Try as he might, the fisherman can never again find Peach Blossom Spring. Upon hearing of the fisherman's discovery, a famed scholar plans another expedition but soon dies from a mysterious illness.

No further attempts were ever again made to find Peach Blossom Spring. Until now.

In "Peach Blossom Spring," the fisherman who chances upon the Arcadian community is from the small town of Wuling. In my research I have learned that Wuling is now known as Changde and is in southern China in Hunan Province.

The poet himself lived near the beautiful Lushan (Lu Mountains) in what is now the neighboring province of Jiangsi. In his retirement, T'ao Yuan-ming was given to roaming the beautiful landscapes he loved, and his farm was not so far away that he could not have come upon the mysterious village nestled in the magnificent mountains which are now part of western Hunan province. It is my theory (the reader might here wish to place the word "crackpot" before the word "theory") that T'ao Yuan-ming actually found Peach Blossom Spring and, as a poet, felt compelled to write about it. But to keep others (such as myself) from finding it and thereby changing it forever, he wrote his discovery as fiction, a tall tale of a remote, idyllic, isolated utopia so that none but the most unbalanced lunatic would actually believe it exists. Well, I believe it exists.

Preparation

Before I moved to New York, I lived in Hong Kong for 17 years, and I have been into China several times. So I know a few things. But as the experts on China say "there are no experts on China; only varying degrees of ignorance." Very true. But one thing I do know is that Chinese adore their children and it is always a good idea to bring something for the kids of anyone who does you a kindness. And since just about everyone in China has children and is constantly searching out ways around government regulations to have more, toys are always well received.

So, as part of my preparation for traveling in China, I find myself at the tiny gift shop on Manhattan's 17th Street Pier, South Street Seaport, and I spot two perfect gifts to bring into China. One is an American "flag sparkler" for $3.95. The other is an American "flag yo-yo" for $2.50. What kid wouldn't like his very own yo-yo or a gadget so cool that, as you push up a metal lever, a circle spins and sparks fly out? And both have been painted with the red, white and blue colors of the American flag.

But on my way to the cash register I look them over more closely and spot the line in tiny letters on both: "Made in China." Probably the sparkler factory is right where I'm going. Or maybe they tore down Peach Blossom Spring to build the East is Red yo-yo Factory. I drop the tainted items back into the baskets and move on.

If I have any hope of finding Peach Blossom Spring, I decide that it is important to do as much research on Hunan Province as I can. I walk to a Barnes & Noble Bookstore and while searching for material on Hunan spot a copy of *Daily Life in China on the*

Eve of the Mongol Invasion. While paying for it, I say to the clerk: "I guess someday we'll be reading about Daily Life in America on the Eve of the Barnes & Noble invasion." That's when I realize not everyone appreciates a jocular sense of humor.

I purchase and pour over maps of China, peruse guidebooks and spend a great deal of time on the Internet. I learn that Hunan means "south of the (Dongting) Lake" but the section on Hunan in the *Lonely Planet* guidebook is not encouraging. It begins: "Most people pass through Hunan on their way to somewhere else, but the province has its attractions."

It seems that every explorer who ever made it to Hunan felt compelled to comment on the clannishness of the people. In the 1870's, the writer John Thomson wrote that "the natural routes to the great consuming districts of (Hunan's) interior are kept jealously sealed against external traffic."

According to the *National Geographic Magazine*, by the year 1900, all 18 of China's provinces had been explored and mapped by foreigners except Hunan. One of the magazine's writers in that year seemed irritated: "The (Hunanese) are the most clannish and conservative to be found in the whole empire, and have succeeded in keeping their province practically free from invasion by foreigners or even foreign ideas." (Gosh darn those dull-witted Hunanese – don't they know gunboats and missionaries and foreign concessions are all the rage in China?)

And a decade later things were no better. In 1911, William Geil wrote that the capital of Hunan (Changsha) "keeps up its reputation as the most anti-foreign city in China."

I know the province was the birthplace of Mao Tse-tung and that people there clung to his teaching and honored his beliefs longer than elsewhere in China. Hell, for all I know, the Cultural Revolution is still going on in Hunan. Maybe I should pack my little red book of Mao's quotations. (But not the one with an introduction by Lin Biao.)

On my first trip ("first" assumes I don't find what I'm looking for the first time and will have to return; rather negative thinking, I know) I will be in Hunan for part of June and much of July. According to what I find on the Internet, July in Hunan is the month of rains, storms, floods, heat and humidity. A typical comment: "Hunan lies in the path of cyclones that pass from west to east along the Yangtze Basin in summer, bringing with them at times long periods of heavy rain, resulting in extensive flooding of low-lying lands."

I decide in the face of this negative publicity I need to speak to someone from Hunan. As I'm in Manhattan, and as most provinces of China probably have an association in Chinatown, I grab the Manhattan phonebook. After all, in the old days, Chinese had associations for everything: cotton hongs, cotton yarn hongs, dealers in cotton fabrics, gold shops, silver shops, rice stores, black tea companies, green tea companies, kung yee tea hongs, king yee tea hongs, yee jin tea hongs, satin ribbon hongs, raw silk hongs, dealers in fish maw, silk piece good hongs, sandalwood hongs, wet nurse hongs, dry nurse hongs, bird's nest shops, rattan dealers, compradore hongs, lead and tin shops, paper hongs, fur shops, wood hongs, tea box makers, matting shops, linguists guilds, new clothes shops, old clothes shops, Chinaware shops – well, you get the idea.

I search the phone book. Restaurants galore: Hunan Chef, Hunan Cottage, Hunan Delight, Hunan Delight II, Hunan East, Hunan Garden, Hunan Inn, Hunan Pan, Hunan Park, Hunan Royal. Alas, no Hunanese Association. But I do turn up a Hunan Commercial Bank in the World Trade Center. Unfortunately, the harried woman who answers the phone has never heard of a Hunanese Association. I am tempted to ask if she has ever heard of Hunan but she hangs up.

Which means, I suppose, that in June's 95 degree heat, I'll have to mosey about New York's Chinatown until I spot a Hunanese Association plaque on a building. First, I take clothes to my local

Chinese dry cleaners. The middle-aged owner, Gong Yuan-chang, is from Shanghai and his wife's family name is Chu and since everyone at the hospital where she works as a nurse calls her to come quickly by repeating her name, the dry cleaners is named in acknowledgment of this repetition: Chu Chu Cleaners.

While the owner has me sign in the book for yet another lost ticket, I casually mention that I am about to leave for China.

Him: "Where you going?"
Me: "Hunan Province."
Him: (slight scowl): "Why?"
Me: "I'm going to try to find Peach Blossom Spring."
Him: (more scowl): "What?"

I switch to mandarin and explain about the poet and his most famous work. The owner's face immediately lights up. "Yes, of course, T'ao Yuan-ming. A wonderful poet."

He then half speaks, half chants two lines from the story of "Peach Blossom Spring" and tells me how when he was once injured and didn't know what to do an American lawyer helped him without charge. The dry cleaner wanted to do something for the lawyer so he bought a painting of bamboo and used a Chinese brush to write the two relevant lines on the painting. The lines refer to that moment when the fisherman in the story could go no farther as the stream ended before a cliff. Just as he thought there was no way in, he spotted the opening and entered Peach Blossom Spring; and a wonderful new world opened up to him. The lines, according to the dry cleaner, are often used by Chinese when a situation looks hopeless but something unexpectedly shows the way; as the lawyer did for him.

Then he squints his eyes, looks at me skeptically and slightly tilts his head. "Are you really going into China to find Peach Blossom Spring?"

I reply in the affirmative.

He holds out his fist with his thumb up, a gesture among both Chinese and Americans acclaiming happy accord or outright admiration. "Good," he says. "Very good."

Of course, what he has to say to his wife over dinner that night might be something else. Perhaps more along the lines of a crazy, long-nosed, green-eyed, foreign-devil on a wild goose chase in search of a mythical utopia found only in a fourth century poem. Still, I am greatly encouraged by his reaction. It was not one of ridicule or disbelief. In fact, I am quite certain I detected more than a bit of wistful desire in him. It was almost as if he was wishing he could whip off his apron, turn off the lights, lock up the shop and go with me.

A friend points out that if I find the place, I'll most likely be known as The Man Who Found Peach Blossom Spring. I like the sound of that. It's right up there with The Man Who Broke the Bank at Monte Carlo and The Man Who Shot Liberty Valance. Although the thought occurs to me that if I don't find Peach Blossom Spring will I be known as The Man Who *Didn't* Find Peach Blossom Spring? But I don't think so because, to the best of my knowledge, no one has ever been called The Man Who *Didn't* Break the Bank at Monte Carlo or The Man Who *Didn't* Shoot Liberty Valance.

And it's not as if I have to worry about someone else getting there first. It's not as if several teams of famished explorers and their snowbound dogsleds are rushing to be the first to reach the South Pole. This is not a contest between tall ships with sleek bows and all sails spread racing from China to London with their precious cargoes of tea. As far as I know, other than myself, no one is rushing to discover Peach Blossom Spring. And that is one of the great benefits of being the only one to believe something exists: no competition.

I continue searching the Internet. One of the sites I find is "The Changde Adoptive Families Forum" put up by people who adopted babies from the city of Changde, exactly where I need to go to start my search for Peach Blossom Spring. The site explains why babies adopted from Hunan are known as Chili Babies: "The Hunan Province is known for the spicy and flavorful dishes that they create with hot peppers. Since everyone eats these dishes, the babies that are born there take on the characteristics of the hot 'chili' peppers. So the wonderful little girls we have taken home as our daughters will have the same hot and spicy personalities of the peppers. (Local guide) Daphne said that from now on, we should think of this story when our daughters are 'exhibiting' some spicy behavior!"

No mention of sons, only daughters. I e-mail one of the persons listed on the site and ask if they know of a hotel to stay in in Changde. The next day I receive an e-mail from a woman asking how I knew they had been in China ending with: "Have you been reading my mail?" Talk about "hot and spicy personalities." I reply to reassure her that I have not but that I am in fact a psychic. I never hear from her again.

Late on a Friday night, outside my East Village apartment, the streets are swarming with apple-cheeked, beer-guzzling New York University students, and wannabe cool dudes from New Jersey ("bridge-and-tunnel crowd") with green hair and rings embedded in their eyebrows, noses, lips and tongues, and local punks and skinheads with multi-colored Mohawks, kinky young women from Japan, their apricot eyes partly covered by glowing pink-and-green strands of once-jet black hair, Hari-Krishna people tapping on drums and banging cymbals and dancing themselves into a state of giddi-ness, sleepy-from-working-two-jobs male and female cops, who seem to be waiting patiently for Godot and most of whom have traded in their revolvers for semi-automatics, insouciant dog walkers neglect-ing to pick up after their Chevy-sized pit bulls and German Shep-herds, and – giving new meaning to a former mayor's "gorgeous mosaic" – bored Mexicans sitting in front of Korean greengrocers to ensure that no one of *any* nationality snatches up the buckets of flowers or baskets of fruit from the outside display without paying, and the few hookers and their pimps who haven't yet got the word that our puritan mayor doesn't like them.

Ensconced inside my semi-basement apartment, on the Internet, still searching for anything connected to Hunan province, I stumble across the "Hunan Yiyang Mosquito-Repellent Incense Manufacturing General Factory" and the "China Mosquito-Repellent Incense Industrial Association Directory Office." This is good because Yiyang is a town between Changsha, the capital of Hunan, and Changde, formerly Wuling, home of the fisherman who started all this by getting lost, and I want to know if there is a train between the two places or not. The factory manufactures "coil mosquito-repellent incense, Cat brand insect-repellent spray, electric mosquito-repellent incense, quick-acting mosquito-repellent tablets, cockroach-repellent tablets and fragrant incense." So who takes the tablet – the cockroach or me?

I don't like the sound of all these mosquitoes and cockroaches running around Hunan province especially since New York is on the alert for West Nile Virus-carrying mosquitoes (so the mosquitoes that migrated to Manhattan from the *East* Nile are harmless?) but I console myself with the thought that all of this battlefield artillery might be for export. It probably ends up in New York City.

I e-mail the Director and General Secretary. The e-mail is returned: "user address unknown."

But while checking for that e-mail, I find another. My 81-year-old mother in Vero Beach, Florida, has sent up a note purportedly from my 89-year-old stepfather. On a recent visit, I had told them about my search for Peach Blossom Spring and explained why it will be similar to Don Quixote's adventures in Spain. Over an Early Bird Dinner with no fewer than 71 items in its salad bar, I spoke to them of how in *Don Quixote in China*, readers would travel with a writer as besotted with the spiritual riches of China's literary landscape as Don Quixote de la Mancha was besotted with of the ideals of chivalry. Whereas for Don Quixote, windmills and powerful magicians became the unbeatable foe, in *Don Quixote in China*, I would be facing an even greater adversary: modern China's unbridled and unashamed passion for getting rich combined with its post-Cultural Revolution ignorance of traditional literature. Of course, I didn't bother to mention that a foreign traveler searching for a quite possibly mythical utopia in a very materialistic, money-minded, China may well find more than his fair share of Cervantes-style punishments.

During several grueling shuffleboard matches I explained how I intended to be serious in my quest, but not to take myself too seriously; how I would draw parallels to the adventures of Don Quixote de la Mancha, as I too might with justification be described as tilting at windmills and possessing a mind "crazed by reading;" as one whose "overexcited imagination blinds him to reality," and described as an "idealist frustrated and mocked in a materialist world." (In fact, the Chinese would have called Don Quixote a *shu-tai-dz*, a fatuous fellow who knows nothing of the world except through books.) And, of course, I explained all about Sancho Panza, the hapless squire to Don Quixote, whose only goal was to be governor of an island. Whatever it was in the early bird specials, by the time I leave Florida, I have a toothache.

My stepfather had shown no particular interest in my tale. But by some kind of bizarre coincidence, shortly after I left, they watched a TV version of Don Quixote starring John Lithgow as Don Quixote and Bob Hoskin as Sancho Panza, and since then my stepfather has been keen to accompany me to China as my squire. Almost insistently keen. This is his e-mail:

"To: Don Quixote de la Mancha from your friend and Squire Sancho. I have a few questions in my mind. I am thinking about riding the donkey. I assume that we both face the same way. Right? But how do I get him to start? Do I hit him on the back end (soft or hard?) Or whisper in his ear (right or left)? Then how do I get him to stop? This requires a lot of planning on my part even if I get a tall donkey. I don't want my feet to be dragging as I might go barefoot. Let me know the answers and where I can get a donkey. You see I want to be all ready when called. Your good friend and Squire, Sancho."

The tone of the message sounds more like my mother than my stepfather but the wackiness in my family long ago rubbed off on my stepfather so who knows. And the thought occurs to me that if an 89-year-old man serves as my squire in China while searching for Peach Blossom Spring, that would almost guarantee a write-up in *Modern Maturity* magazine of the American Association of Retired Persons. So the question is: Do I have it in me to sacrifice my elderly stepfather in order to reach millions of readers and sell lots of books? I decide to put off the soul-searching question but I respond to the e-mail by pointing out that one of the Eight Immortals used to ride a white mule which he would fold up and put in his wallet when not needed. When needed, he would sprinkle water on it and it would reappear. I suggest that my stepfather check out Vero Beach travel shops for something like that. I don't bother to mention that the Immortal is said to have ridden the mule backward.

The woman at the post office to whom I hand my Hold the Mail card is Chinese as is my mailman. But both are from Hong Kong and neither has been to Hunan. And if I read their attitude correctly, neither has the slightest interest in going to Hunan. Ever.

One of the many translations of Peach Blossom Spring I have is from a book devoted to the poet by Professor Tan Shilin of Jinan University. It is entitled, *The Complete Works of Tao Yuan Ming* and is in both Chinese and English.

I find an e-mail address for Jinan University on the Internet. The response informs me that professor Tan retired from Jinan's Foreign Language Department in Kwangchow (Canton) and now resides in Chongshan. I try the number several times; AT&T operators try the number several times. Nothing quite works.

The following morning a dentist informs me the aching tooth will have to be pulled. Lisa, the dental assistant, asks if I would like to have "twilight sleep." She explains that she can place a nosepiece over my nose and, as I breathe in the twilight sleep, it will make me high and disassociate me from what is going on. As a child of the 60's, of course I want to get high. And, as the dentist points out with a wink, "It's legal."

As we wait for the dentist to reappear with his tools, Lisa adjusts the machine behind me and says, "Let's get you higher," a beautiful phrase I hadn't heard since the late 60's student riots at San Francisco State College.

I smile and say, "Lisa, let me take you away from all this." No, wait, did I say that or just think it. No, I couldn't have said it; I've got too many things in my much numbed-over mouth.

Lisa explains how far twilight sleep has come: that unless a patient is a rubber fetishist he will get tired of the smell of rubber from the nosepiece so twilight sleep now comes in various scents and Lisa offers a choice of three: mint, french-vanilla and – I kid you not – peach. So while the dentist is busily extracting my second pre-molar or pre-second molar or something like that, I ascend into the Land of Peach Blossom Spring, this time with a little assist from nitrous oxide. The dentist office gradually transforms and I find myself on a skiff gliding along a sparkling stream covered with peach blossoms. The peach trees end and I step from the boat onto the bank where, with very little trouble, I locate the eerie light coming from a narrow opening in the mountain. I squeeze through the opening and come face to face with the dental assistant dressed in the skimpiest of native sarongs. She hangs a garland of peach leaves about my neck and hands me a succulent peach. I realize I am about to experience pure happiness. But as she leads me off toward a thatched hut surrounded by vividly beautiful flowers I hear a strange cracking noise behind me. I turn to see my dentist emerge though the crevice. He says, "It's out!" And I am taken off nitrous oxide and given pure oxygen and then the nosepiece is removed altogether and Peach Blossom Spring is no more.

When I return from the dentist, I spot what appears to be an extended family of excited Asians gathered in front of my building. They are using long bamboo poles to reach up into the branches of a gingko tree and shaking the tree for all they are worth; elderly grandmothers, middle-aged couples and plenty of kids. A few are pushing on the tree while one young man has even climbed on top of someone's parked van in order to reach higher.

Having lived in Hong Kong for 17 years, I know immediately that A. these were Cantonese, probably from Hong Kong, B. whatever part of the gingko tree they were after would be used in soup in Chinese restaurants or as medicine in Chinese pharmacies or both and C. they were extremely pleased to be getting it.

New Yorkers pass by and cast wary and suspicious glances at such goings-on and one actually stops beside me and asks, "Why are these people trying to push that tree down?"

The truth is the City of New York in its wisdom realized that even New York exhaust fumes cannot kill this hardy tree and so they planted them on every bare spot of ground. The problem is they were supposed to plant *male* gingko trees because the female gingko trees bear fruit (or whatever it is) and it is messy and, frankly, it stinks. And, to tell the truth, the smell of the gingko fruit is not nearly so bad as certain other odors around my neighborhood, about which the less said the better. In any case, right in front of my apartment is a *female* Gingko tree, which each season never fails to be a beacon and a bonanza for extended Chinese families.

Meanwhile, back at the Chu Chu Dry cleaners, I learn that the owner's father left China in 1946 and eventually taught Chinese at an American university for many years. But when he left China, he left his children behind and never returned to see them. Then, in 1972, his mother turned 90, an important birthday for Chinese, and so the dry cleaner's father was about to return. Then Nixon went to China and suddenly everybody in America became a sinophile and wanted to learn Chinese and play the butterfly harp and watch kung-fu movies from Hong Kong, so the college persuaded him to delay his trip for one year. In March of 1973, the year he would have returned, he died of cancer. Although the dry cleaner did not tell his grandmother of her son's death, she had a dream in which the son said they should both go together. She died in May of that year.

I ask where his father is buried and he says New Jersey. I mention the tradition that the bones should be buried in China and he quickly turns over a laundry ticket and sketches out a tree and jots down a Chinese saying about a very tall tree that sends down its seeds to the earth, meaning: no matter how important or how distant, one must always return to China. But he says if they had sent his father's coffin back to China there would be no one to tend the grave. Here they can visit every year during the Ch'ing Ming Festival.

Then I learn the dry cleaner had been in China until the late 70's and was still a boy when in 1946 his father left for America. He looks away and lowers his voice as he tells me he never saw him again. At that, I pry no further, but I have seldom spoken to a Chinese of any occupation without, over time, learning of some sad tale or even horrible tragedy just beneath the surface of his or her seemingly ordinary life.

My friend, Robert Lin, drops by. Robert is a fine actor who played Chairman Mao in Martin Scorcece's film on Tibet, *Kundun*. I first met him when he tried out for my musical set in 1857 Hong Kong, *Fragrant Harbour*. But Robert is 6' 2", half Manchu, very scholarly, Chinese opera-trained, and with the broad face of a Northerner. My musical needed typically skinny and smaller

Cantonese and we couldn't use him. But we became close friends.

I casually mention to him my desire to find Peach Blossom Spring. He mentions the Chinese phrase, "*Hua fu chui jih*, (Hua Fu Chases the Sun). In other words, the Chinese version of a wild goose chase. We discuss it and he says that he hasn't heard of any sightings of a remote, idyllic community like Peach Blossom Spring but has heard of several villages in one area of China in which women are in control and all is based on matriarchy. Having once been married to a Chinese woman, I have no doubt that despite surface appearances Chinese women are in control *throughout* China, but I ask him where this place of Women in Command is. He says he'll try to find out but he warns me if I go there that I might become – he hesitates, groping for the right phrase in English and finally finds it – "a copulation tool."

God, I wish my mandarin were as good as his English, but I hasten to assure him that I was in fact *born* to be a copulation tool of beautiful Chinese women in villages in the middle of China; that it has always been my destiny, my fate, my karma, and that I can easily swing around to the female-dominated villages on my way back from Peach Blossom Spring, kill two birds with one stone, and all that. He promises to try to find out more about them.

But shortly after, I hear that he has gotten his American citizenship and, after many years in the States, is going back to visit his parents. Reading between the lines I understand that his portrayal of Mao might not have gone down well with Beijing authorities and he decided to become an American citizen before heading back to China. Obviously, his mama didn't raise no fool.

Meanwhile my own mother is inundating me with any and all newspaper clippings that have the faintest relevance to China. One of them involves a Florida schoolteacher who is going to live in China for a year with her husband. She has already begun studying Chinese culture as well as the language and, "the next step, she said, is to tackle the alphabet so she can read the language, as well." My mother underlines that sentence. My mother knows the Chinese language doesn't have an alphabet. In fact, my mother knows I will find Peach Blossom Spring before the Florida schoolteacher finds a Chinese alphabet.

I receive a notice in the mail that China desperately needs English teachers and several groups working in China will be speaking and recruiting nearby. I attend the meeting and learn that English teachers are in such demand that in one case a homeless man was sent to some remote province to teach. No one is quite certain what happened to him. A slightly embarrassed woman from Shanghai does her best to tactfully explain to a young Chinese-American woman that Chinese parents actually tell them they want "white" American teachers to teach their children English. To say the least, this information does not go down well with the young Chinese-American woman.

After the meeting, I take one of R.H. van Gulik's Judge Dee mysteries and head for a Chinese restaurant where I have the famous General Tso's chicken. I forget which, or rather, who came first, Judge Dee or General Tso, so I am not certain whether General Tso read Judge Dee's murder trials or if Judge Dee ate General Tso's chicken. A puzzlement.

When I return home and check the mail I find a "China for Children catalog" offering such items as Yang Ge dance fans, Tianjin folk Art T-shirts, silk longevity scarves, Year of the Dragon lapel pins, and "cute and fuzzy" panda bear slippers. "A portion of the proceeds supports the work of Our Chinese Daughters Foundation, Inc." Not knowing what might eventually develop from my trip to China, I decide to file the catalog for future reference.

I check the website of Hong Kong's South China Morning Post and do a search of recent articles on "Hunan." Time to see exactly what kind of place I am heading for. I find this:

4 February 2000: China residents of a Hunan village refused to help victims of a bus crash, instead they stole valuables, cash and clothes from survivors. The victims said the villagers asked them if they had money to pay for assistance, then looted the bus.

20 February 2000: A six-year-old girl was beaten to death by a 12-year-old boy in a Hunan village after she threatened to tell on him for setting off fireworks.

25 February 2000: A natural gas explosion in a workshop in Hunan province killed 13 people and injured 54.

8 April 2000: Two suspected murderers, members of an armed gang from Hunan province, were killed by police in a shoot-out in Chechiang province.

18 April 2000: An explosion on Thursday at the Liaowangping coal mine, near Chenzhou city, Hunan province, killed 11 miners, one missing.

24 May 2000: Mystery yesterday surrounded a helicopter crash which left two people dead and three injured in Hunan province, as investigators continued to probe why the mainland's first corporate helicopter went down.

7 June 2000: A pontoon bridge crowded with spectators watching a dragon boat race overturned and threw 130 people into a Hunan province reservoir, drowning 13 people.

11 June 2000: A traditional dragon boat festival in Hunan turned into tragedy last week when a dam gate was opened, dragging a boat into a reservoir and killing 11 participants.

During a checkup I mention to my doctor that I am going to Hunan Province during the rainy season. He briefly disappears and then hands me some anti-malaria pills and the National Center for Infectious Diseases "Health Information for Travelers to East Asia." Its list is as impressive as it is hair-raising: "Travelers' diarrhea (E. Coli, Salmonella, cholera, and parasites), fever (typhoid fever and toxoplasmosis, liver damage), Malaria, yellow fever, Japanese encephalitis, leishmaniasis, plague, Hepatitis A, Hepatitis B, rabies, and Dengue. As Deng Hsiao-ping is deceased, I assume "Dengue" is not some strange romanization of his name or a misspelling but, whatever it is, it sounds ominous. I leave the malaria pills home but, just in case word arrives from Robert about the location of China's matriarchal villages, I pack a few Viagra....

My First Encounter with
Don Quixote's Freston the Magician

New York to Hong Kong on board Hong Kong's Cathay Pacific Airlines. Sixteen hours plus a one-hour stopover in Vancouver. While 33,000 ft. up in the air, I decide to brush up on my rusty mandarin, both written and spoken. I also draw up a list of useful phrases, phrases which I hope I never have to use:

✗ I think I dislocated my shoulder when I fell from the cliff.
✗ Are you sure this flimsy boat can make it through those roaring rapids?
✗ Shouldn't there be a pillow on my bed?
✗ Shouldn't there be a bed in my room?
✗ I think I lost my passport/glasses/wallet/sanity when the boat tipped over.
✗ You don't reuse the needles, do you?
✗ I'm sure it's great medicine but I'm allergic to toad eyebrows and mosquito dung.
✗ But I had no idea this was illegal in China
✗ But I thought the officer in charge said this could be resolved without a prison sentence?
✗ Isn't it prejudicial for the judge to call me a 'barbarous, out-of-province, long-nosed, foreign-devil'?
✗ But shouldn't the verdict come *after* the trial?
✗ Please don't pull the pin out of the grenade until I'm off the bus/ferry/boat/train/balcony.
✗ The gentleman says to tell the customs official that he is *not* smuggling Chinese coins in his chest; he has a pacemaker.
✗ Excuse me, there must be a mistake: This isn't my laundry/luggage/wife/husband.
✗ But before I took your pills I wasn't coughing/vomiting/seeing double/unable to walk.

It wasn't long into the flight when I learned that there was a child in the seat directly behind me. I learned this because of his almost constant habit of kicking the back of my seat. This in turn prevented me from sleeping and gave me horrible jet lag which was to cause several problems.

It is embarrassing to relate that I checked into the wrong hotel but it was not entirely my fault. To get a lower rate, I had booked through an Internet site and the Internet site had the Hong Kong hotel in Kowloon, Hong Kong at a very good rate. There was some confusion between the hotel and the Internet site about my reservation both on line and when I arrived in Hong Kong but I was given a room. Seven hours later, I was asked to come down to the front desk with my paperwork and thereupon discovered that instead of checking into the Hong Kong Hotel in Kowloon, Hong Kong, I was supposed to have checked into the Kowloon Hotel in Kowloon, Hong Kong. Although I was told I would have to leave there would be no charge because it was obvious that the hotel and the Internet site had missed obvious signs also.

I pack and walk over to the nearby Kowloon Hotel. A sweet, young Chinese woman behind the desk looks at my passport and checks her computer.

Sweet, young thing: "Oh, we have you down for an early check-in."
Me: "I did check in early; I just checked into the wrong hotel, that's all."
Sweet, young thing: "Oh."
Me.: "But I am in the former British Crown Colony of Hong Kong, right?"
Sweet, young thing: "Yes."
Me: "Well, there you go, then, I'm in the right city, at least, so no harm done."

I could see the Caucasian lady in charge trying unsuccessfully not to laugh. She probably thought I had never been to Hong Kong before when in fact I had first arrived in Hong Kong before anyone behind the hotel desk had been born. So there.

I call my former secretary and suggest we have lunch so I can get her (Chinese) reaction to my search for Peach Blossom Spring. She says to meet her in the Sogo Department Store in Causeway Bay.

Me: "But where, exactly?"
Former Secretary: "At the Cosmetics Counter."
Me: "Why the Cosmetics Counter?"
Former Secretary: "Because it's by the front door."
Me: "But what if they try to sell me lipstick or something while I'm waiting?"
Former Secretary: "Then be sure to get the right shade."

Ha, ha. Everyone in Hong Kong is a comedian.

My former secretary has put on a few pounds, but the brown eyes in her still youthful face have the same cynical gaze I remember from years before; the one she reserves for when listening to the madcap schemes of foreign-devils. Over a Thai meal, I barely finish outlining my plan of finding Peach Blossom Spring before she makes her views clear: "I don't think you will find it." Honesty, not tact, has always been her strong suit. "Anyway, why didn't you go in the spring when the peach blossoms were out?"

A good question, of course. A *very* good question. The truth is I didn't have my act together enough to get there by then. But there is something else: T'ao Yuan-ming said the fisherman found peach trees in blossom lining both sides of the river's source and that there were no other trees; but he never said which month it was. My belief is that the poet meant that the fisherman found a magical place where the peach trees are in bloom whatever time of year. My former secretary finds that very funny. In fact, every now and then throughout the meal she covers her mouth with her hand and laughs and repeats her belief that she doesn't think I will find it. Ah, ye of little faith. I let her pay for the lunch.

I learn from a newspaper report that the American Ballet Theatre will soon arrive in Hong Kong to present a spirited version of *Don Quixote*. According to a press report, the ballet will be "enhanced by the wholesome American style of dancing, and will no doubt offer a splendid evening, and send everyone home happy after its joyous ending." In the various translations of Cervantes' *Don Quixote* I have read, the ending was anything but happy, in mood falling somewhere between Beckett's *Waiting for Godot* and Margaret Mitchell's *Gone with the Wind* but I'm a firm believer in giving people what they want.

The message lights in my hotel room do not work properly and I miss several calls. Finally, I realize there is a problem and call friends who assure me that they had in fact left several messages. The assistant manager sends up a bottle of red wine as compensation.

While walking through the streets, heading for dinner, I notice that Hong Kong is as vibrant and bustling as ever. The dramatic skyline seems to have still more and even higher buildings; the shipping in the magnificent deep water harbor teems with as many craft as ever.

While crossing the harbor on the Star Ferry, an English businessman sitting beside me is speaking into his cellphone: "Well, we would have no problem in monitoring their assets inside China…well, when you say 'asset disposal program,' what do you mean?…Yes, that would be the typical transaction cycle." I change my seat.

At dinner, friends complain of the poor economy, growing unemployment and of an economic slowdown, but with the exception of certain Manhattan neighborhoods there is not a more dynamic place on earth.

I first saw Hong Kong in 1967, fell in love with it, and came back to live in 1970. I arrived from Taiwan with just under one American dollar in my pocket and when my contact failed to meet me at the airport, I allowed a van driver of one of the small hotels inside the notorious Chungking Mansions to take me there. There are many stories of Chinese arriving in Hong Kong with no money but leaving as multi-millionaires. I at least accomplished the first half–the arriving with no money part. But I've always wondered if there was ever a case of the opposite: someone arriving with lots of money who left a pauper. I suppose not; Hong Kong, "Fragrant Harbor," is not that kind of place.

Chungking Mansions is a short walk from my hotel and I am pleased to see that it is still here and is every bit as tawdry, unsavory and down-market as before. As soon as I approach, an Indian man steps in front of me to offer me a suit and a Chinese man approaches to sell me a watch. In the garishly lit hallways, beyond the money changers and sari shops, energetic, enterprising and ever-restless people from Africa, China, the subcontinent and the Middle East are haggling, bargaining and making deals. The hum of human activity seems to be as steadfast and relentless as the hum of fluorescent lights above their heads. Odors of exotic dishes and sweating bodies flood my nostri s. I stand before several of the building's lifts to read the signs: "The Delphi Club mess, Pakistani mess (Pakistan and Indian halal food), Khyber Pass Club mess, Ashok Club (Nepali food), Sher-T-Punjab Club and Mess (Indian and Muglai food), Everest Club (best Nepali and Indian food), Gurung Army Store, New Hawaii Guest House, New Peking Guest House, New Asia Guest House, Super Guest House, Tom's Guest House, Himalaya Guest House, Tokyo Guest House, Welcome Guest House, Fortunate Guest House, Ocean Guest House, London Comfort Guest House, Hollywood Guest House, Columbia Guest House, Happy Guest House, Shanghai Guest House, New Washington Guest House, Dragon Inn, Hang On Tailors, and (ominously) one of the signs simply reads, "Big Brother."

But, of course, the city has changed. In the 70's my friends had middle-aged amahs with green jade earrings and black *samfu*; now their maids (as well as the "Suzy Wongs" in Wanchai) are young women from the Philipp nes. And in the 70's, before diesel engines changed their fishing methods, Hong Kong residents could look out upon the South China Sea and observe fleets of

Chinese junks with their beautiful, butterfly-wing sails returning from their fishing grounds. Now one is more likely to spot a container ship. And, of course, the British Flag is no more.

There is an old saying I have always liked. It goes something like: "Decent girls don't go to Hong Kong; nor do respectable youths travel by the Fatshan boats." An admonition probably created well over a century ago but I wish I had been in Hong Kong at the time the warning was thought necessary, and I have spent an inordinate amount of time imagining what went on on board those Fatshan boats.

At last I manage to track down professor Tan Shih-lin on the phone. We talk mainly in English and he tells me he is "in the picture" as "they" have told him about me. I assume he means the people at the university in Guangchou (Canton) but, being a paranoid writer, I realize he and "they" could be part of a group opposed to anyone finding Peach Blossom Spring, just as Don Quixote's powerful enemy Freston the Magician dogged him at every turn.

But I have a few questions for him. The story of Peach Blossom Spring is told in story form but in Professor Tan's book he includes a short poem about Peach Blossom Spring, also by T'ao Yuan Ming. However, his is one of only two books I have ever come across which includes the poem. His answer is what I had suspected: the story of Peach Blossom Spring was actually a preface for a poem of the same subject, but over the centuries the Chinese have chosen to include only the story in their "gems of Chinese literature," not the less favored poem, which in any case, basically just repeats information from the beautifully written preface.

However, in the story version, it is said that the clothes of the people living in Peach Blossom Spring are "not unusual" but in the poem it says the clothes were "of an ancient cut." I ask Professor Tan if he can shed any light on this discrepancy. He tells me that the poet's implication regarding the dress both in the prose and in the poem seems to be that the people of Peach Blossom Spring were of Han stock, i.e., they were neither of ethnic minority stock nor were they immortals or other-worldly beings. The settlers had an abiding adherence to traditional Han culture, without having, in the course of five or six hundred years, even slightly altered established rituals and fashions in dress. It is a very clear explanation, one that solves an age-old mystery other translators have grappled with.

He warns me that there is a Peach Blossom Spring set up for tourists near Changde (the former Wuling) begun in the Ch'ing Dynasty, as well as several others in other parts of China, all more recent; all claiming to be the real Peach Blossom Spring. (Not unlike here in New York City, the long simmering dispute over which of several is the *real* Original Ray's Pizza.)

Before I hang up, I decide reluctantly not to ask Professor Tan the question I would really like to have an answer to. The back cover of his book mentions that he was born in Nanjing "with a German background on his mother's side....Only after the ten years and more of great upheavals across the nation did he settle down to teaching at Jinan University (Guangzhou)."

Of course, the phrase "great upheavals across the nation" refers to the Great Cultural Revolution of 1966-76 when, during the years of fear and madness, millions of Chinese were denounced by one another and tortured and murdered. It is not difficult to imagine the horrors Professor Tan, with his "German background," must have suffered before it could be written, "did he settle down to teaching."

That is why I understand perfectly when he hesitates to give me his address. He mentions he is "hopelessly out of touch with life around me" and that it would be difficult to reach him there and instead gives me a name of someone in the United States who can relay letters. Much like those who retreated into Peach Blossom Spring, Professor Tan may well have had more than enough of his fellow man. And this is the unasked question I had: why had he chosen to spend several years of his life translating the complete works of this particular poet; a poet "unstained by worldly dust," a poet who refused to bow to a "country bumpkin" official for "five pecks of rice a month," who quit officialdom to retreat to a life of farming and nature and wine and poetry? Was it because it is the lesson the horrors of modern China has taught him as well? As his introduction says, "In a culture predominantly Confucian, where rank and emolument were the coveted reward for scholastic pursuits and where promising scholars were expected to distinguish themselves in public life, T'ao Yuan-ming's complete break with time-honored conventionality was without precedent." And on the same page the quote from Tao's *Back to Country Life*:

"A captive in the cage for years, Back to nature I've found my way."

I can't help but wonder if the above quote reflects the view and the experience of both men.

The China Travel Service is practically around the corner from my hotel. The businesslike, middle-aged woman there takes my picture, attaches one to my application for a visa, and hands me back three copies. I soon learn that The China Travel Service has perfected a technique to ensure that photographs taken there never dry.

She carefully peruses my application. This is the fifth time I have traveled into China and I am not a complete fool when it comes to indicating my profession on official forms. For example, I know better than to write my profession as "journalist" or "writer" or "novelist" or anything involving the reporting or divulging of information. Smuggler, scoundrel, ne'er-do-well, even serial killer, perhaps, but never "journalist." Be it ever so humble, no government anywhere in the world likes a journalist or – God forbid – a foreign correspondent. A smuggler, at least, is a kind of businessman. So I have written what I regard as the most innocuous of professions: "Musical Theater Lyricist." I also know enough about Chinese psychology to know that they would lose face if they had to admit that they don't know what a musical theater lyricist is, and, thus far at least, no one has ever questioned me on it.

In the place for Purpose of Trip I have written "To find Peach Blossom Spring." The woman stares at that sentence for several seconds without blinking (but the wrinkles on her forehead increase each second), then picks up an ominous looking black pen, draws a line through the five words and above them writes "Tour."

If Don Quixote de La Mancha himself showed up and wrote in his reason for entering China as "I, Knight of the Lions, bravest knight-errant ever to unsheath a sword, the man for whom the greatest dangers are expressly reserved, and wondrous adventures, and brave deeds of fearless daring, the undoer of wrongs and injustices, wish to enter the Middle Kingdom to joust in tourneys, to quest for grails, to undo injustice, to terrorize giants, to succor widows, to protect damsels in distress, to perform the most remarkable deeds of knighthood ever in this world seen, or which could be seen, and to treasure the fairest lady of them all, the beautiful damsel Dulcinea de Toboso," I have no doubt that this woman would simply pick up her black pen, draw a line through it all and write "Tour."

A man at another desk checks the train schedule for me. I explain I want to travel by train to Changsha, capital of Hunan province. The price one-way from Hong Kong to Changsha is HK$545 (about US$68). He tells me that the only train to Changsha leaves at three in the afternoon and arrives at Changsha at 2:40 the next morning.

Me: "Two-forty in the morning? I didn't know there was a two-forty in the morning."
Man behind desk: "Ha, there is! And don't sleep too much."
Me: "Why not?"
Man behind desk: "Because the train stops in Changsha for just a few

minutes. And no one will come around to wake you."

Me: "So what happens if I sleep through the stop?"

Man behind desk: "Ha, then you wake up in Beijing."

Me: "Beijing?"

Man behind desk: "Yes, that's where this train is going."

Me: "Then what happens?"

Man behind desk: "Ha, then you pay more."

When I stop at a camera shop for new batteries, the salesman points out that my camera is old, the batteries will cost half as much as a new camera, and China probably doesn't sell that type of battery if I need one. He offers to buy my camera for his collection of old cameras. I buy the new camera and sell him mine, but the way he looks my camera over – as if it is a relic from the Warring States period – makes me feel like a relic as well.

After I pack my bags I have time to look over the local paper. There is an article about wives from China being beaten and called "stupid China women" by their Hong Kong husbands. Another article reports that a Hong Kong-based TV company will pay compensation to a woman from mainland China who works in their London office. Her colleagues are from Hong Kong and they apparently referred to her as their "country cousin" and "subjected her to months of slurs." Menial tasks which no one wanted to do were described as having a "Chinese smell." It seems the Chinese tendency to look down on outsiders –"out-of-province-people"– did not die out with the Ch'ing Dynasty.

The sign in the Kowloon Railway Station for Train K98 reads: "Dongguan/Guangzhou East/Guangzhou/Shaoguan/Changsha/ Wuchang/Beijing." The female conductors' uniforms and kepi caps with rear sun flaps remind me of the French Foreign Legion as portrayed in old movies. The one in charge of my car hands me a small metal tag which I must return before I get off the train. I have no doubt that in this bureaucratic system, should I lose that tag, there will be trouble.

I find my compartment of four bunks, two upper and two lower, and sit on a lower bunk. An old Chinese woman comes in, checks my ticket, and motions that that is her bunk. I apologize and sit on the lower bunk opposite. A slender, young, bespectacled, Chinese man enters, checks my ticket, and explains that that is his bunk. Nevertheless, he encourages me to sit on it for now. No need to climb up yet. His name is Cham Yen and he is a Hong Kong Cantonese who is off to Beijing to spend the summer with his grandmother. He won't arrive in Beijing until 7 p.m. the following day. He is a mere 19 years old and an only child. He has a large case of food that his mother packed for him and while we are talking she calls him on his cell phone to make certain he is OK. His father is a salesman in cloth material and buttons, in Hong Kong and China.

Just before the train starts to move, the fourth member of our compartment enters. He is a 20-year-old American from California named Brendan who is heading to Beijing to teach English in north China. He is sporting two small earrings in his right ear and wearing a cap. He could fit right in in Manhattan's East Village.

Brendan has taught in China before and enjoys it. He mentions that he has only 500 renminbi (about US$55) left because he spent all his money in Hong Kong, so he plans to pass through Beijing and go right to his school without staying overnight in Beijing. He also passes on the advice to me that I should drink only bottled water in China but that since beer in China is cheaper than bottled water, I should drink only beer.

The compartment is cramped but all are friendly and soon we are on our way, heading for Changsha, approximately 900 miles to the northwest. We pass through the newly developed town of Shenzhen where married Hong Kong businessmen buy apartments in which to keep their girlfriends, and past concrete houses which give way to longer and longer glimpses of rural countryside.

Later, Brendan, Cham Yen and I persuade the workers in the

dining car to let us sit in one of the booths a bit before they officially open. A major accomplishment on a Chinese train. Cham Yen explains that the way he pronounces his name is Cantonese and that when he goes to Beijing the characters for his name are read in mandarin as Chen Hsin. In China, the same Chinese character is pronounced differently in different dialects, so a Mr. Ng in Hong Kong would be called Mr. Wu in Beijing. It is as if someone from Tennessee named Gore arrives in California and his name is pronounced Bush.

I find both young men likable and unpretentious. Brendan also mentions that teaching in China is great except for some of those in administration, "the know-it-all 30-year-old's." Something about Brendan's attitude toward 30-year-old's makes me feel ancient.

The dining car fills up and at other tables just about everyone talks or rather shouts into a cellphone. At some point we briefly discuss the 1979 conflict between China and Vietnam which, according to Cham Yen, China won; and then with an expression of sorrow he adds, "but more Chinese died than Vietnamese."

I have decided not to mention my mission in China unless someone asks what I am doing in China. As Chinese are a curious people, I am almost always asked. Cham Yen is no exception. I especially like Cham Yen because of all the Chinese I meet in China he seems the only one whose belief that I will in fact find Peach Blossom Spring is genuine.

Cham Yen has just seen "Mission Impossible 2" and gives it a glowing review. This leads to talk of the late hero of Chinese martial arts films, Bruce Li, and how he died so young. The year was 1973 and I was living in Hong Kong at the time. Cham Yen says he wasn't born then. Whenever I talk to young people about something I did in the past or about something that happened in my youth, they almost invariably say, "I wasn't born yet." Young people are beginning to piss me off.

I ask Cham Yen if he knows who killed Bruce Li. He looks at

me and wrinkles his brow in puzzlement.

Cham Yen: "He died a natural death."
Me: "No, he didn't."
Cham Yen: "He didn't?"
Me: "What was his nickname?"
Cham Yen: "I don't know."
Me: "*Li Syau Lung.*"
Cham Yen: "Yes, that's right!"
Me: "And what does *Syau Lung* mean?"
Cham Yen: "Little Dragon."
Me: "And what does 'Kowloon' mean?"
Cham Yen: "Nine dragons."
Me: "Right. Don't you see? Bruce Li was living in Kowloon at the time and The Nine Dragons were jealous of the fame of the Little Dragon and so they killed him."

Cham Yen laughs. But over a quarter of a century ago, at the time of Bruce Li's death, every Chinese in Hong Kong repeated that version of the event, and everyone suspected that Bruce Li's being born in the year of the dragon in the hour of the dragon also had something to do with his feud with the nine dragons. A new, less superstitious, generation has forgotten. I tell Cham Yen I still remember a handmade tribute to Bruce Li hanging in a Wanchai alley just after he died. A large photograph of him was bordered in black and beneath the photograph were four Chinese characters: *Ching Shen Pu Sz* ("A Pure Spirit Never Dies"). It always amazed me how deeply Bruce Li was loved by the people of Hong Kong, especially the young. But it is not surprising that in a colony in which Chinese had no king or queen or flag of their own, the fighting spirit of a never-say-die Bruce Li underdog would become popular.

Cham Yen has a lovely innocence about him, which would not be surprising if he were from the mainland but is unusual for a Hong Kong Chinese. After we discuss a beautiful Hong Kong movie star who killed herself in the 60's, I ask him if he can name the four classic beauties in Chinese history and he admits he can't. I name them – Hsi Shih, Yang Kuei-fei, Diao Chan and Wang Chao-chun – and point out that they all had tragic endings so it may be best not to be too beautiful in China. He says he is not interested in old beauties, only modern ones. He asks me if I like Chinese women.

I hesitate then decide to confess to him what I seldom tell anyone else. How when I was about nine or ten years old, I would sit in front of the television set in Groton, Connecticut, "Home of the Nautilus, Submarine Capital of the World," watching cowboys and Indians fight it out. And how my parents always thought I wanted to be a cowboy when I grew up. And how the truth was I didn't want to be a cowboy nor did I give a damn who won the battles. I only wanted to get a glimpse of Indian women. Living in Connecticut at the age of ten I didn't even know *what they were*. I only knew every time I saw one of those young women emerge from a teepee I felt an inexplicable frisson of excitement pass through me. Something about the long braided jet-black hair, the high cheekbones, the almond eyes, the smoldering looks, the curvaceous form filling out the buckskin – I was already, even then, a Caucasian male moth to a Mongoloid female flame and, had I been able to crawl inside the TV set, no doubt would have.

It was about that time that adult westerns were popular on American TV and my favorite was *Cheyenne* starring Clint Walker. On one of the episodes a beautiful Indian woman, trying to prevent him from turning her in to the authorities, gave him a doe-eyed look and said, "I can give you pleasure." But Cheyenne wasn't having any of that and he turned her in. That's when I knew that that boy had some serious problems. Definitely a spur missing there somewhere. I never forgave him for that and I never watched him again.

Anyway, I tell Cham Yen that many years later I learned two more things about those beautiful "Indian maidens." First, most of them weren't Indian at all; rather, Italian- or Spanish-American actresses with makeup and blush or highlighter or whatever it is that clever women use to give the impression of having high cheekbones. Second, I learned that most experts still believe that twelve thousand years ago there was a land bridge between Alaska and Russia and that Asians crossed it and populated the Americas. Which explains why so many Native Americans resemble Koreans, Manchurians and Mongolians. Which means that at the age of nine or ten I was already afflicted with Yellow Fever. And before he can respond I tell him, as Americans would say, "I'm sick, I need help, but *I'm* the victim here."

Cham Yen obviously thinks I am mad but he seems to enjoy my company. He says I am very humorous and wonders why Chinese can't be humorous. Perhaps he hasn't seen Jackie Chan movies. Or read the sayings of Chairman Mao.

When a lovely Chinese woman sits at a table a few seats behind us, I tell him that since he likes Mission Impossible so much, I shall give him one. I ask if he can see the woman behind us. At first he doesn't understand the mandarin expression for "behind." Finally, he understands, looks in her direction, then asks in English: "What did she do?"

Brendan and I crack up. I explain that she didn't *do* anything. Like a crystal clear lake surrounded by China's magnificent mountains, she is beautiful; she doesn't have to *do*; she just has to *be*. I explain that his Mission Impossible is to put the man she is with out of the picture and get her over to our table. Cham Yen completely blows his mission.

He does get up to ask for more bowls for his noodles and is abruptly told by a member of the dining car staff to sit down. He complains that northerners are rude. I mention that northerners think southerners are loud. He ponders that a bit then says, "Maybe so, but they are *rude*."

Outside the window a strange mixture of Chinese houses passes by, resembling nothing so much as Pueblo Indian homes. Or is it my Yellow Fever kicking in again? Before long, the train reaches the "Frontier Inspection," where everyone and his baggage must leave the train and line up to present his passport. The lines are long, the June day is typically hot and humid, and the somewhat disheveled Chinese officials have their hats off and their shirts outside their trousers. I pass through the passport line and head for the luggage inspection. The Chinese officials hardly glance at my large plain brown bag but they take notice of my shoulder bag. On it is a cow, a barn, and the slogan, "Bouchercon '99 – Mischief in the Midwest."

Bouchercon is the world's largest convention of mystery writers and mystery fans wherein hotel waiters gradually and rather nervously get used to middle-aged writers and fans and librarians sitting around discussing how to commit the perfect murder. Its last convention was held in Milwaukee, hence the slogan. However, I now realize, assuming the Chinese customs officials read English, they might be thinking that I mean to create mischief in *their* Midwest. And, indeed, a case could probably be made that anyone entering Hunan Province to search for Peach Blossom Spring is most likely up to mischief. But they wave me through and I pass outside the building.

While waiting for the others to exit customs, I notice a dark-complexioned vendor in blouse and well worn trousers selling a selection of Chinese vegetables. She is probably in her mid-thirties but, like so many Asian women, appears much younger than she is. She is one of those women you sometimes glimpse in Asia and other parts of the world where people are still struggling with concerns in life more practical than the enigma of feminine pulchritude: incredibly beautiful but enmeshed in a poverty which has allowed her no opportunity to use her beauty to better herself. Had she been born inside a palace during one of China's dynasties, she would have been a woman with the power to, in the Chinese phrase, "overturn a kingdom." She knows nothing of what Thomas Mann wrote of the "profound leaning which those who have devoted their thoughts to the creation of beauty feel toward those who possess beauty itself."

She wipes her brow and she stares toward the doorway of the shabby customs building, hoping for more potential customers. What I feel toward her is almost a form of worship. That which I can never achieve in words stands before me in the flesh, her beauty a form of taunting; a goal forever beyond my reach. I wonder what she would say if she knew that for one week with her, one night, one *hour* – I would give her *anything* she wanted; my soul, my honor, my freedom, my entire collection of John D. McDonald's Travis McGee.

A conductor passes by and I strike up a conversation. I ask what Changsha is like. He says he has never got off the train at Changsha. He doesn't know anyone who ever has got off the train in Changsha. He asks me what I want to go to Changsha for. I explain that from there I will take another train to Changde and from Changde check out the Peach Blossom Spring built for tourists in the Ch'ing Dynasty and then start my search in the mountains and valleys and rivers for the real one. He nods, clears his throat with great zest and spits into the dirt, then ambles off, obviously sorry he asked the question. By the time he leaves, the lovely vendor is gone.

Back on the train it soon grows dark, the dining car closes at 9:30 and we return to our bunks to continue desultory conversations while listening to the click-clack of the wheels on the rails. There is no space for luggage except on the bed itself so I make myself as comfortable as possible but again and again check to make certain the alarm is properly set and the clock is beside me.

I have snatches of strange dreams in which farmers and fishermen welcome me to Peach Blossom Spring, lift me up and carry me toward a picturesque thatched cottage surrounded by peach trees in full bloom. I rock from side to side and seem to be slipping from their grasp when suddenly I wake up dangerously close to the edge of the upper bunk. I check the hands of my clock. According to the clock there is still an hour to go but then I realize I can't hear the ticking of the clock. The clock has stopped!

And then it suddenly hits me: this is the work of Freston the Magician, powerful and persistent nemesis of Don Quixote and now me as well, and he has done his work well. With hindsight it is painfully obvious: What at the time I thought was merely an obnoxious, annoying, pesky, obese kid kicking my chair all the way on the flight from New York to Hong Kong was in fact Freston himself. How else to explain the fact that for the first time in my life I checked into the wrong hotel, the fact that the message lights were mysteriously not working in the right hotel, and the fact that jet lag from lack of sleep on the plane may cause me to miss my train stop in Changsha? All of which leads me to be more and more convinced of the presence of a Vast Conspiracy of Black Magic working against me as I try to find Peach Blossom Spring. Don Quixote was right: there are powerful enemies out there.

I jump up, frantically slide the compartment door open and run through the train. It is early morning and no one is around. In my frenzied rush I bang my knee on a sliding door but continue on, now with a decided limp, like Chester on Gunsmoke.

Finally, I find a slumberous, disheveled worker kind of sleepwalking out of his compartment on the way to what might euphemistically be called a men's room. I rudely grab his arm and check his watch and find that it is the same as my clock which I realize I am still clutching in my hand. I place the clock close to my ear and then I hear the ticking. I give the worker a broad smile. The worker seems to think I am as strange as the foreign devils his grandfather probably warned him about and he quickly brushes past me.

I gather up my bags from the compartment and slide the door

shut as quietly as possible. Now there is nothing to do but wait. I walk slowly along the worn red carpet lining the cars, beneath the fluorescent lights, listening to the roar of the train and occasionally looking out into the darkness of the Middle Kingdom. Signs on the train are everywhere: "Keep Quiet," "No Throwing," "No Spitting," "No Smoking," "No Peaches." No peaches? Christ, I'm starting to imagine things.

A sign with a finger and three red drops of blood pouring from it reads: "Taking care of your hands." They apparently mean not to get your fingers caught in the train door. I study the schedule on the wall for awhile, curse the communist use of impossible-to-read and horribly unsightly simplified characters, then pull down a seat and sit facing a wall a foot away. Considering that the windows are *behind* me, I wonder if perhaps the Chinese Frank Lloyd Wright-types who designed these cars placed the seats on the wrong side of the aisle. Not exactly the way the Jet Set travels but it will do; I concentrate on the fact that the train is speeding me through the darkness closer to my goal of finding Peach Blossom Spring.

Cham Yen appears, sleepy but unable to sleep. I don't envy him his journey: it will be a tiring one. He reminds me that before I can leave the train I have to give back that little metal tag to the conductor in charge of our car. I search my trouser pockets – I can't find it. I don't know what the punishment is for losing it but I know there will be one. In the dynastic penal code of the Chinese empire, they would specify how many strokes of the bamboo for each offence or how long iron chains and various wooden or iron fetters should be left on or how far from Peking those found guilty should be exiled or if a prisoner should be branded. *Branded!*

I begin frantically searching my luggage. And what if they regard the metal tag as some kind of seal or official stamp of office? In the Ch'ing Dynasty penal code it says, "All persons guilty of having been principals or accessories to the crime of stealing the official seal of any magistrate or tribunal, or any seal or stamp whatever issued by the Emperor, shall be beheaded." Jesus Christ! Or what if they assume I want to resell it and simply call it robbery? Even then the penal code says, "...he shall not suffer death, but receive 100 blows of the bamboo, and be sent into perpetual banishment at the distance of 3000 lee (from Peking)." *One hundred blows of the bamboo*?! That American kid in Singapore was bitching about *four*! Wait. Calm down. Think. Three thousand lee from Peking would be about one thousand miles. Where would that put me? Probably in Hunan province. Right where I'm going. But it would be perpetual banishment. I turn my shoulder bag upside down and spill out the contents. Where the hell is that damn tag? And if I can't find a metal tag how the hell can I hope to find Peach Blossom Spring?

Or what if after they find my copy of *Don Quixote* and read about Freston the Magician they consult the Penal Code and conclude that I'm one of those "magicians, who raise evil spirits by means of magical books and dire imprecations, leaders of corrupt and impious sects, and members of all superstitious associations in general?"

And what of all those even more horrible punishments that weren't mentioned in the Ch'ing Dynasty Penal Codes? Like strapping someone tightly to a cross facing east and cutting off his eyelids so that when the sun rises he will go painfully blind? Help! Or forcing a tightly bound naked man to sit squarely on the sharpened tip of a bamboo that can grow several feet within 24 hours? Heeeeeeeelp! Or what about how they used to send men to a room they called the "Silkworm Chamber," because newly hatched silkworms and recently castrated males both needed a heated room in order to live? A eunuch! Jesus Christ Almighty!

Naturally all agreed that Ah Q had been a bad man, the proof being that he had been shot; for if he had not been bad, how could he have been shot?

—Lu Hsun's *The True Story of Ah Q*

I check my trouser pockets for the fourth time. Wait a minute, what about my *shirt* pocket? Yes! I find it! I find it! My eyelids are safe!

I wipe sweat from my forehead and begin stuffing clothes, books and sundry items back into my luggage. As I finish, the train is pulling into Changsha, and Cham Yen helps me with my luggage, shakes my hand, and wishes me luck. "You will find Peach Blossom Spring," he says.

Changsha

From the train platform to the front of the station is a journey through a long, dimly lit tunnel. At this time in the morning all is surreal and strange: disembodied voices, strange smells, faces made grotesque by flickering lights and dark shadows, something out of the ninth circle of Dante's *Inferno*. In 1868, an American geologist, Raphael Pumpelly, managed to reach Changsha by boat but the inhabitants refused him permission to land and he had to turn back. Indeed, the residents of Changsha managed to prevent foreigners from entering the city until the end of the 19th century. A typical account tells of a foreign traveler arriving on a steam-launch: "The students beat the wooden fish and assembled; they upset the soup-cauldrons so that if any would not join the demonstration neither should they eat…they went to the governor and demanded the expulsion of the foreigner." My fate is less dramatic: people are staring but at least no students are upsetting soup-cauldrons and no one is shooing me away.

I throw my bags into a taxi and tell the driver a hotel name, a name I found in a guidebook as being new and clean and reasonable. The book said it also has a western cafe as well as a Chinese one; this is important because if there is one thing I have learned while traveling in China it is that I do *not* want to start the day with a bowl of beef-blood congee with white cubes of bean curd floating in the reddish broth. It always reminds me of the remains of swimmers attacked by sharks in the movie "Jaws."

The driver warns me that is not a good hotel and the road is being torn up. We cannot even reach it. I should go to a better hotel. In my travels in Asia, I am used to taxi drivers getting kickbacks from certain hotels, so I insist on that hotel but, for once, a driver was telling the truth. The road is being widened and is all torn up. The hotel is all right but not one of Changsha's best. The small, poorly lit, lobby is deserted, mysterious and just a bit spooky – a scene from a novel written by Stephen King based on the writing of Lao Tzu. Worst of all, as I will learn in the morning, the western café is closed.

People appear seemingly from nowhere. In China, people always seem to be appearing from nowhere. Anyway, I am checked in. My room is small but relatively clean. On the dresser I find this:

The Sobering Peppermint Spray

Initiate at home; beware of imitation. Xiamen Leixin Industrial, Ltd. produces a high biological and technological product which has been reaching international advanced level. It can get rid of the odors in one's mouth and it provides fragrant smell and moist throat. It is necessary for all drivers, shareholders and writers. *Ingredients*: High quality tea, peppermint, natural essence, fragrant liquid, organic sugar.

I have no doubt the Sobering Peppermint Spray does all it claims to do but, as a writer, I cannot help but wonder why writers and shareholders and drivers were singled out as especially in need of this product. Did someone do some testing and find that writers and shareholders in particular have halitosis? How was the testing carried out and how many writers were in the test group? And did the test include *all* writers and *all* genres, both fiction and nonfiction, both romances and mysteries, both Nora Roberts and John Grisham?

But it is now nearly four in the morning and all I want is a shower. After which as I reach over to turn out the light my hand brushes a 6 inch by 4 inch box beside my bed. It has a photograph of a muscular but gayish looking Chinese boy about 20, naked except for a pair of tight, white briefs.

Men's Health Briefs

Specific - It is a traditional replacement designed specially for sound men with many effects on health. It can swiftly absorb and evaporate the remains of urine and sperm and sweat. It can keep the skin of private parts dry and well-ventilated, and prevent the accumulation of odor-causing dirt and prevent or treat infection of the skin. Keeping penis clean is the most effective measure to prevent penis cancer. Wearing close-fitting it longterm in the light of demand, you can get advantage of shrinkage of phimosis.

Directions: Place your penis between the low front of briefs and the P-S spacer (if you have Phimosis, withdraw it). Facilitate the extraction of your penis through either opening formed by the low front and the P-S Spacer.

Not being a doctor, I am not certain if I want to take "advantage of shrinkage of phimosis" or not, but as I drift off to sleep I realize my room is a virtual cornucopia of interesting and healthful items all carefully selected for my benefit.

I am woken in the manner many travelers to China are woken. A phone call about 7:30 in the morning asking in rapid Chinese for someone who must have checked out the day before. The fact that this is constantly happening in every hotel in every province makes me wonder if China is full of scam artists who are always one step ahead of their customers. Perhaps the caller is calling to complain about the unexpected results he obtained when using Men's Health Briefs or the Sobering Peppermint Spray. I can't tell because he is using the local Changsha dialect which even native Chinese mandarin speakers would not understand. I mumble something in mandarin about his having the wrong number. He hangs up. From the street below I hear the sounds of construction. That I could hear outside my East Village apartment.

I briefly check the TV to see what's on. The game on a children's program consists of several adults arranging themselves on the floor in the form of a Chinese character while a bunch of excited kids try to guess what the character is. The kids never miss but what bothers me is that the characters are the *simplified* characters to which I have taken a personal dislike. Yes, I know it takes years to learn the traditional, more complicated characters, but at least many of them give clues to their meaning and sound. And over the centuries writing eventually achieved such refinement that calligraphy became an art form half way between writing and painting. It was said that Chinese practiced their characters to improve their character. The simplified characters look like the random scribbling of a demented eunuch who indulged in too much sobering peppermint spray. And, as I constantly point out to Chinese on the mainland, no Chinese uses short forms (well, at least none outside of the 1.3 billion Chinese in China).

(Of course, it is only fair to point out that the complicated and difficult classical language underpinned the ruling classes in China in that the overly worked peasants had no time or opportunity to learn the complex characters let alone the endless classical allusions a scholar was expected to know. But who wants to be fair?)

Across the street from my hotel, a construction worker is 24 stories up on bamboo scaffolding, balancing dangerously while putting up some advertising bunting. His daring act reminds me of nothing so much as a sailor moving precariously along the ropes of a tall ship, desperately trying to furl sails in a squall. He steps out onto a huge Chinese character which I notice is also a simplified character. There are fewer strokes in the simplified character he is on than in the traditional one, making it more difficult for him to get into a safe position; and it occurs to me that if he falls to his death, that will be good ammunition in my campaign to convince the Chinese to abandon the simplified characters and return to the beauty of the traditional ones. However, not one to oblige arrogant foreigners with agendas, he finishes without falling, leaving me to find other, less dramatic, examples of why simplified characters should be discarded.

From my window, it is already obvious that Changsha, a city of almost six million, is vibrant and bustling. Not, perhaps, when compared with Beijing or Shanghai, but vibrant nonetheless. The early morning sunlight reflects intermittently off the yellow safety helmets of workers atop several buildings, as if sending coded signals, and cranes are perched on top of buildings in all directions. It is almost impossible not to feel that this is a city with money to spend. This sense of a vibrant city was reflected in the notes of travelers nearly a century before. William Geil described Changsha as "one of the best in China. It presents few of the usual features of narrow alleys with noisome smells and poor lights, and the houses are well-built and well-kept, while the people are vigorous and alert. From coolie to philosopher, every class seems self-respecting and dignified."

The Xiangjiang River runs through the entire province of Hunan, and Changsha, about a hundred miles from the Yangtze, owes much of its prosperity to its location on this river and to the fertile plains surrounding it. Geil writes of how "valley after valley has its own dialect, differing in both idiom and pronunciation, and in the streets of Changsha may be heard a Chinese Babel."

The city is well situated for export but is especially known for its manufacturing, such as machine tools and aluminum products, and, across the river, Hunan University specializes in geology, mining and metallurgy.

It is also an old city, one which has existed in one form or another for 3,000 years and was once the capital of an independent state. On a hill across the river, a youthful Mao Tse-tung observed the fall scene and wrote his poem describing the future he wanted for China: "A multitude of mountains and rivers will be as red as the forest below...." The city also boasts several sites connected to the life of Mao including the Hunan No. 1 Teachers' Training School where a teenaged Mao studied and then, in the early 1920's, later taught. It was in the beautiful and unspoiled hills of Hunan that a young and penniless Mao traveled about as recorded in the book, *Mao Tse-tung and I were Beggars*. And, of course, the house in Shaoshan in which he was born is less than three hours by train.

The street my hotel is on, *Wu Yi Lu*, or, May 1st Road, runs from the train station to the east all the way to the river in the west, dividing the city into north and south. Now the capital of Hunan, Changsha was rebuilt since it was practically razed to the ground in fires during the devastating battles of World War II. And now those buildings are in turn making way for taller, more modern skyscrapers.

I well realize the Mao era is over in China, but that knowledge doesn't quite prepare me for the elevator music which, incredibly, during a hot, humid summer, consists of a medley of Christmas carols including "Frosty the Snowman," "Rudolf the Red-nosed Reindeer," and "Santa Claus is Coming to Town."

After a futile search of nearby streets and alleys for a restaurant serving what might be described as a western breakfast, I enter a small Chinese restaurant. Although I am told they do have a western selection, the so-called western breakfast entries are few and uninviting and to quite an extent unrecognizable. However, my eyes light up when I spot a bowl full of lichees, known in Chinese as *lichih*. There are certain fruits in Asia which can make even the most grueling trip bearable. In Thailand, for example, who could resist the delicious pulp of the rambutan or the combination of mango and sticky rice with coconut sauce? And in China, it is the lichee that revives the tired traveler's spirit. Its bright crimson color, its delicate scent, its succulent crispness and its rich sweet flavor make it irresistible.

On the table, the leathery outer covering has been removed and the translucent white fleshy pulps of the fruit are piled up in a bowl. As far back as the Han Dynasty (221 B.C. - 220 A.D.) China's poets were praising the lichee. The most famous story of the lichee is how during the T'ang Dynasty (618 - 907 A.D.) the emperor Ming Huang set up a seven hundred mile hang-the-expense relay system to ensure that his imperial concubine, Yang Kwei-fei, would have fresh lichees. As the famous poet, Tu Mo wrote, "The red dust rising as the swift horse arrives brings a smile to the face of the Imperial Concubine; she alone knows that the lichees have arrived." This extravagance was no doubt partly responsible for her ultimate fate – strangled by a red sash of silk at the foot of Ngo Mei mountain. A tragedy written up over the centuries in poetry, plays and film: "Heaven and Earth will one day end; but this unending sorrow will last forever."

A pudgy waitress with her hair pulled back into a braid passes by carrying a set of circular bamboo trays containing steamed pork buns. I compliment her on the lichees.

Me: "This is really wonderful!"
Waitress: (suspiciously) "What?"
Me: "I didn't expect lichees for breakfast!"
Waitress: "What lichees?"
Me: (pointing) "There."
Waitress: (pouting) "Where?"
Me: "In the bowl."
Waitress: "Those are melon balls."

I place a few pieces of the round white pulp on my plate and take a bite. So they are. Melon balls a shade of white so lichee-like that, without my reading glasses on, I saw what I wanted to see. The waitress gives me a look as if to say "If you can't tell a lichee from a melon ball you probably can't tell your ass from a hole in the ground." Then she sets the bamboo trays down and walks off no doubt to tell her friends about the crazy long-nosed foreign devil who thinks he's getting lichees for breakfast. (Who does he think he is – Yang Kuei-fei?) Well, OK, but I never claimed to be an expert on Chinese fruit.

I head out for the Xin Hua Bookstore, hoping to find a few dual-language editions so I can improve my Chinese. There are none. But they have a collection of maps including one of Hunan Province and I buy one. The salesgirl seems a bit old for her Lolita-braids and smiling-panda blouse but she does try (unsuccessfully) not to giggle while serving a foreigner. As I shall soon learn, the farther west I travel in Hunan, the more giggles my presence will provoke.

I cross the street to the Friendship Store. Near the door women customers are sitting quietly while waiting for the heavy layer of white facial make-up on their faces to work its magic, and earnest clerks stand ready to ambush and spray whoever walks in with whatever is inside the containers they hold. Once a quiet backwater for tourists who needed a carved soapstone mountain scene or an embroidered silk pillow cushion, Friendship Stores have evolved into a kind of down-market Bloomingdales. The only foreign faces I see are on advertisements for Esprit, Pierre Cardin, Yves St. Laurent, Santa Barbara, Polo and Racket Club.

As in Japan, there are young women stationed at the escalators to welcome customers. Unlike those in Tokyo, however, these women are obviously not worried if the customer knows how bored they are with their jobs. From experience, I know that most of the clothes and anything else in this kind of store will be too small for me, so I quickly make my way to the top floor and, before leaving, mosey over to the liveliest corner of the store – the game department.

A rotund mother and her equally rotund young daughter are playing a game in which each time two crocodiles make their way out of their caves, the mother and daughter hit them on the head with rotund rubber hammers. Each time the hammer connects, the crocodiles emit a peculiar pain-filled cry of agony and slowly retreat back into their caves. The mother and daughter seem to enjoy the game immensely. Whether or not there is some kind of behavior displacement going on here, I don't know. Bop – agghhh! Bop – agghhh! Bop – agghhh!

The scene reminds me of my two boxes of rubber toys I bought in Hong Kong in 1971. They are Cultural Revolution toys of Little Red Guards sitting on the head of an American Military Policeman and when the toy is squeezed the Little Red Guard hits the MP on the head with his fist. Having had some run-in's with military policemen in the Army, I liked what I saw. Twenty years after I bought them I took some to Sotheby's auction house in New York, certain that Sotheby's would confirm that these cultural items from a past era were now worth their weight in gold.

Me: "These were made for Chinese children during the Cultural Revolution."
Sotheby's: "Were they made for tourists?"
Me: "No, no, I bought them at Commercial Press, not China Arts and Crafts."
Sotheby's: "They're interesting, it's just that we have no market for them."
Me: "No market?"
Sotheby's: "We don't sell items we can't place a value on and we have no market for toys from the Cultural Revolution."
Me: "So what should I do with them?"
Sotheby's": "Hang onto them. They will definitely be worth something some day."

Great advice if I were getting younger every year.

Two teenage girls about 15 or 16 dance on platforms in front of a game screen which flashes the word "Danger" every time they make a wrong step. It's not clear to me how the game is played but games like these were not created to be understood by anyone over twenty. Both girls have wholesome faces with pretty pigtails and red cheeks, the kind of girls once seen ubiquitously on propaganda posters all over China with Red Guard slogans urging everyone to be vigilant in the war against moribund, decadent, bourgeois, Capitalist imperialists.

But as both move uninhibitedly about in their clinging dresses they reveal every post pubescent curve of their bodies. A mind less pure than mine might see them as sexy and erotic but fortunately, "Purity" is my middle name and the thought never occurs to me. Despite their best efforts and extremely fast dancing, the screen lights up to tell them they failed. They laugh and step off. As I head for the exit, I pass by the mother and daughter still engrossed in their tussle with the crocodiles: Bop – agghhh!

While I am in Changsha I decide to visit the Hunan Provincial Museum, the local university and the Martyrs Shrine. But first I have to go to the China International Travel Service and make sure I can book a train to Changde. Assuming there is a train to Changde.

I jump into a taxi and find that the driver is a woman. I love women taxi drivers. Women taxi drivers anywhere in the world are always fun to travel with and they usually bring good luck. Kind of like a rabbit's foot. In Beijing I fell madly in love with one named Autumn Orchid and invited her to New York where we could paint the town red, so to speak. I gave her my card but I haven't heard from her yet. That was 1996. Maybe she lost it.

Me: "Hi, there. How are you today?"
Cute Chinese Taxi driver: "Good. Where do you want to go?"
Me: "Lotus Hotel. You know it?"
Cute Chinese taxi driver: "I'm sorry, that is zone two."
Me: "Is that bad?"
Cute Chinese Taxi driver: "I am a zone one taxi."
Me: "So you can take me to hotels in zone one?"
Cute Chinese taxi driver: "Yes."
Me: "So what hotels are in zone one?"
Cute Chinese taxi driver: "T'ungch'eng (Dolton)."

Me: "OK, let's go there."

✔ *Peach Blossom Spring Note Number One:* When in a Chinese taxi with a cute woman driver, if she cannot take you to your destination, change destinations.

To my way of thinking, there is nothing shameful in rearranging one's schedule to be with a good looking woman. In my career, I have to this end changed not only destinations but even political philosophies. Where I grew up in Groton, Connecticut, whenever a submarine was launched, the Citizens Anti-Communist Committee of Connecticut would picket across the street from the Committee for Non-Violent Action. Not having anything better to do, I would pick up a sign that said something like, "Better Dead than Red," and stand with the anti-Communists facing off against the pacifists.

But then I noticed the women in the Pacifist group had long black hair framing oval faces and long, loose-fitting, clothes and seemed almost, well, *Asian.* And so it was that one day I put down my "Better Dead than Red!" sign and, much to the disgust of the anti-Communist group, walked across the street and picked up a sign that said something like, "Unilateral Disarmament Now!" It was the smartest thing I ever did. Not only did they invite me up to their farm in Voluntown for supper but one of the young women there taught me how to use the Chinese *Book of Changes,* the *I Ching.* And since, despite my apostasy, we still managed to win the Cold War, I don't see that any harm was done.

Anyway, I begin a conversation with the driver and learn that she is Mrs. Ch'en, married with one child and that Chinese in the cities can have one child while Chinese in the countryside can have two. I also notice the plastic, red-and-gold, good luck charm with red tassels and tiny bells and Chairman Mao's picture hanging from the rearview mirror. I ask her if she likes Chairman

Mao. She laughs and says Mao's picture hanging from the mirror helps to avoid accidents and even to avoid financial problems. When alive, Chairman Mao formulated and implemented wacky policies that killed about 30 million people and caused disastrous financial problems in China, but now his image has become retro-cool, not to mention commercial, and his picture is on charms hanging from automobiles all over China. In life, he was a disaster; in death, his image is considered auspicious. What's wrong with this picture? I want to tell Mrs. Ch'en that Chinese are inscrutable but I can't remember the Chinese word for "inscrutable."

When Mrs. Ch'en asks me what I am doing in Changsha, I tell her about how I will search high and low in China's mountains and valleys and caves and caverns and leave no stone unturned while trying to find Peach Blossom Spring. When I finish I ask her what she thinks of my plan. She says it sounds good but it's going to be hot and I should drink lots of water. Mrs. Ch'en is obviously the practical type. I tell her that if she were single I would invite her to go with me. She laughs again and studies me in the rear view mirror. She says she doesn't have enough days off. I catch her looking at me again in the mirror. I begin to suspect Mrs. Ch'en may avoid foreign passengers in the future.

As we pass through the streets, I try to get a sense of the city. The traffic is chaotic, the drivers don't know how to drive, the bicyclists don't know how to bicycle, the pedestrians don't know how to walk. No one seems to look before acting. It is as if they think they are in some kind of game and if anything goes wrong they can start over. Bop – agghhh! Traffic in other Asian cities is bad but it has a rhythm to it; not here, although there are almost as many women riding on the backs of motorcycles as in Bangkok.

Whenever I travel, I try to look at women not as sex objects but the way other women look at them, i.e., clothes objects – what are they wearing. A male travel writer has to make a determined effort at describing how women dress, and not knowing much about women's dress, it is therefore one of the hardest things for me to write about. But as the women on bicycles and on the backs of motorcycles pass by, I make an important discovery. Although at first glance their legs appear bare, many of the women are actually wearing flesh-colored socks up to just above their ankles, no doubt for protection against dirt.

✓ *Peach Blossom Spring Note Number Two:* Find out if *Vogue* or *Women's Wear Daily* needs a stringer in Hunan Province.

As I figured, having a woman driver proved lucky. The T'ungch'eng or Dolton Hotel is the best hotel in Changsha, and had I not changed my destination I might never have found it because it is so new that guidebooks and maps don't have it listed. Not only that, but they have an Internet room or "Interwang" or "wangba" as the Chinese say, "wang" meaning net. They also have a game room, bowling alley, recreation room, snooker room, and a coffee shop full of waitresses dying to learn English. I didn't know it at the time, but with one night's exception, I would not be seeing a foreign face for seven days.

In a men's room I come upon the most modern urinals I have ever seen. There is without question a urinal gap between China and the United States. There are two lights on the urinal, a green "power" light and a red "sensor" light. As I crowd up to the urinal, they blink. I feel as if my groin is getting a cat scan while I whiz. The truth is that this ultramodern urinal contrasts so greatly with the street urinals I have used in China that the difference is almost a metaphor for the uneven pace of development in China.

Outside the hotel, the inner street is crowded with over one hundred Chinese enjoying western ballroom dancing. There are young couples, middle-aged couples, old couples and several women practicing their dance steps with one another. In some cases, the steps seem to be a cross between Chinese *t'ai chi* and western dancing. During the Great Cultural Revolution such activity would have no doubt resulted in serious consequences. I have seen this in other Chinese cities but whenever I come upon it, it still strikes me as being delightfully incongruous.

At the Martyrs Shrine I meet two Chinese students whose Hunanese-accented mandarin is almost unintelligible. I mention that I have seen the Martyrs Shrine in Nanjing as well and ask if those are the same people being honored. They say they are not. Here they were killed by the Kuomintang, there by the Japanese. Chinese history is full of martyrs and if the losing sides in all battles and wars could erect their shrines as well, there might not be enough room for them in all of China.

The nearby Hunan Provincial Museum is known for its exhibition of treasures from the Mawangdui tombs found on the outskirts of Changsha and especially for the well-preserved 2100-year-old female corpse of the Western Han dynasty excavated from the ruins. There are robes "as thin as a cicada's wing," embroidered silks, musical instruments and weapons, painted coffins, cosmetic boxes and carved figures. But it is this woman that people really come to see: "The body is moist and rich in fat under the skin and its tissue still maintains a certain elasticity."

But she has been pumped full of formaldehyde and her open mouth resembles nothing so much as a scream and her facial expression suggests a horror beyond anything Poe ever imagined. I notice that her internal organs have been removed and preserved and placed on rather ghoulish display, and I feel like a voyeur at the apartment of Jack the Ripper.

I head upstairs and roam through a small exhibition of painting and calligraphy. Over the years, I have learned many legends about Chinese who spent their lifetimes practicing such refined art forms. There was the ancient painter, Chang Seng-yao, who did not dare paint in the eyes of the dragons he drew as he said it would then be so lifelike it would awake. When ordered to do so by the emperor, Chang did paint in the eyes and the dragon spread its wings and flew off into the sky. As for calligraphy, it was said that Zhong Yao of the Wei Dynasty would enter his bathroom and become so engrossed in contemplating calligraphy that he would often forget to come out. (Chinese sources are unclear as to whether or not he went blind from contemplating calligraphy in his bathroom.)

Wang Hsi-chih would become so engrossed in his work that he often neglected to eat. In more modern times, the famous calligrapher, Weng Tong-he, was thrown into prison where a vengeful eunuch, desirous of his calligraphy, gave him squares of toilet paper only after making him write "I need to go to the bathroom" so he would have some samples for his collection.

As for paper, itself, about the time T'ao Yuan-ming was tending his garden, a writer living in Luoyang had his work copied to such an extent that again and again its popularity raised the cost of paper and, even today, every Chinese can quote the expression, *Luoyang chih kuei* or "the price of paper is soaring in Luoyang." (If this book becomes a runaway bestseller, Americans will say, "the price of paper is soaring in America.")

As I exit, three Chinese women at a table hand me a Chinese brush and ask me to sign my name in their guest book. I tell them that my calligraphy is horrible, and Chinese can always tell when I write something that it was written either by a Chinese child or by a foreigner. But they insist and I write my name in Chinese. They act as if I have just invented the wheel and give me a bottle of water. I'm not certain if that is a consolation prize or if every visitor receives a bottle of water but the heat and humidity are getting to me so I am pleased to take it.

I have had serious problems in the past in Asia with heatstroke and so I relax under some shade outside the museum and quickly finish off the bottled water. The first incident in a long series of incidents was when I arrived in Bangkok with the Army Security

Agency in 1966. I had been in-country no more than two days when I began to collapse. I was put in a van and taken to a local hospital where I was immediately treated for VD. Of course I didn't have VD, I hadn't been in Thailand long enough to do anything that might have resulted in VD, but medical personnel always assume that a GI who has been sent to a hospital must have VD because everyone knows GIs don't get heart problems or kidney problems or hernias, etc., so it must be VD. The treatment was successful (since I didn't have it anyway) and I was sent back to my unit. But, not having any wish to visit a Changsha hospital (they might assume all foreigners must have VD), I try to stay cool.

Yuelu Academy, now part of Hunan University, is across the river and into the trees, so to speak. The river bridge stretches over an island which has given the city its name, "Long Sand," or Changsha. The Yuelu Academy is one of four famous ancient academies in China. It was founded in 976 A.D. during the Northern Sung Dynasty and in 1903 transformed from a school of Confucian learning into one which offered modern subjects on its curriculum and then in 1926 into Hunan University. It is a wonderful place to roam about in and some of the beautiful calligraphy was written or carved by great scholars and even emperors. But whenever I visit something like this I can't help wondering how much was destroyed by Mao's Red Guards and then later restored. It may be that they left this place alone; it may not be. Nothing in the official literature mentions the Red Guards and those now running the place are, to put it mildly, keeping their own counsel.

The academy prepared scholars to sit for the Imperial Examinations. I have always had great admiration for China's traditional dynastic educational system. It was partly responsible for stultifying their way of thought and leaving them unprepared to deal with western ideas and encroachments, and it was not open to women, slaves, boat people, embalmers, criminals, actors, etc., etc., but, whatever its flaws, it was a system which *honored learning.*

In an America which worships people with the IQs of dying breadfruit trees simply because they can throw balls through hoops or kick balls into nets or hit balls over a fence and which scorns the learned as "egg-head professors" in "ivory towers," it is difficult to imagine a society in which special riders on the fastest mounts galloped to the villages of those who placed highest in examinations and posted notices of honor on the door. And while American presidents call and congratulate the quarterbacks of winning football teams, in China, for those who succeeded at the highest level of learning, triumphal arches were built in their home villages.

I linger at the Academy, sitting on an ancient wall, while listening to an unseen musician playing an *er-hu,* a kind of two-stringed violin, and trying to imagine how the world looked through the eyes of these scholars during the dynastic cycle when the written word was so revered that there were special receptacles in which to discard writing – written and printed characters which would eventually be burned in special brick-lined containers. A world in which civilian mandarins were held in far greater regard than military mandarins giving rise to the saying: "Good iron does not become nails; good men do not become soldiers."

Whatever the faults of their system, I cannot help but be envious of the beauty and wisdom of their civilization and, although no expert on Chinese culture, I know just enough to understand and, more importantly, to *feel* how, in the eyes of a mandarin official, westerners would have indeed appeared as barbaric, uncivilized savages who knew nothing of the *Book of Rites* and *Confucian Analects,* or the Way of the *Tao* and the *Book of Mencius.* People who crudely grasped one another's hand when meeting, whose women walked openly and shamelessly beside their men arm-in-arm, and whose huge, ungainly noses were like those of demons from the underworld. And the huge *unbound* feet of their women who no doubt wore those bulky crinolines to hide deformed bodies! And their barbaric eating utensils that resembled some sort of exotic weapons, and their custom of separating animal meat from bone *at the dining table* rather than preparing it before serving. People so wicked and so blasphemous toward the ceremonies and traditions of their own lineage that they actually left their country of birth while *their parents were still alive.* And the people in the Land of the Flowery Flag (later *Meiguo* – Beautiful Country – America) whose emperor stepped down every four years to live among the common people only to be replaced by another!

I love to see photographs of the old walls that once surrounded Chinese cities but most of the walls are long gone. Changsha's wall is no exception but a small section is still standing within the city itself. It is now known as the Tianxin Pavilion and its crenellated walls are decorated with colorful flags. Inside the walls are a few antiquated cannon and several clusters of old men playing Chinese chess. There is a small park and, long before I reach them, I can hear the *er-hu* players and their lady singers. I find that they are almost all late middle-aged or elderly practitioners of traditional art forms. The er-hu players sit on small wooden seats with their instruments resting on their left thighs, and playfully and expertly run their horsehair bows over the two strings, imitating everything from excited ducks to quarrelling concubines to gusty winds in a tower. I have seldom seen Chinese in China enjoying themselves as much as these people obviously are and I linger awhile.

In the 1800's, the sound of the two-stringed er-hu was the most detested sound to foreign travelers in China, and they spared no effort to convey to their readers the horror of this instrument's affront to western ears; but I have heard er-hu players from China inside the subway station under New York City's Times Square play with such melancholy beauty that even the muggers were moved to tears.

As I walk through the park I am assaulted by a deafening din;

the stridulation of what must be an incredible number of over-sexed crickets. Which is strange because I thought crickets only did their thing in the evening. And this is where I shall share a little known secret: Travel writers are divided into two groups – those who know the difference between crickets and cicadas and kadydids and those who don't. Of course it goes without saying that I am in the latter group. But I do know that the male cricket rubs his wings together to create a sound that attracts the female, and, to attract *his* female, the male cicada rubs his wing against his abdomen or his antenna against his backside or his leg against his thorax or something like that (and anyone nerdy enough to know what a thorax is can kiss mine) and anyway who in their right mind cares about the sexual lives of bugs anyway?

Much of my knowledge of China comes from my study of past dynasties, particularly the late Ch'ing period, and when traveling in modern China such knowledge almost always proves useless. What I have learned about crickets and their habits is no exception. While it is true I don't know exactly how they make their racket I do know that (according to a Ch'ing Dynasty source) I can find out the day's temperature by counting the number of chirps the field cricket makes in 15 seconds and adding 38. The problem is: how do I know if these are "field" crickets or some other kind of cricket simply passing through? And once I come up with a figure out in the field, how am I supposed to find out if it is correct or not?

The same Ch'ing Dynasty source also says that to determine the number of field cricket chirps per minute, multiply the temperature by four and subtract 160. Excuse me, but why the hell would anyone want to know the number of field cricket chirps per minute? At a time when Manchu officials had their pick of beautiful Manchu women and gorgeous Chinese concubines, they were meandering about in the woods trying to find out how many times a minute field crickets chirped. No wonder the Ch'ing turned out to be the last of the dynasties: the Manchus had obviously wigged out.

(Other than their unhealthy interest in crickets, Manchu officials spent much of their time trying to decide how many blows of the rattan someone would get for committing various crimes, such as, "quarreling and fighting within the imperial palace," "marrying female musicians and comedians," "shooting or throwing missile weapons toward an imperial palace," "defacing or destroying the marks with which thieves had been branded," and "murder, with an intent to mangle and divide the body of the deceased for magical purposes." Officers of the government who frequented the company of prostitutes and actresses received sixty blows of the rattan. Now you know why your mother warned you to beware of actresses.)

The last site I visit was suggested by one of the waitresses in the coffee shop of the hotel. It is called Windows on the World and is a long taxi ride past tall buildings and then nondescript housing and then small ricefields but when I get there it looks like a deserted Disneyland-on-the-Cheap wilting in the enervating heat. I believe it is the one owned by the popular Hunan Satellite TV, a station which dared to offer people the lively, racy, fun-filled and propaganda-free shows they prefer; a decision which has made it the most profitable television station in China. Regardless of who owns it, I stay in the taxi.

That night, due to the oppressive humidity, I cut my stroll short and sit at a small bar in a lounge/coffee shop of the Lotus Hotel. Bars in Chinese hotels are often right out in the open, as part of a coffee shop or lobby lounge. They are very unlike the dark, moody, atmospheric, smoke-filled bars in the States wherein one can get quietly and nobly drunk, and stare back at one's face in a beveled mirror framed between bottles of Maker's Mark and Wild Turkey. To say the least, Lawrence Block's Matt Scudder would not feel at home in what passes for a Chinese bar; there are no "sacred ginmills" in China. The inviolable seclusion taken for granted by all habitues of American barstools simply does not exist. It is difficult to fondle mellow, whiskey-flavored musings, to nurture gin-flavored self-righteous resentment or to caress vodka-flavored what-might-have-been's in lobbies full of chattering tourists, screaming children and bright, white fluorescent lights. Perhaps in China, anything introspective is suspect: Turn up the lights! Drinking wine beneath the gossamer moonlight until one enters into a creative rapture, or drinking whiskey beneath a flashing Rolling Rock sign until one enters into a lethargic stupor: different strokes for different folks.

The bartender and his lady cashier and I have long conversations about everything from the Cultural Revolution to American movies to Chiang Kai-shek's military mistakes. Our conversation is interrupted by the only foreigners I will see for some time: eighty-one American practitioners of *shaolin*, both young and old, who are touring China to show the Chinese what they can do. Well, what they can do is get sick and throw up on yak butter in Tibet which is what they did do. All have the exact same shirt on with a dragon across it. Rick from Colorado hands me a namecard with three Chinese characters on it which translate as "shaolin west." He mentions that his wife is involved in the adoption of Chinese children.

I know there has been some criticism of the thousands of Americans who arrive in China to adopt a Chinese baby but I mention to Rick that there used to be in China something called "baby towers." Nineteenth century travelers to China wrote that they first knew they had come upon one because of the unmistakably repugnant odor. These towers often resembled small pagodas with dug-out pits underneath. People would come to leave their unwanted children (usually girls, of course) or else children who had died before one year old and were therefore not considered a person. In some cases, baby girls were abandoned in the open to be adopted by passersby or to starve. The people who abandoned them were often "kind" enough to affix the infant's personal eight Chinese characters of birth to their clothes so that the child would not inadvertently be matched in marriage with someone having an incompatible horoscope.

In his beautifully written book on China, *On a Chinese Screen*, W. Somerset Maugham describes the type of tower in which people placed the unwanted child in a basket and lowered it by rope into the pit below; people too considerate to roughly throw the child down, but cruel enough to allow it to starve to death. Maugham too was confronted with the odor of putrefaction.

Fortunately, baby towers are long gone, and today it is a choice between growing up in a Chinese orphanage watching adults arrange themselves into simplified Chinese characters or growing up in an American family watching the "Sopranos" and "Sex and the City." Although, for female babies, the modern counterpart of the baby tower may be the ultrasound test to determine the baby's sex. Parents desperate for a son, and who can have only one child, might be willing to bribe a back-street doctor for an abortion. Practices such as this have actually led to a shortage of women in certain remote areas of China which, in turn, has led to women being kidnapped and forced to travel to those remote areas.

The shaolin practitioners are far more daring than I am in that they are flying about China on local planes. This despite a picture in the paper of one which recently crashed killing all on board. Eventually they go off to dinner and, under the influence of a few beers, I mention to the bartender that before I hung up my sword for good I was known as the First Sword Under Heaven. I then begin throwing a great deal of nonsense dialogue right out of Chinese martial arts movies which, as a young man, I would line up to see in American Chinatowns. Unfortunately, those areas of Chinese I am most fluent in are precisely those which are most useless when traveling. In my student days in San Francisco and Hawaii, I loved watching Chinese swordfighting movies, always bloody, always bizarre, but always with lovely Chinese women in traditional tight Chinese clothing. "The Ice Snow Maiden," "The One-Armed Swordsman," "Dragon Inn" – I saw them all. And so I became fluent in expressions such as, "Twenty years ago, you murdered my mother and father, and now I will have my revenge!" "I am known as The First Sword Under Heaven!" "How dare you speak to the Iron Fist Without Sympathy in that tone of voice!" "If you think the Goddess of Mercy will save you now, you can forget it!" "Kill them all!" Slash-and-gurgles, as we used to call them.

The bartender says that the reason Rick and the other shaolin practitioners didn't kneel to me was because they didn't realize I was the First Sword Under Heaven. The cashier picks up the drift and says that had they known who I was the shaolin people probably wouldn't have dared even speak to me. One thing I'll say for the Chinese: they know how to humor a drunkard.

We talk about the famous people who were born in Hunan, including Ch'u Yuan, the tragic poet who committed suicide over 2,000 years ago thereby beginning the tradition of the dragon boat races, and Tseng Kuo-fan, the 19th century Confucian scholar, general and mandarin official. Tseng was born not far from Changsha and it was he who built modern arsenals in China and did his best to modernize the country. He and his Hunan Braves were about the only Chinese with courage and training enough to fight the Taipings during the Taiping Rebellion of the mid-19th century.

The bartender speaks of how the communists portray the Taipings as early land reformers fighting against a feudal society. Of course, the communists seldom mention that the Taipings were also fanatics who practiced a bizarre form of Christianity and who destroyed every Buddhist and Taoist temple, prostitute and opium-addict they came across. But the bartender tells me a long and interesting story about how the much-feared Taiping armies surrounded Changsha and how they packed gunpowder in coffins under the city wall and ignited it. But the wall held and after nearly three months of siege, the Taipings finally gave up and moved on.

When I ask the bartender if he realizes that more people died in that conflict that in any war in history with the exception of World War II, he comments that I seem to know a great deal about the Taiping Rebellion.

Of course I do: As with cowboys and Indians, I had no particular interest in who won, but tended to side with the Taipings because they had all female units of beautiful, young Taiping women known as the "silken armies." They wore gorgeous uniforms of silk or satin, no doubt looted from Hangchow and Soochow, and just the thought of them riding their hardy China ponies through the Chinese countryside makes me wish I'd been a young man during the time of the Taipings. I know damn well which side I would have been on.

The entire time I have been in the bar, a waitress has made occasional and half-hearted attempts to chase a wandering sparrow out of the lounge and back out the door. Out of the corner of my eye, I have noticed the sparrow staring in my direction. I find this of interest because a mandarin scholar named Chia Yi was banished to Changsha about 200 years before Christ. (I don't mean to indicate Christ was banished from Changsha, I mean, hell, you know what I mean.) I don't know what the scholar was banished for but he was already in ill health when a hoot-owl flew into his house and perched near him. Chia Yi took this as an ill omen, even one suggesting death of the master of the house, and wrote a poem which, in its opening, implores the owl to let him know the meaning of his arrival. Two thousand and nineteen years later, Edgar Allen Poe wrote of his own travails when a raven flew into his studio. He too demanded answers. Unlike Poe's raven, Chia Yi's hoot-owl didn't even bother to respond with an enigmatic answer. Real writers get owls and ravens; I get a fucking sparrow.

But the sparrow reminds me of my visit to the Poe House in Philadelphia, when I noticed they had a beautiful statue of the raven outside. I mentioned to the folks running the place that I really liked their statue of the Maltese falcon. That's when I found out that Poe people aren't any more fond of a jocular sense of humor than clerks in Barnes and Noble.

Having seen the sights of Changsha on the first day, on the afternoon of the second, I decide to check out the billiard room of my own hotel. I get off on a floor and follow the signs and enter a nightclub. The rooms are fairly dark and in a creepy, cavernous room several young Chinese women are watching an American movie on a screen. The place looks more like a dungeon but a woman in charge leads me through the club, down a dark hallway to the billiard room the door of which is actually *chained*, not just locked. (What don't I know about this hotel?) The tables are set up for English snooker, not American pool, so I thank the woman and return through the nightclub. I pass a heavily made up young woman about 20 whose cherry red lips part to reveal the tip of a pink tongue after which she gives me a very sexy Mae West-style "Hello."

I still need to buy my train ticket to Changde. As always, anyplace mentioned in the guide books has moved but I finally locate the office near the railway station on a street being torn up and widened. It may seem strange that within throwing distance of the train station, I am willing to pay a travel agency a bit more to buy my train ticket for me. However, if one sees the long lines and feels the heat inside the station, one understands.

The "travel office" consists of one small room in which four young people are sitting behind a long table. There are a few faded posters of Hunan tourist sites on the wall and a water cooler that seems to be leaking water all over the floor. Nothing else. I explain what I need and they quote a price. I agree and wait while someone bicycles over to get my ticket. When I give the woman my name she asks if I have a Chinese name. The three characters I use for Barrett are "Bai Rei De." When she sees my name, she smiles and says in broken English that she saw the movie I was in.

Me: "What movie?"
Girl: "Um...
Me: "A recent movie?"
Girl: "Um...
Me: "Was it a funny movie?"
Girl: "Um...you know, he had a mustache too; like you."
Me: "Oh, *that* movie. The one where a guy had a mustache. Sure."
Girl: "Um...Gone with the Window!"

She is so pleased that she remembered the movie title I decide not to correct her. But as my mother always taught me honesty is the best policy I have to say right up front that I did *not* exactly appear in the film, "Gone with the Wind;" however, Clark Gable's name in the film was Rhett Butler, transliterated into Chinese with characters exactly as mine: Butler Rhett, Barrett, *Bai Rei De*. I may not be a Clark Gable look-alike but I am a Clark Gable sound-alike, so there.

The ticket arrives, I am given a not-too-informative pamphlet on Hunan Province and I head back to the hotel. It will soon be my last evening in Changsha and I have to say that the nightclub of the hotel looked godawful but in an interesting way. Should I actually go there and as the only foreigner sit in a dark, dingy, club just to see what goes on? Whenever I travel, I always try to ask myself one question: "What would Paul Theroux do in a case like this?" No doubt about it – he would check it out. (If I understand his travel method correctly, Paul basically checks out dark corners of places he visits as a way of confronting the dark corners of his own soul. Or did I dream that?)

During the afternoon, I spend the day retrieving my e-mail at the Dolton Hotel's Interwang and then reading some newspapers in their business center. The China Daily is an English language newspaper published in Beijing. It is usually pretty boring and always full of carefully composed articles about the proper use of the Internet in China as well as bubbling-over-with-enthusiasm stories about the wonders of joint ventures, but it's getting better. I find this entry in the classifieds:

> Young Chinese girl, good English and education, sweet, beautiful, IT business, would like to meet single overseas Chinese gentleman, Asian or Western, engaged in IT business preferred.

An article mentions that it is now illegal to collect, sell, process or export *fatsai*, a kind of vegetable, because it is over-picked and overpriced. Chinese have been demanding high prices for this sand-fixing plant because in Chinese "fatsai" sounds like the expression "getting rich." Chinese take their homonyms very seriously indeed as anyone can attest who has seen the astronomical prices Chinese pay at Hong Kong auctions for license plates with numbers considered to be auspicious.

Another article mentions that the name of Viagra in Chinese has been changed from *wei ge* ("strong man") to *wan ai ke*, an expression which has no meaning. The government hopes this will correct the common misunderstanding among the thousands of men who line up for it and who mistakenly believe that Viagra is an aphrodisiac.

But as I skim the rest of the paper, I come upon an article and photographs that make me want to jump out of my chair. The article is about a farmer in Shensi (pinyin: Shaanxi) Province who happened to see a televised version of the famous Chinese novel, *Romance of the Three Kingdoms*. The author of the *Three Kingdoms* took great liberty with history but did base his material on the warfare and warriors who lived during the Three Kingdoms period (A.D. 220-280).

Similar in a few ways to Arthurian legends or even more to our own American cowboy era, it was a very short period of time but a period which gave birth to a myriad of legends of great men and daring deeds. Chu-ko liang, the great military strategist, Ts'ao Ts'ao, the talented but evil enemy, and, of course, the three heroes and sworn brothers of the Peach Garden – Kuan Yu, Chang Fei and Liu Bei. Kuan Yu would over many centuries be elevated by emperors into the Chinese God of War, a fierce, bearded, red-faced god whose shrine is often found in restaurants and shops throughout China and in Chinese restaurants abroad.

The article says Mr. Guo is attempting to recreate the *muniu liuma*, "wooden oxen and running horses" which, according to the novel, Chu-ko liang invented. These were a kind of wooden mechanism in the shapes of oxen and horses which could walk automatically and therefore assist in transporting military supplies. "Guo believed in Chu-ko liang's wisdom and decided to try and reproduce the ancient robotic mechanisms, after careful study and countless experiments." This inspired Chinese farmer has turned part of his farm into a workshop, and enrolled in study programs to learn about physics and mechanics. So far, each of his oxen and horses can carry loads up to 165 pounds and run forward, although only when pulled by men. Guo is still attempting to make them walk on their own.

But the sentence that pops out at me is: *"Even though some take it as a product out of the novelist's imagination, Guo thought of it as a fact."* And I realize I have found a like-spirit; a madman, an eccentric, a crackpot, a Chinese Don Quixote. I am searching for a utopia described in Chinese literature 1600 years ago and this eccentric Chinese farmer is trying to reproduce a technique found in Chinese literature 1800 years ago. Guo Tongxiao can also be described as tilting at windmills and possessing a mind "crazed by reading;" as one whose "overexcited imagination blinds him to reality."

The article puts me in a high-spirited mood for the rest of the day and, come nightfall, I am ready to try out the dark, dank, mysterious nightclub in the bowels of the hotel. I get off the lift about 8:30 and head for the nightclub. A well dolled-up woman with cheeks sprinkled with glitter greets me with a sultry Lauren Bacall smile and leads me into the rear of the large room where men and women are watching a man play a lute of some kind. Not what I expected. Even more surprising, rather than seat me, she continues to lead me through the large room, down a hallway and into a small room. It is easy to follow her: her glitter glows in the dark.

The room has a TV set and video, a "No Smoking" sign on the door and (this being China where last year they smoked 1.7 *trillion* cigarettes) an ashtray on the table. The woman smiles and leaves. There is silence all around me. There are two microphones on the table. I have a horrible feeling I am in for some karaoke. I have never been to karaoke as I always thought of it as a place where drunken businessmen go to make fools of themselves while singing to girls who, for a price, show great appreciation for their talent. Now it may be my turn.

I see what looks like a popcorn container in the corner, the large bucket size the salespeople in the movie theaters like to push on you and with which you get a free soft drink. I could use some popcorn about now. I pick it up and read the English side of the "popcorn" container.

Filtering Fire Self-Rescue Respirator
(Filtrating fire escape Breath Salvator)
RZL-15 Filtering fire self-rescue respirator is a personal self-rescue helmet from fire that can prevent smoke and toxicant. It is suitable for hotel, restaurant, supermarket, cinema, nightclub, sky crapper (sic) and larger scale transport facilities. The standout character is that the Respirator can becombined with other mask with the technician's direction.

So where is the technician during a fire? Under "Attention" it says: "It can't be used in which the density of the oxygen is lower than 18 percent." How do I know what the density of the oxygen is if a room is filling up with smoke? And what I really don't like about the Filtering Fire Self-Rescue Respirator is that the fourth and last line of directions says, "Select the road and run."

I light up a local *Baisha* "White Sand" cigarette, "manufactured by Changsha Cigarette Factory, Hunan," and decide that somehow this combination of "no smoking" sign on the door and ashtray on the table sums up modern China better than any long, erudite essay.

Then the door opens and a young woman in a white sweater and white slacks enters the room and says, "Hello!" It is the Chinese version of Mae West I passed by previously. Her name is Miss Hu and she is nibbling from a black lump inside a small transparent package which she says is a chicken leg. It looks more like beef jerky run amuck. The hostess reappears behind her with slices of water melon and asks what I would like to drink. I ask for Chinese Tsingtao beer and am told they have Budweiser. Obviously, some Budweiser representative has done some hustling and bustling here in Changsha.

The girl sits beside me and says other than "hello" she speaks no English. She says she is from Hengyang, another city in Hunan, and when I ask her why she didn't take a job there, she says she would be too embarrassed to do nightclub work in a city where her family lives.

I have heard this kind of thing many times before in China: young people working in nightlife entertainment industries far from their homes in areas where they are not known. Most often, they seem to be working in the next province over. This is a growing phenomenon which I don't think western observers of China have paid enough attention to: that everybody in China will soon be working in the next province over. We have bedroom communities; China has bedroom provinces.

While I talk with her, I decide to raise the subject of the disappearing Chinese woman. I explain that, as so many families still prefer sons, newborn females are often abandoned or fetuses aborted. Hence, not surprisingly, there aren't enough women to go around and so many are now being kidnapped and sold to lonely farmers in remote areas. Miss Hu tells me she has heard of this but no one she knows has been kidnapped. (She tells me this while painstakingly reapplying her lipstick, a chore made necessary because Lilliputian bits of cherry red lipstick rubbed off on the dark black chunks of beef-jerky-like chicken now being assaulted, besieged and bombarded by ravenous digestive juices somewhere inside Miss Hu's belly.)

Without further ado, Miss Hu picks up a remote and begins fussing with the video. She asks me what songs I would like. I see they have both western and Chinese songs. I choose a few including Bill Haley's "Rock Around the Clock." She begins with a Chinese song which she sings along to. I drink my beer. She encourages me to sing to "Rock Around the Clock." I start to sing and then notice the subtitles. It has been a long time since I heard Bill Haley and the Comets sing "Rock Around the Clock" but I am quite certain the line was "put your glad rags on and join us, ho, we're gonna have some fun when the clock strikes one." What I see on the video is "put your red flags on."

I try to picture the harassed Chinese translator assigned to doing the subtitles listening dozens of times to the song trying to make heads or tails out of what Bill and his friends are singing, and finally giving up in frustration and going with the old "red flags" line. It might not be accurate but it is safe. It is true I have a terrible memory, but if kids dancing on Dick Clark's American Bandstand had worn red flags, I'm sure I would remember it.

The door opens again and Miss Hu's sister enters. She is wearing a white sweater and short white skirt. She is 22 years old and has apparently decided to come see how her younger sister is getting on with the foreign-devil. She sits beside her sister and sings along to a horrible version of a Taiwanese love song. Next, a shockingly youthful Dustin Hoffman appears on the screen in scenes from "The Graduate" and the two Miss Hu's and I sing along with the "The Sounds of Silence," or at least our East-West acculturated version of it.

Then I notice there are songs listed from the Cultural Revolution and I ask Miss Hu to program a few of those. When they come on, I happily sing along with "East is Red" and other favorites of the 60's (at least in China). The sisters seem to know the words to modern pop songs much better than those of Cultural Revolution songs. But in these old films I see wonderful scenes of Mao and his colleagues (some now in disgrace) and am fascinated not only by the historical footage but by the fact that a quarter of a century after the Great Helmsman's death, a Capitalist running dog is sitting with two pretty Chinese sisters drinking beer and eating watermelon slices and singing along to his (now) funky lyrics such as "Chairman Mao's Thoughts are like a Never-Setting Sun." Yes, history does repeat itself as farce, but I'm not certain this is what Mao had in mind and, above all, is all this really going to help me find Peach Blossom Spring.

After a few more songs, Miss Hu's sister opens the door to leave. Miss Hu hears something outside in the main room and quickly asks for ten *renminbi* (about US$1.10). I give it to her and follow her as she scampers out to the nightclub. On the floor of the nightclub people are throwing foam dice the size of cardboard boxes. After each throw, the crowd expresses its approval or disappointment. Miss Hu runs into the crowd, picks up a die and throws it. She loses. I decide it is time to go and I pay a very reasonable amount for a pleasant if somewhat bizarre evening. The woman and Miss Hu have a quick exchange in Changsha dialect which I don't understand, but I believe they are discussing whether or not the foreigner will be taking the lady home for the night and the general feeling is no he won't be but that's OK. I had no plans in that direction to begin with but the thought of the beef-jerky-chicken lumps ensconced inside Miss Hu's digestive tract being forcibly transformed into nutrients solidifies my decision.

I say goodbye to Miss Hu, the well dolled-up lady with sparkling cheeks leads me out, and I return safe and sound to my room. I take a sleeping pill to ensure a sound sleep. Tomorrow is the train ride to Changde. And two hours south of Changde is Peach Blossom Spring.

Changde

The train from Changsha leaves for Changde at 7:58 in the morning and will take five hours. On this train I sit beside two passengers and across a short table face three more passengers. Fortunately, I have a window seat and can look out. The five passengers around me are students in Changsha heading back to their families in Changde for a visit. The two girls are quite pretty which makes sense because Chinese say Hunanese men and women are very attractive, which is true, and the Hunanese believe the Tujia minority women in western Hunan are very attractive, which I shall in due course also find to be true.

At one point, one of the students asks to see my ticket. I show it to him. Although it is only 37 *renminbi*, about four American dollars, he shows me his ticket which is exactly half that price. He apologizes for the fact that China has charged me a "foreigner's price," and asks me if in America that is how we treat visitors. I tell him we charge everyone the same but we get back at foreigners in our own way, such as making them listen to the speeches of Hilary Clinton.

As always, I am asked if I am married. As always, when I say I am divorced, I am asked how many children I have. As always, when I say no children, Chinese look a little surprised and ask why. Over the years, I have tried to come up with the perfect answer to this question, but other than blaming my ex-wife, I have found nothing that satisfies them. It seems having children, especially a son, has been so important in China for so many thousands of years that even modern Chinese find it difficult to relate to someone who might not want to have a child. I have been toying with the idea of making up a family for myself, based on old reruns of "Leave It To Beaver."

Across the aisle, a dark-complexioned woman with a tired, haggard face lifts up her simple blouse, clearly revealing her pendulous breasts, and begins breastfeeding her baby. This most natural of acts causes an immediate change in the atmosphere. The students are uneasy and somewhat embarrassed, but the peasant-types in other booths around us are not. It is as if the act of breastfeeding in public has revealed different stages of development between classes.

Eventually, one of the students gets up the courage to ask me what I am doing on a train in the middle of Hunan province. I explain about how I am searching for the real Peach Blossom Spring but will first check out the one for tourists near Changde. And then proceed from there.

They discuss this among themselves for some time then seem to reach a conclusion. One of the girls says that if such a hidden community does exist in some remote spot, it would most likely be in the misty mountains of Zhangjiajie, in the western part of Hunan. At first, trying to pronounce "Zhangjiajie" is a bit like asking a Chinese to say, "Bob's black-backed bathbrush," but as I practice saying it, I check *Lonely Planet*. It says, Zhangjiajie, part of the Wulingyuan scenic area of Northwestern Hunan, "offers some of the most bizarre mountain scenery in China." Yes, that is certainly a possibility.

At Changde they get off the train with me and all but one takes a bus to their final destination. They wave goodbye as if to an old friend and I find myself sorry to see them leave. The boy who showed me his ticket price insists on helping me by getting me a taxi and taking me to the hotel. As I know nothing about Changde, I am happy to have his help. He takes me to what he says is the best hotel in the city and we enter the lobby. Although the hotel doesn't look like much, immediately I realize it is the right choice because the plaque behind the reception desk says, "Assigned Reception Hotel for the 8th Asian Canoe Championships and the 2nd Youth Canoe Championships."

Inside my room, I unfold my map of Hunan and indicate to the student where I plan to go.

He advises me not to go to certain areas and to stay on the main roads. Staying on the main roads is not the way to find Peach Blossom Spring and I begin to wonder if this isn't yet again one of Freston the Magician's men, or perhaps Freston himself in disguise. But the boy has gone out of his way to help me so I unpack the bottle of red wine given to me by the assistant manager of the Kowloon Hotel when I missed messages and meetings because of the faulty message board in my room no doubt caused by Freston the Magician. The boy says he will give it to his father. I thank him for helping me and he leaves.

I shower and head for the revolving restaurant to get a view of the town. During the half hour I am there, I seem to see exactly the same scene so if the restaurant actually revolves it is certainly the world's slowest revolving restaurant. From up top I spot the Yuan river, once the main thoroughfare from the hills of western Hunan to the plains. Logs floated down this river to Changde and then to Changsha, and junks with exotic sails carrying cotton and salt and "tong oil junks" with high prows and square sterns crowded the river.

The rivers in this area stretch out from the Tungting Lake to the northwest and like so many lakes and rivers in China the Tungting once boasted a magnificent spectacle of Chinese junks. In 1868 Albert Bickmore wrote in the *Royal Geographical Society Journal*:

As far as the eye could see before us and behind us and for several miles on either side the surface of the lake was perfectly feathered with white sails, some in sunshine, some in shadow, and some in the dim distance apparently gliding on a thin film of air over the water. Twice I counted nearly 440 boats in sight at one time, and with the aid of my field glass fully 100 more could be distinguished. Many were loaded with tea, many with coal, and many were just swimming along under huge deck loads of round timber.

I try to imagine the dreamlike quality the river must have had as exotic junks with magnificent sails passed by the high walls of the city. Now there are very few boats of any kind and the walls are gone. Not for the first time when contemplating the beauty of a lost China, I feel a kind of *Weltschmerz* descend upon me.

And then I remember it was along a stream from this very same river that the fisherman in the story came upon Peach Blossom Spring. And, as suddenly as it came upon me, my sense of depression at the loss of China's past glory dissipates, and I feel the smug excitement of a hunter who has his long-sought quarry in sight. I can see a park near the river that looks interesting but the town looks a bit boring. From below, it will look worse.

Downstairs I ask a friendly bellboy if he can arrange a car and driver for the two-hour drive to Peach Blossom Spring. We set it for 11 o'clock the following morning.

Inside the park by the river, elderly men and women are shouting in unison as they exercise. The day is extremely hot and humid and I find it difficult to walk very far but there they are moving energetically about like young people. For whatever reason, the park doesn't open out to the river and I walk back through it, sweat running down my face. An elderly man is sitting on a bench, arms at his sides, legs crossed, apparently delighted to broil in the sun. He has very alert eyes beneath bushy white eyebrows and his intense gaze follows me as I walk. He asks me in mandarin where I am going. I tell him back to the hotel; it's too damn hot. Then

I ask him how he knew I could speak mandarin. He says, "I can see it in your face."

This is the third time traveling in China that someone has told me that. I suppose the truth is that they simply assume because I am alone without any guide I speak the language. Still, it is interesting to hear that my mandarin-speaking ability, such as it is, can be seen in my face.

✓ *Peach Blossom Spring Note Number Three:* When traveling in China, if people often look at you and assume you speak Chinese, ask your mother for more details about your father's ethnic background.

When I return to the hotel, although it is still early evening, already businessmen-types are gathering in the lobby with young women from a nearby nightclub and heading for the elevators. I have a quick drink and then force myself to walk around the town. Most Chinese towns are not built to be walker-friendly and in the height of summer even a walk around one long Chinese block can be exhausting.

Mao's picture is hanging in some of the shops. But so are more traditional Chinese couplets. I walk through a noisome market-place displaying bloody carcasses and animal entrails and come upon a sign with a drawing of a dog that says, "Live Dogs." I'm not sure what they do with those live dogs but I have a hunch they won't be live for long. Hundreds of frogs in baskets stare out at me from beneath wire mesh and the odors of the marketplace, enhanced by the stifling heat, make me almost dizzy.

I walk to the river but no craft of any description is moving upstream or downstream. Nearby is doubtlessly the most modern street in town: a street lined with shops offering clothes for the young. The western names are big, the Chinese shops are small, and there are very few people about in the heat. I enter one just for the sake of enjoying a bit of air-conditioning, chat briefly with a Chinese man and woman, neither of whom has been to Peach Blossom Spring, then cross the street to buy yet another bottle of water.

Near my hotel are four-story apartment buildings, obviously new, set one after another like a row of toy blocks. In Changde, these new buildings are probably considered a wonderful place to live, but the small areas of lawn appear as lifeless and deserted as the architecture is tasteless and unimaginative. Unlike Changsha, there are almost no sounds of construction; what sounds there are here are traffic noises. The wide road in from the train station is lined in part with trees and boasts several modern roundabouts but the attempt to glamorize the main road makes the rest of the rather shabby town seem even more depressing; like an aging demimondaine with a slash of bright red lipstick. Changde is a very old town which seems somehow to have given up any real attempt to modernize. At least during the hot season.

One of the few things I do like about Changde is the quiet and peaceful setting. It is obviously a safe town for travelers; a town in which one can be reasonably certain nothing much will ever happen. (Less than two months after my stay in Changde a branch of the Agricultural Bank not far from my hotel will be the scene of what the *South China Morning Post* will call "one of the bloodiest and most spectacular bank robberies in the history of communist China." Eleven men and three of the gang leader's "mistresses" will eventually be executed for a Bonnie and Clyde-type, five-province crime spree in which 28 people were murdered.)

On my way back to the hotel, I spot what appears to be a clone of McDonald's called Mekinmu's. I walk in the door and enter a large and quiet room, similar to a McDonald's but without all the bright colors. There are only one or two customers and a few children playing on some large wooden toys in the far corner and a few employees in red-and-white striped uniforms. I order a soft drink from the clerk, a pert young woman with an abundance of hair pulled back in a bun. She has what traditional Chinese poets described as "apricot eyes" as well as "moth eyebrows," i.e., similar to the gracefully curved antennae of that insect. And the same poets would have praised her teeth as being "even and regular like melon seeds." She asks where I am from and I tell her.

When I sit down at a table, she leaves her post and sits down facing me. We converse in mandarin and a bit of English. Her name is Miss Pong. She is 20 years old, the daughter of a rice farmer and she hopes one day to become a private secretary. She gets up at 6 every morning to go to school, then at 5:30 she comes into work at McDonald's, sorry, I mean Mekinmu's, and works until midnight.

Miss Pong is very pretty and, as we talk, one thing is very clear: Miss Pong is not simply interested in practicing her English; truth to tell, Miss Pong is a flirt. And Miss Pong obviously enjoys being flirtatious. Which is OK with me because, as Kurt Vonnegut asked in his novel, *Jailbird*, "And what is flirtatiousness but an argument that life must go on and on and on?"

Although I have seen no other foreigners in the town, Miss Pong says there are two young foreign male English teachers at her school. I wonder how they and their raging hormones deal with this gorgeous, coquettish creature without going out of their minds. Perhaps they wear Men's Health Briefs and take advantage of shrinkage of phimosis. Perhaps they take cold showers. As I will soon find out when I head farther west, most people in western Hunan take cold showers by necessity, including me.

In traditional Chinese culture there are five signs of a classic beauty: cheeks as red as the almond flower, mouth like the bloom of a peach, eyes bright as autumnal ripples, a waist as slender as the willow leaf, footsteps like the flowers of the water lily and hair as black as a raven's wing. (Actually, that always seemed like six to me but perhaps the Chinese Ancients counted differently.)

Miss Pong definitely has cheeks as red as the almond flower and a mouth like the bloom of a peach. Her eyes certainly sparkle the way a pond does when the winds of autumn blow across its surface. Her waist is as slender as a willow leaf, at least the ones I've seen in Brooklyn Botanical Garden. Her hair is as black as a raven's wing although the damn bird that keeps me awake in New York these days is a crow, not a raven, so I can't be positive. It's just the part about the footsteps like the flowers of the water lily that I'm not sure of.

And then I realize something else about Miss Pong: she is not simply flirting; she is testing the potency of her burgeoning sexual power. She is at the age when she is passing from girlhood into womanhood, and she has that fascinating mixture of lingering uncertainty and growing confidence in her ability to attract men, and there is no doubt this young enchantress enjoys testing her charms on an American male, even one old enough to be her father, and then some. Still, this being Asia, age differences don't matter so much. And, after all, Dante was head over heels in love with his Beatrice when she was 9 and Petrarch went gaga over his Laureen when she was 12. So by the standards of several great love affairs, this succulent soubrette is already over the hill. Still, do I really want to be known as the Humbert Humbert of Hunan Province? The Woody Allen of Wulingyuan? The Don Quixote de la Mancha who transformed into Don Juan de la Mekinmu's?

In Changsha, a coffee shop waitress thought I was 40. Miss Pong guesses my age to be 30. I notice that the farther west I travel in Hunan, the younger people think I am. I set out trying to find Peach Blossom Spring and have apparently found the Fountain of Youth instead.

Miss Pong studies and works from early morning until midnight with only one day off a month and I can only hope that, rather than wasting her youth, she is at least using that one day wisely, such as having a roll in the rice with one of the local lads.

As I'm thinking this she smiles just enough to reveal her dimples-to-die-for and asks me what type of woman I like. The truth is I always wanted to have an affair with a woman like the one Bret Harte described in *The Luck of Roaring Camp*: "Cherokee Sal...Perhaps the less said of her the better. She was a coarse and, it is to be feared, a very sinful woman." And of course I have often fantasized over the woman described in the immortal words of Raymond Chandler in *Farewell, My Lovely*: "I like smooth shiny girls, hardboiled and loaded with sin."

Or perhaps a tryst with Khubla Khan's niece Khutulun, who wagered one hundred horses that she could out-wrestle any man. According to Marco Polo, she accumulated ten thousand horses and never married. At San Francisco State College during the student riots of the late 60's, we would have called Khutulun a 'far out chick'. But I skip all that and simply tell Miss Pong the God's honest truth: that, like my paladin Paul Theroux, I have always been fascinated by the beauty of Chinese women. She looks away and glances back at me.

In the 17th century erotic classic, *The Carnal Prayer Mat*, Li Yu describes a woman's glance flashing "as vividly as lightning amid the mountain crags." Indeed, as far as lightning amid the mountain crags goes, this Hunanese Lolita is the sensual counterpart of *The Perfect Storm*.

As Miss Pong effortlessly and expertly flirts like some Chinese version of Scarlett O'Hara, I try to imagine what it would be like to be married to a beauty like this and to live in the States with her. I try to picture the two of us pulled off the highway somewhere near Santa Monica, facing one another across the tacky green-and-purple imitation marble tables of a Taco Bell, she munching on a Big Beef Burrito Supreme and me tucking into my "crispy, flaky, chewy, tasty" Nacho Cheese Chalupa, while tapping our feet to the latest Rap sounds and casting occasional glances at the kids crying nearby because their daddy (busily digging into his Double Decker Taco Supreme) won't buy them a talking Chihuahua and a Dr. Pepper.

Or perhaps we could live in Manhattan where Miss Pong could buy her tank tops and jeans from Screaming Mimi's, eat her burgers and fries at Stingy Lulu's, get her body piercing and tattoos done on St. Mark's Place, and enjoy a cappuccino at the Pick-Me-Up Café while watching East Village crazies being arrested across the street at Tompkins Square Park.

Or we could live in a small southern town and enjoy countless hours of pushing shopping carts through endless aisles of irresistible ambrosial temptations at Winn-Dixies and Walmarts, then head out for our favorite video store. In the beginning, during her adjustment period to American cultural values, it might be best to start Miss Pong off with something of an uncomplicated even vacuous nature, something like *Dumb and Dumber* and *How Stella Got her Groove Back*, and a bit later maybe even pick up a copy of *Hannah and Her Sisters*. (Much later, when I think she's ready, I'll introduce her to the "adult" section of the store and pick up a copy of *Hannah* Does *Her Sisters*.) We'll make a video/feast all-nighter of it and start our very own Munching Marathon greedily devouring oodles of Kellogg's frosted strawberry pop tarts ("free pop-tarts carrying case with two proofs-of-purchase"). Wearing very few clothes indeed, we'll sprawl comfortably on our luxurious latex (made in China) waterbed devouring Nabisco's Teddy Cheddy baked cheddar crackers, Pringle's nutter butter bitys peanut butter sandwich cookies and Comic Blaster's chocolate crème cookies "with exploding candy bitz!" Once we've polished those off, we'll ratchet ourselves up to a new plateau, a totally wired, sucrose-induced, junk-food high, diligently working our way through bags, bowls, boxes and cartons of Laffey Taffey, Twizzlers, Munchos, Zonkers, Crazy Dips, Twinkies, Pinwheels, Hohos, Ding Dongs, Devil Dogs, Zingers, Ring Dings, Yodels, Funny Bones and Snowballs. And we'll wrap up a never-to-be-forgotten grand finale by pigging out on mammoth-sized dollops of Blue Bunny's "fat free brownie fudge fantasy frozen yogurt."

I don't see how an intelligent Chinese lady from a remote area of Hunan province could fail to be attracted to a man who can offer her a chance at obtaining a much coveted green card and a pop-tarts carrying case and an unlimited supply of Cap'n Crunch's crunchy chocolate flavored cereal. Even at the height of the Ch'ien Lung emperor's glorious reign, it never got better than that.

I think of friends I have known who have planned their lives carefully, worked two jobs to put children through college and sacrificed to make a decent living for their families; and here I am in Hunan province – no jobs, no kids, no family, no plans whatsoever except, God willing, to have a romp in the rice with Miss Pong, to find Peach Blossom Spring, and to eventually present myself to the women in charge of the matriarchal villages and hope that if I am selected for duty as a copulation tool they have a nearby pharmacy where Viagra is dispensed without a prescription.

I speculate for a moment as to whether or not Miss Pong could serve as my chivalric ladylove, an essential requirement of any Don Quixote-type adventure. After all, in reality, Dulcinea del Toboso was but a hardy and simple peasant lass who had never even spoken to Don Quixote, so surely someone as lovely as Miss Pong could pass any chivalric quest for a worthy feminine ideal, Mekinmu outfit or no. Although, of course, Don Quixote rode about as a medieval knight-errant searching for adventure during his own modern time whereas I am a modern knight-errant searching for an idyllic community unchanged from ancient times.

My reverie is interrupted by Miss Pong who says she admires my plan to find the real Peach Blossom Spring and asks what I am doing now. I am showing enormous self-control in the face of great temptation, is what I'm doing, but I keep that to myself. I tell her I wish there were an Internet bar in town so that I could check my e-mail but the hotel people said there isn't any in

Changde. Miss Pong says she thinks there is one on the second floor of the building right across the street from my hotel.

That is good news indeed, but it is difficult to take my leave of Miss Pong. If I were a younger man I would say something to her like, "Excuse me, I don't mean to be rude but you are so beautiful that if you won't have dinner with me, I will drown myself in the Milo River like the poet, Ch'u Yuan, and they'll have to start yet another Dragon Boat festival for me as well." But I'm not a younger man and, besides, the need to check my e-mail is just strong enough to disentangle me from this *yin-yang* of sexual dynamics that Miss Pong's charms and my own weak nature have enmeshed me in. I thank her and get up to leave, but not before telling her that I will certainly be back to see her again. She walks me to the door and smiles. As Li Yu would describe that smile: "With ruby lips apart, (she) looks as pretty as a flower that understands speech."

I walk up the street and over to the building across from my hotel. It is now getting dark and there are few lights on the ground floor of the building. The building is like many of those in China – it looks as if it is being torn down or perhaps just being put up or perhaps it has been as it is since the Sung Dynasty.

I walk through a dark empty space and up some stairs to the second floor. I see some lights from a store of some kind. There are boxes of what seem to be computers in the windows. Several young Chinese are talking in the hallway outside the store. When they realize I am looking for an Internet cafe, they explain that this is where computers are sold or fixed but they will take me to where I need to go.

So I follow these people, three men and a woman, for several blocks through streets and alleys of the town. They ask if I have eaten and I say I just had a milkshake at Miss Pong's, I mean, Mekinmu's, and am quite full. We meet up with a friend of theirs, a Mr. Lau. They enter a small restaurant and say goodbye while I follow Mr. Lau down several more shabby streets and poorly lit alleys. It is now very dark, the narrow, dingy lanes are neither well populated nor well lit, and I no longer have any idea where I am or where this stranger is taking me.

Eventually, we come to a nondescript concrete building and walk up to the second floor. The stairway is dark and cluttered. I try to remain alert for whatever might happen. We enter a bedroom which has nothing but a bed and several posters of Western and Chinese guitarists and music groups on the wall and, in the corner, a computer. Mr. Lau leads me to the computer, turns it on, and tells me to go right ahead. Suddenly, "Windows 2000" appears on the screen which is about two levels ahead of where I am in New York with my Windows 95. During the 20 or so minutes I spend on the computer, Mr. Lau gives me a bowl of plums, a nice gesture but considering how sticky I get his keyboard, a bad idea.

A girl enters the room and I tell her how smart her brother is but I will learn later that she is the girlfriend of Mr. Lau's brother. When I am finished, Mr. Lau says his server is very cheap and absolutely refuses to take money. Then he invites me to dinner and we walk to a kind of house/restaurant with a few tables outside and with very little on the menu unless one likes very hot Hunanese food laced with peppers while sweating profusely in the oppressive heat out-of-doors.

Mr. Lau senses my discomfort and says he has a better idea and we hail a taxi. Within minutes I am once again outside Mekinmu's. Apparently, when it comes to Western cuisine in Changde, (I believe the Chinese characters for Changde mean "eternal virtue" – if so, Elvis has left the province) Mekinmu's is Spago's and Four Seasons combined.

We head to the counter and once again I am speaking with Miss Pong. Only now, with a third party present, we are on a more formal, polite basis. As most relationships move in the opposite direction, it is a bit awkward to pretend to know someone less the second time than the first time. It is as if we had engaged in an illicit love affair and her husband had suddenly walked in with me. And, come to think of it, how do I know Mr. Lau isn't her husband? It wouldn't be the first time I've been suckered by a pretty face.

Mr. Lau and I talk about China and America and the Internet. When I ask him how much time he spends on the computer, he smiles sheepishly and says, "very much, but it is cheap." I ask him what he likes best about it and without a moment's hesitation he says, "the freedom!" I think it is at that moment that I truly realize what a revolutionary invention the computer really is, and what an insidious threat it must represent to officials in a closed society desperately waging a losing battle to manage and conceal information.

Mr. Lau insists on paying for my meal and I foolishly ask for two pieces of chicken. He orders two wings for himself. In American dollars the price is inconsequential, but I realize the amount he paid would be about three times what he would have paid in the outdoor restaurant and I feel guilty about the money he spent. Probably half a day's pay for him. I give him my namecard and tell him I will lose face if he can't think of something I can do for him in New York.

Mr. Lau doesn't wish to leave China but he does hope to eventually work with computers in a larger city. While we talk my eyes water: even the fast food chicken legs have been spiced up to suit Hunanese tastes.

When we get up to leave Miss Pong accompanies us to the door. She politely asks us to come back again but, as Mr. Lau turns away to leave, she favors me with the same kind of smile as before. The kind of smile that Tadzio gave Gustave Aschenbach in *Death in Venice*, the one that made Von Aschenbach internally admonish Tadzio with, "How dare you smile like that? No one is allowed to smile like that!"

So that the reader does not reach the erroneous conclusion that I am the only traveler who has commented extensively on the beauty of Chinese women, be they imperial concubines or

Mekinmu clerks, let me quote Marco Polo on his 13th century visit to Hangchow: "The women of Hangchow show extraordinary expertise in beguiling men, and without effort can converse with people from all walks of life, so that men, once having been enticed by their feminine charms, become bewitched, and are so captivated with their beauty and allurements, that it is impossible for them to think of anything else."

Worse yet (or, better yet, depending upon one's point of view), even the emperors themselves were often much distracted by the beauty of their women. Again, from Marco in Hangchow: "The people of this land had neither interest nor ability in the arts of war; their pleasure was provided by women, and only women, and the most indulgent in this was the emperor himself, as for him there was nothing else but women...."

When I was a younger man I would have frowned upon such behavior. At that time, I admired the great Chinese and Manchu emperors who built great walls, dug grand canals, and sent out expeditions to conquer the "barbarians at the borders of the empire." Now that I am older, and have a better appreciation of the exquisite loveliness of Chinese women as well as how brief life can be, I completely empathize with those emperors who, surrounded by hundreds of Miss Pongs, seldom if ever got out of bed and quite happily left the empire to be run (and ruined) by the constantly scheming, bed-wetting eunuchs. If that is the classic case of an emotionally immature man afflicted by Yellow Fever then several Chinese emperors themselves had Yellow Fever. So if my hand has been caught in the fortune-cookie jar, theirs was there first.

I head back to the hotel and take a quick shower and read a bit before I fall asleep. The book is *Real China: From Cannibalism to Karaoke* by John Gittings. The author also traveled to Hunan and mentions that the late Shen Tsong-wen, a writer from Hunan, was criticized (no doubt during the Cultural Revolution) for praising the beauty of the Hunanese people, both men and women.

But the writer and translator Robert Payne wrote that "those who have been in Hunan can testify that they are as beautiful as he (Shen) has described."

During the Cultural Revolution, Shen Tsong-wen gave up writing and hid within his own Peach Blossom Spring by burying himself in the safe and sane world of museum cataloguing. I wonder what he would say if he had seen Miss Pong. In his novel set in Hunan, *Border Town*, he describes the type of women who wear "artificial silk tunics, flowered print trousers, and have long, arched eyebrows, and big lavishly scented chignons." (Sounds like the Chinese version of Cherokee Sal.)

But, strangely, I do not dream of Miss Pong or any of the four great beauties of Chinese history or of women with long, arched eyebrows. I dream of Chu-ko liang, the master military strategist of *Three Kingdoms* fame. I see him in the midst of one of his most famous tricks of all, "The Ruse of the Empty City." He is sitting on the wall of a city calmly playing a lute and burning a stick of incense. All the gates to the city are open. When the enemy armies arrive, they see Chu-ko liang and are aware of his reputation for caution. They are certain that he has hidden a great army inside the city and is trying to inveigle them to enter and be slaughtered. And so the armies retreat.

There was no army inside the city. It was one of Chu-ko liang's great bluffs.

In the morning, why I had this particular dream isn't clear to me. It soon would be.

Peach Blossom Spring

The next morning I decide to try breakfast at a local restaurant. The only breakfast available is Chinese breakfast. I order from a vivacious and sprightly waitress who says her name is Zooey although I doubt she has read J. D. Salinger. Zooey is unusually short and stares at me through a pair of glasses with very thick lenses. She likes practicing her English and she wants very much to go to America. The way things are going with my breakfast, *I* very much want to go to America.

There is a huge if somewhat tacky golden dragon at the front of the room, saccharine Taiwanese loves songs are playing over a scratchy tape machine, and most of the teenage waitresses are hiding behind pillars, giggling about having a foreigner in their restaurant.

The chairs are made in such a way that when I get up to get more food they fall over backward. It takes speed and timing and practice to get up, turn, reach out, and steady the chair before it falls over. Eventually I get the hang of it and I think I earn the respect of the waitresses; after all, it is not easy to master this skill.

Along a wall, there are watery glass tanks of various catches from the sea: crabs with pink strings still attached to their midsection are dancing about without a care in the world; shiny black eels are slithering between obviously dying fish; squids are jumping up and banging their heads against the glass as if trying to get out; curious lobsters are pushing and shoving and maneuvering against each other to get a front row seat against the glass – after all, how often do they get to see a New Yorker desperate for coffee and granola with fresh fruit eating beef congee and pork dumplings with soy sauce at seven in the morning and trying to make small talk to a young woman in a checkered uniform named Zooey who would love to get out of China the way the squids are dying to get out of their tank?

When I check out the Chinese buffet, I watch a middle-aged man speak (shout) into a cell phone with one hand, and ladle out pork blood soup into his bowl with the other. Without spilling a drop.

Back at my hotel I wait in the lobby until the bellboy informs me the car has arrived. I get in the back seat and we're off. The car is of Chinese make with a red, police-type cherry light on the top. When the driver finally gets off the cell phone, I introduce myself. The driver is a well-built, middle-aged man with a closely cropped haircut and certainly looks like a policeman but he turns out to be the manager of an automobile company in Changde. The car apparently belongs to a friend of his. I wonder if the fact that he has time to drive me to Peach Blossom Spring means business is slow.

He asks if it would be all right to bring his wife along. I assure him that would be fine. I'm always happier if a driver has someone up front to talk with because there is less chance he will fall asleep. We pull up in front of his house, his wife jumps in the front, and in no time at all we are on the yellow brick road to Peach Blossom Spring. The wife is chatty and I quickly learn that she and her husband are not going in with me as they've been there before but will wait for me outside. I tell her I may be quite some time. She tells me that is no problem. She hesitates and then asks why I didn't come when the peach blossoms were in bloom.

The drive is not a particularly picturesque one and some of the risks the driver takes seem almost suicidal but no more so than other drivers take as they barrel straight for us around dangerous curves. I lean forward to suggest to the driver's wife that just possibly they might want to actually use the seatbelts which I have noticed the car has for them. The suggestion is greeted with a smile of incomprehension.

The time passes quickly and at last I arrive; my goal has been achieved – after all this time, effort and expense, I am standing in front of Peach Blossom Spring. Or at least in front of several souvenir stands. I pay 50 renminbi (about US$5.50) and enter beneath the ornate memorial arch. I pass a sign announcing a "pink flower forest." The peach blossoms are of course not in bloom and as I walk through the trees I pass very few tourists. Anyone with any sense visited the area during March and April.

Eventually I climb a series of steps and I come across about two dozen men relaxing beside covered bamboo chairs with poles. The men are bearers and offer to carry me up the steep steps and around Peach Blossom Spring. At first I refuse; despite the enervating heat being carried in a chair might make me feel like a 19th century colonial. But they are insistent and complain of not having customers, and I remember in Hong Kong when the last few active rickshaw-pullers sat by the Star Ferry with their rickshaws they had placed a sign nearby that said: "Don't feel sorry for us; use us."

And so I climb into a chair, place my feet on the wooden rung, the bearers – one in front and one behind – lift the two long bamboo poles, and we're off. When I see the steep incline of the steps set into the hills I wonder if I have made the right decision:

Read all about it: *Bamboo pole breaks sending tourist tumbling to his death at Peach Blossom Spring! Police say they are mystified as to why he didn't come in March or April when the peach trees were in bloom.*

But bamboo is incredibly tough and the men are extremely surefooted and soon I am able to relax in the rhythmic sway of the chair. As we travel up and down hills and I occasionally exit to enter temples or to climb the steps of pavilions, I catch glimpses of distant rivers, any of which could hide the real Peach Blossom Spring. But despite the beauty of the rolling hills, the area does not seem to be the ideal place to hide a community. Construction of temples here began in the tenth century but it was only in the Ch'ing Dynasty reign of Kuang Hsu (1875-1908) that building was planned and carried out to approximate the poet's story. The area is usually divided into four: Taoyuan Mountain, Taoxian Hill, Tao Yuan Hill and the village of the ethnic minority known as Qin. I need to check them all.

At one point I spot an opening in the side of a bosky hill and ask the bearers to stop. I walk up above to the narrow entrance and a roly-poly, irrepressibly jolly woman appears, offering to rent me a flashlight. She looks like a wannabe salesperson who has just that morning completed a home study course on "how to make money in your spare time by renting stuff to foreign-devils." I take the flashlight and ask if there are any snakes inside the tunnel. "No," she says. Then when I have paid her her money and am well into the tunnel, I hear her say, "*Yehsyu you yeh yen.*" ("Night swallows, maybe.") Night swallows? That rings a dull bell. Right – it's time to play the favorite Chinese game again: "let's use a pretty word to describe not-so-pretty-things." Night swallows are what Chinese call – you guessed it! – *bats.*

But I'm determined to explore the area and, ignoring all rustling sounds overhead, I begin my crouched walk through the tunnel which eventually comes out to a clearing where I expect I might find the real Peach Blossom Spring. What I find instead are my bearers already waiting for me at a tea house. (They give me the same look that Trigger used to give Roy Rogers after a long, hot chase, i.e., "Why didn't you ask me; I could have told you where the shortcut is.") How they got there ahead of me perhaps only Freston the Magician can answer. This is said to be the tea house where T'ao Yuan-ming had his tea while enjoying the peach blossoms. That may be but the tea is the worst I've ever tasted.

I buy the bearers tea and refreshments and ask them if there are mountains and valleys in China, especially in Hunan, where no one has ever gone. They say there are many places like that. I explain my mission and ask them if they wanted to hide a community from the outside world, what part of Hunan would they go to. They mention the mountains of Zhangjiajie. It is beginning to sound like Zhangjiajie is the most likely place to hide a remote community.

Inside the first temple, someone asks me to write my "honorable name" in a book. I don't like the sound of that because in the East whenever someone wants me to write my "honorable name" in a book, it costs me money. It does here too. There will be more so-called temples where I will be asked to write down my "honorable name." Looking at the names and considering the suggested donation, I assume places such as these have two sets of books, one for Chinese and one for foreigners. But at least I learn from the woman working in one that there are no fewer than *seven* other places in China claiming to be the real Peach Blossom Spring.

In one temple, two elderly men begin to dress in Taoist robes to perform a ceremony for me but I explain I lived in Hong Kong for 17 years and have seen such ceremonies many times. However, we do have a lively discussion of Lao Tzu and the *Tao de Ching*, a classic I have not seen on sale in any bookstore in China.

At the ethnic village, there are no villagers, let alone tourists. I seem to be one of the very few visiting Peach Blossom Spring off season in the height of summer. But some of the traditional farm implements are on display including stone rice grinders which were once pulled by oxen or even by men walking in a circle. There are also chain water pumps sloping down into a lake and the chair bearers happily untie them and demonstrate how they work. With the larger types of these water wheels, men throughout China would place their arms over a horizontal rod of bamboo and use their feet to turn the wheels which in turn moved water along a chute up onto the fields in need of irrigating. These water wheels could transfer an amazing amount of water in a short period of time.

The treadwheels designed for punishing prisoners in England and even in Hong Kong's colonial prison were very similar in nature and men greatly feared them; only no one told the Chinese farmers that the English considered this type of wheel-turning to be an insufferable punishment so Chinese farmers didn't seem to mind using them in the least.

Later, as we sit drinking still more tea atop a hillside pavilion, I begin to appreciate the quiet beauty of Peach Blossom Spring. It is not a spectacular, untamed beauty, boasting large swathes of cloud-shrouded craggy cliffs; rather a series of rolling hills and shallow valleys covered with copses of pine and cypress, clumps of magnificent bamboo and lush green banana plants, with an occasional splash of yellow-tiled roofs amidst green trees, sloping gently toward the Yuan river in the distance. And seeing Peach Blossom Spring without the peach blossoms is like seeing a woman *d'une certain age* without her makeup.

I think of the enormous influence this poet had on Chinese literature. He has come to be regarded as China's first great landscape poet; a man loved for his character and behavior as well as for his poetry. Unlike some of the highly embellished poetry which had been in favor and would be again, T'ao's prose and poetry avoided flowery words, false emotions and, for the most part, learned references. The scholar, Liu Wu-chi, suggests the Chinese love this poet above all others for "his warm personal insights and the spontaneous flashes of his candid heart."

In the T'ang Dynasty, Li Po, Tu Fu, Wang Wei, Han Yu and Po Chu-yi all paid homage to the Gentleman of the Five Willows. In the Sung Dynasty Lu Yu, Wang An-shih and Su T'ung-po did the same, with Su T'ung-po even modeling one hundred and nine poems on T'ao's work. Lu Yu even insisted that poetry could not be learned without studying the work of T'ao Yuan Ming.

I think of this sensitive and well educated poet from a Confucian family in decline struggling to make a living during a chaotic and unpredictable period of China's long history; attempting to serve officials near home as well as generals in such far away places as Chien-k'ang (present-day Nanjing), the capital of Jin. And then eventually resigning and returning home to eke out a living on his farm, finding solace and joy in wine and nature and friendship. And, of course, in poetry. But while the poet praised his beloved wine for its ability to "conquer melancholy, prolong life and exalt the spirit," his five sons seemed to have disappointed him. It appears that not one of the five was interested in or capable of a "literary career." (The Chinese line might be translated as "no intellectual gift for paper and pen," or, as in Peter Tan's translation, "But none goes in for the writing brush.")

There are times when I read some of his poetry and find that Robert Frost is indeed the right poet to compare him with; at other times, when reading of his unconventional, Bohemian nature and his love for "filling his cup (of wine)," I would say Charles Bukowsky or Lawrence Ferlinghetti would be the closer in temperament and outlook.

References to him in other poems are often expressed in subtle ways: Li Ch'ing-chao, of the late Sung, regarded as China's greatest woman poet, alluded to T'ao in her poem in which she "drinks wine by the eastern fence." T'ao loved the chrysanthemums which grew by his eastern fence. Unlike so many flowers which bloom in spring, chrysanthemums are independent enough and hardy enough to bloom in the frost of autumn, and Chinese poets have often seen that flower (along with the pine) as a symbol of the unbending recluse, a man who spurned fame and glory to heed only the call of his cottage, his wine and his poetry. There is even a scene in Shen Fu's 18th century classic, *Six Chapters of a Floating Life*, in which his wife is stared at and interrogated by country folk prompting her to say that she feels "just like the fisherman who happened upon Peach Blossom Spring." And, in this lovely atmosphere, I reflect for some time on my journey in search of the ultimate unspoiled community, possibly real, possibly the product of a poet's imagination.

Chinese have long regarded the peach as something very special and T'ao was no exception. This "fairy fruit" symbolizes both marriage and springtime. In paintings one comes across the god of longevity holding the "peach of immortality" or sometimes emerging from it. The "fairy peaches" found in the garden of the Royal Lady of the West offer immortality to those who eat them (but they ripen only once every three thousand years so timing is crucial). Children were protected from evil spirits by the string of peach stones worn around their neck or by an amulet of peach wood. A type of chrysanthemum (no doubt loved by T'ao Yuanming) is known as "drunk with wine made from peaches of the immortals." Both Taoist priests and Chinese doctors place high value on the fruit, flowers, and bark of the peach. The brotherhood oath made by the heroes of *Romance of the Three Kingdoms* was made in a peach orchard. Pupils and disciples were referred to as "peaches and plums" and rosy cheeks of a lovely maiden were known as "peach cheeks." The head of the Eight Immortals is often portrayed holding a peach, and it was right here in Hunan province that a shopkeeper's daughter ate a supernatural peach and became an immortal. Problems with wandering spirits escaped from untended tombs? Just chop a branch from the east side of a peach tree, taper it as a wedge, and force the V-shaped wedge into the tomb. After this, no spirit will ever be able to leave the tomb again.

But my tranquil thoughts on peaches and poetry are interrupted by a small boy sitting on a rail below the pavilion playing a flute. As I watch him play it suddenly hits me; I finally understand exactly why I had the dream of Chu-ko liang and the "Ruse of the Empty City." Chinese love clever tricks. And what better way to hide the *real* Peach Blossom Spring than by dressing it up and presenting it as a tourist attraction! The brilliance and daring of their plan is equal to anything Chu-ko liang ever thought of! Of course no one has ever found Peach Blossom Spring; precisely because the incredibly clever Chinese, no doubt with the assistance of Freston the Magician, have been hiding it *in plain sight* for God-knows-how-long! The residents of the real Peach Blossom Spring have become ticket takers, souvenir hawkers, noodle vendors, chair bearers and tea house waitresses, a Houdini-like slight-of-hand so audacious it takes my breath away.

But, unfortunately for them, I didn't just fall off the nightsoil wagon yesterday. And now it's no more Mr. Nice Guy. I dismiss the bearers and begin walking about on my own. People I passed previously smile at me as before; but now I'm onto their little game. And if I'm right, and they've been trying to put one over on me, I'm going to bring truckloads of cameras and webcams and microphones up here and hook up Peach Blossom Spring on round-the-clock Internet feeds for so-called Reality TV.

But after retracing my steps and looking for clues, the truth is I can't be sure if this is the real Peach Blossom Spring camouflaged to look like a tourist attraction or if it is simply a tourist attraction built to resemble the real Peach Blossom Spring. Or as the philosopher Chuang Tzu put it after waking from his butterfly dream: "Am I a man dreaming I am a butterfly, or a butterfly dreaming I am a man?" I get out my notebook and write:

Possible Peach Blossom Spring Location Number One:
Peach Blossom Spring

I decide to check out the mountains of Zhangjiajie and, if need be, I can always come back to Peach Blossom Spring and continue my investigation. Besides, a relaxing train ride will help me reflect on my new theory. And if these people have been pulling a fast one all these years, they should know that in the age of the Internet and Lonely Planet guidebooks it won't take much to turn this place into just one more gated suburban community desperately trying to keep visitors out. They may have to learn the hard way that PBS stands for more than Peach Blossom Spring; it also stands for Public Broadcasting System.

Zhangjiajie

"Why did you bomb our embassy?"

My train conversation with the three middle-aged women in my seating area had begun innocuously enough. Where was I from, where had I learned Chinese, where was I going, what did I think about China, how many kids did I (not) have, etc., etc.

We briefly discuss my search for Peach Blossom Spring and although they say they admire the poetry of T'ao Yuan-ming, they admit not having read any of his work for many years. When I mention that during the worst of the Mao years, "Peach Blossom Spring," like just about everything else, was considered "reactionary," there is a kind of embarrassed silence. Whatever they privately think of the Great Helmsman, this is the province in which Mao was born and they will not openly criticize him.

Then somewhere along the line our conversation takes a perceptible turn. One woman begins complaining about how Chinese are treated at the American embassy when they want to visit America and, speaking of embassies, why did you bomb ours? Fortunately, I am ready for them. With a perfectly straight face I tell them that the plane that bombed their embassy in Kosovo wasn't an American plane; it was a Japanese plane. That it was a Japanese attack.

At first, they don't know how to react. What I have said is absurd but on the other hand the Japanese have done so much damage in China, who knows? Maybe one last kamikaze pilot had been up there all this time since World War II and at last decided to give his all for the emperor. I look at their intent but immobile expressions and they remind me of TV correspondents in foreign countries who have just been asked something by the station anchor in New York but who, because of the several-second delay, have not yet heard the question.

The woman directly facing me is older than the other two and more wizened. Deep lines etch her forehead and still other lines form a pattern of almost perfect squares on her stubborn chin. Emanating outward from her very alert, dark brown eyes are rivulets of intricate lines known in the West as "crow's feet" and in China as "fish tails." Finally, she wags a finger at me in admonishment and says, *hu shuo pa dao*!

Hu shuo pa dao is an interesting Chinese expression which literally means, "empty talk (on) eight roads," or, figuratively, "the shit is flying in all directions."

Well, OK, maybe it was an American plane but all the world knows it was an accident. *How can it be an accident when everyone knows Americans have the latest and smartest weapons?* Because it takes smart men to work those weapons. *But the American military is smart!* Don't tell *me* the American military is smart; I was in the Army for four years! Besides, this kind of thing happens in all wars. Didn't we kill several British soldiers during the Gulf War? You think Americans just kill Chinese? Look at our history: we've killed Chinese, Japanese, Vietnamese, Koreans, Cambodians, Laotians, Thais, Filipinos, lots of people!

They mull this over in silence. Eventually, our conversation on the subject tapers off and, without acknowledging it, we agree to disagree.

What I really want to tell these women is that their news is censored so how would they have a clue as to what is going on, anyway? For example, not one word of foreign or domestic criticism of the Yangtze River dam project appears in the Chinese press. And I want to ask them why Chinese so easily believe their government unlike, say, the Russians during the communist period who knew enough to read between the lines. No doubt because of China's long dynastic history, everyone simply obeys everyone else, especially the "silken sounds" of the emperor and, as Mao's era proved, emperors have yet to go out of vogue.

These women seem to have no inkling that their government wanted to use their anger against America because those in power were trying to get them to forget the Tiananmen massacre. In the embassy bombing Beijing bureaucrats saw a wonderful opportunity to play the patriotic card and to cleverly redirect their wrath toward Americans. I want to scream at them: Why are you so naive?

But I say none of that because trains have ears and I don't want to get the women in trouble nor do I wish to be thrown out of China before I find what I've come for. No doubt that is precisely the trap Freston the Magician has set for me.

After a short silence, once again as friends, we speak of other subjects. One of the subjects is how much President Clinton and Chairman Mao resemble each other in their love for young women. This makes them smile and, looking at one another, they laugh like schoolgirls who have just shared a naughty joke.

I tell them about the current fad of American young people in New York's East Village for tattooing Chinese characters on their skin; how I have seen such characters for "Bad girl" (*huai nyu jen*) on young women in Miami and in New York; and how Mike Tyson has Mao's picture on his shoulder. This interests them and they discuss this among themselves.

At one point, I ask one of the women what tattoos she has. She is astonished that I would think she has a tattoo and places the tip of her forefinger to her nose and says, *Wo*? ("Me?") And this is something I have noticed about Chinese. When they want to indicate themselves they place their forefinger on their nose whereas an American places it to his chest. I have spent decades trying to interpret the significance of this difference as well as its implication for American foreign policy but so far I've drawn a blank.

The closer we get to Zhangjiajie, the more picturesque the scenery outside – beautifully terraced rice fields, quaint red brick farmhouses with black-tiled roofs and rolling hills. I like to think of the numerous green shades of ricefields as being similar to Chinese dialects; emerald green is mandarin; bright yellow is Cantonese, and all the permutations of yellow-green shades in between represent all the other dialects.

I would like to tell you that water buffaloes turn the dark chocolate earth of the paddy fields, guided by barefoot farmers with the flick of a bamboo wand. Villages are half concealed behind a thicket of trees. The L-shaped peasant houses have overhanging eaves supported by pillars to provide shelter from the heavy spring rain, and decorated roof tiles to ward off evil spirits. I would like to tell you that because that is what I see.

Unfortunately, that is exactly how John Gittings describes the same setting in his *Real China: From Cannibalism to Karaoke* and, the way it works, when even the most deserving writer tries to pinch a line or two from someone else's work, there is always some officious, nosey Parker reader with too much time on his hands who feels it necessary to drop a note to publishers and editors pointing out the strange coincidence of such striking similarities.

So I will have to tell you instead that red slashes of upturned earth match the red bricks of the houses. The blue sky is heavy with billowy white clouds and all above is reflected in small squares and rectangles of water, making it appear that heaven has merged with earth. Farmers are planting fields using both real buffalo and iron buffalo and a few old men are even fishing in the tiny bodies of water between fields. The broad leaves of lotuses are everywhere and it is clear there will be a bumper crop of lotus roots.

Chairman Mao's personal physician wrote that leaves of trees were dusted before Mao and his wife arrived at their destinations and lush green fields of rice were moved closer to the tracks when Mao traveled by train so he would not notice the famine (which his policies caused).

"But isn't everything here green?" asked Dorothy.
"No more than in any other city," replied Oz; "but when you
wear green spectacles, why of course, everything you see looks
green to you." – *The Wizard of Oz*

These ricefields, however, look real enough.

Chinese of course do not simply have rice. In a rice-growing culture, one must speak specifically of which rice at what stage of growth. *Daily Life in China on the Eve of the Mongol Invasion* mentions: "New-milled rice, husked winter rice, first quality white rice, rice with lotus-pink grains, yellow-eared rice, rice on the stalk, ordinary rice, glutinous rice, ordinary yellow rice, short-stalked rice, pink rice, yellow rice and old rice." I wonder what kind they throw at weddings.

Eighty-five percent of Hunan is still farmland and the land is so fertile farmers can grow two rice crops a year, and, sure enough, the train speeds past field after field of rice ready to be harvested and every so often I see beside these fields the deep green seedlings of the next crop ready to be transplanted whenever the farmers have prepared the field.

Rice and tea are Hunan's major crops but soybean, cotton and wheat are also grown. God, what a boring sentence; anyway, rice is grown in the fields and in the low terraces, and the tea is grown on the hills, a logical arrangement if ever there was one and no doubt implemented only after thousands of years of trial and error. Hunan is in fact China's leading rice producer and is sometimes referred to as "China's granary." The saying (loosely translated) is: "When Hunan, Hupeh, Kwangtung and Kiangsi have rich harvests, all of China will be whistling Dixie."

They also grow something called "ramie" (of course I don't know what that is but it is described as having "dark green, thick, broad leaves;" so what doesn't?) and something called "rape." I don't know what that is either but I do know Americans wouldn't consider it politically correct and I also know those involved in the musical, *The Fantastiks*, decided to change their "Rape Scene" to the "Abduction Scene," and maybe China had better start thinking along those lines with the "rape plant" as well.

Writers on Hunan always mention that the province produces sugar cane, tobacco and other "cash crops." I confess I have never understood the meaning of the expression "cash crops." Does it mean the other crops the farmer grows are just for fun? Or does he use the other crops for barter only? Do Hunanese farmers accept frequent flyer miles and gift certificates in lieu of cash for certain produce? Why wouldn't he take cash for *all* his crops? And by the way Hunan has both "tea oil seed" and "tong oil seed." Maybe Yale's Jonathan Spence can tell the difference, I can't. All I know is one is OK to drink, one isn't, and whenever someone in Hunan offers me a cup of tea, I sip it very slowly.

And there is another reason I sip tea slowly. Let's say you're checking your e-mail in an Internet cafe somewhere in Changsha, and someone places some tea on your table. A nice gesture. However, the tea is in a glass, not a cup, and, unless your hands are as callused as a lumberjack's, the glass is far too hot to pick up. Second, the glass is a kind of tall Tom Collins glass and all the tea leaves are piled up in a dark, ominous, brooding layer about an inch thick on top of the hot water. So by the time the last few leaves fall to the bottom, so that your parched lips can actually touch the liquid inside the glass, the tea is cold. I don't mean to sound like some kind of complaining, condescending, colonial-type foreign-devil, but – and it hurts me to say this – somebody has got to teach the Chinese how to make tea. And when a country reaches the point that the people are not speaking their language properly, nor writing their language correctly, nor making a decent cup of tea – well, let's just say several dynasties lost the Mandate of Heaven for a lot less.

Nor am I the only sojourner to China to bitch about the tea. Nineteenth century travelers to China complained about something they learned about too late to do them any good: *ke cha*, or, "guest tea." Apparently the tea you were served was not meant to be drunk; the custom was when your host (usually a scrumptiously polite mandarin official wearing a hat with a pretty knob and a peacock feather who wanted you dead and would never have granted the interview in the first place if it were not for the cannon lining the decks of your nearby frigate or sloop-of-war) picked up his cup to take a sip of his tea, that meant the interview was over. Of course, long-nosed barbarians didn't know this and they slurped up their tea and overstayed their welcome and never understood why their host never got back to them. Although the guest tea technique is no longer in vogue, Beijing businessmen and government officials have a plethora of more sophisticated techniques by which to subtly insult their foreign partners and foreign diplomats respectively, thereby confirming the superiority of Chinese culture.

The train arrives and just before the women depart the lady with the intricate fish tails tells me we must all keep an open mind and open heart and a few other things I don't quite get. But I thank her and her companions for their friendliness, pick up my bags, and start walking. Near the door of the train station is a sprawling newspaper rack over which is a huge sign that reads in English: "China Post." Beneath the sign an unusually large woman is fanning herself while dozing off in the stifling, enervating heat.

Me: Excuse me. Do you have a copy of the *China Post*?
Nodding off woman: No.
Me: Do you have any English language publications?
Nodding off woman: No.
Me: Have you ever had any English language publications for sale here?
Nodding off woman: No; no need.
Me: (pointing to the sign): Then why do you display this sign?
Nodding off woman: That's what they gave us.

I begin walking away from the station knowing almost nothing about where I am or where I am going. I only know there is an area around the railway station with several streets of not very inviting buildings; there is a Zhangjiajie town one must take a minibus to; and, beyond that, somewhere in tree-clad mountains swarming with flying squirrels and golden monkeys and Chinese tour groups, there is a Zhangjiajie village.

But from out of nowhere comes a young man with an almost copperbrown complexion and a toothy, Slick Willy smile. I thereupon dub him "Slick Willy." He introduces himself and asks where I'm going. When I tell him I've come to see the mountains (I've actually come to *search* the mountains but that information I decide not to impart until I know if I will be using his services or not) he invites me to his office near the railway station where he can show me the area on a map.

Inside his "office," an unpretentious second-story room up some concrete steps, he points to places on a wall map and gives me an understanding of what is here. And what is here are beautiful mountain streams, crystal clear lakes, huge caverns and caves with rivers flowing through them and, most important, a magnificent forest of quartzite sandstone crags, canyons and mountain peaks, the perfect place in which a community could hide itself from the world. I can also go rafting on the Maoyan River, a wonderful way to search for the entrance the fisherman (i.e. the poet) discovered 1600 years before.

I ask him why Zhangjiajie is not on my map and he points to "Datong," the former name of the area. Datong, he says, means something like "nothing here," or "no good place." Apparently, the previous name was given to the area before any local tourist board had begun its operations. And someone decided to name it "the realm of the Zhang family," after a Han Dynasty recluse named Zhang.

I decide to take him up on his offer even before several guides walk in. Among them is an extremely handsome woman whose features and brown skin remind me of Tibetans. (In fact, Chinese I speak to later will confirm my impression that Tujia people often resemble Tibetans.) I silently mutter that if there is any just god looking down from his or her heaven, this lovely woman will be my guide during my days and nights of searching. I choose my words carefully and speak nonchalantly to Slick Willy. "Oh, you have women guides as well."

Slick Willy looks up from the paperwork he is drawing up for me. "Yes, she is my wife."

Curses! Foiled again! I mutter something about her having a lovely smile and curse the gods and goddesses who have pumped up my hopes only to let me down in my hour of need.

Within minutes Slick Willy and I have left his wife and office behind and are bumping about on a minibus into Zhangjiajie town. When we arrive, he picks up the heavier of my two bags and I follow him through several streets and alleys and a marketplace crowded with everything from fly-covered vegetables to fly-covered animal carcasses. I pass by a large window displaying wedding dresses in a shop called "Newly Matron," and in response to my wave, a woman in the window covers her mouth with her hand, laughs and ducks behind a dress.

Slick Willy takes me to a small hotel with dirty rooms which I reject and we eventually arrive at the Dragon International Hotel where he bargains the price down for me. Tonight I pay for the hotel, the following two nights his company pays from the money I gave him. He tells me he will return the following day at six in the morning with my guide.

After a shower, I spend about an hour walking around the town until the heat is simply too much. As I head back, I pass through the town's sprawling marketplace. I watch small boys crowd around cages with snakes and baskets with frogs and then I notice a number of young chow puppies in cages. One in each cage. I stop to look at them. They look hot. A man and woman look up.

Man/woman: You want to buy a dog?
Me: No, I don't think so; Americans don't eat dogs.
Man/woman: You don't have to eat it.
Me: No, really, I don't think so.
Man/woman: We can deliver it for you.
Me: I live in the States.
Man/woman: We can wrap it.

Right, and on the customs form I'll just make a notation that the dog is to be used for food purposes. Actually, I am a dog lover but I try never to judge the customs of others, and the fact that some Asians have eaten dogs for centuries does not bother me. After all, we eat dead cows. My philosophy is: As long as nobody eats *my* dog or *my* cow, I don't care what they eat.

As for eating, I suppose in Hunan I should try an *authentic* Hunanese restaurant but I soon find myself inside the air-conditioned coffee shop of the Dragon Hotel. The menu is in English or at least someone's version of English. In addition to "stewed sizzling bean curd," there is also something called "bean curd thripe in salad." What the hell is a "thripe"? Do they mean the bean curd is "ripe" but they printed a typo? Or did somebody with a pronunciation problem write this menu? I pass over the "faud rip squid silk" and instead order a "Dragon Sandwich" which turns out to be something close to our club sandwich but with an extra unidentifiable layer of meat.

When I checked in, the man at the desk claimed this was the only four star hotel in Zhangjiajie but I will find out later he lied; there is a newer and better one. But as I sit in air-conditioned comfort watching the nearby xylophone player do her best with a very maudlin interpretation of the Everly Brothers' *Dream, Dream, Dream,* I have no complaints. The heat has made me groggy and zombie-like, and even the folding of the napkins by waitresses at a nearby table becomes a meditative experience. I don't recall ever being in a coffee shop which has a xylophone player and before I go upstairs to reread some of T'ao Yuan-ming's poems for clues to the whereabouts of the real Peach Blossom Spring, I applaud her efforts.

Later that evening, I decide to brave the enervating heat and humidity and eat Hunanese food at a local restaurant. A very local restaurant. No English on the menu, no air-conditioning, no fans, lots of flies. With sweat rolling down my face and onto an already sweat-stained wooden table, I peruse a menu with such items as "jellied duck's tongue," "fried white gourd," various kinds of snake and other assorted delicacies which, for all I know, may well be on the endangered species list. And when I realize I may soon bite into endangered species, I have no doubt this ordeal is karma for something I did several years before.

I had come up with a book concept which I was absolutely certain would at last bring me fame and fortune: *The Endangered Species Cookbook.* The basic concept for each animal or bird on the endangered list was a short essay reporting the plight of the animal followed by a how-to-trap-him section followed by a recipe. I had an artist do a sample cover illustration, had a food writer do a few chapters, made up a dummy cover, and flew off to what was in those days known as the American Booksellers Association. I went right to a booth whose company was known for publishing humor/satire books and had in fact done the very successful title, *101 Uses for a Dead Cat.*

I told the man I had a concept I thought their company might like to publish and then held up the cover so he could see clearly the cover title and the cover illustration of several endangered species looking out forlornly from a cooking pot with a fire roaring underneath. What I most remember is his look of stunned disbelief, the way he held his two hands out, palms toward me, and how he actually took a step backward, as if what I was holding was radioactive. And that was the last I saw of him.

In the end, no one bought the book but as I now look at the items on the menu I know beyond any doubt that it is payback time. Travelers to China in the 19th century often quoted the saying, "Chinese will eat anything with four legs and its back to the sky." When I asked a Chinese friend of mine about this, she thought for a moment, and then said, "Actually, it doesn't have to have its back to the sky."

I do my best to make sense of the simplified characters on the menu. The middle-aged waitress with shifty eyes and furtive manner hovers about impatiently and finally suggests I try a dish of soft pork with beans and vegetables. In fact, she seems to be almost pushing it on me. Fortunately, I didn't just fall off the mung bean wagon yesterday: It was exactly after having had a dish of *sukaramaddava*, or "soft pork," that the Buddha fell ill and died. If this isn't proof that the waitress is working with Freston the Magician, and that I have to be alert and vigilant at all times, I don't know what is.

I finally choose fried fish in sautéed black bean sauce and some rice. Needless to say, the fish and the rice will both be spicy. The Hunanese love spicy, richly flavored food the way Ronald Reagan loved jellybeans: hot-and-sour vegetables, spicy deep-fried chicken, cold rice noodles in spicy sauce, spicy prawns, crispy spiced fish, etc. They seem to think if a dish doesn't have heaps of garlic, red chili paste, hot-pepper-and-black-bean sauce, and something called fagara (Szech'uan pepper), it can't be tasted. It is said Mao liked to pop peppers into his mouth and chew them the way we eat pretzels. Chefs from Hunan and Szech'uan will tell you that spicy food aids the body in getting rid of excessive moisture and helps to offset the unpleasantness of extreme humidity. (Perhaps they've never heard of air-conditioning and ice.)

Judge Dee was dismayed. He was not a gourmet, but he liked at least to know what he ate. He forced himself to taste a small morsel of the bean curd fish, and nearly choked. Seeing the abbot's expectant look, he said quickly, 'This is indeed delicious. You have excellent cooks!

The Haunted Monastery by Robert H. Van Gulik

The *Continental Atlas of China* mentions China's "western cuisine" and says, "One famous dish is Mrs. Pockmark's Beancurd, named for the woman who created it. This hot, spicy stew is made with minced pork, bean curd, dried red pepper flakes and Szech'uan pepper."

I have not forgotten that Kuan Yu, the man who eventually became the Chinese God of War, was originally a beancurd seller. And I am not unaware that one of the "attractions" of Changsha is *chou doufu*, stinky beancurd, but I have had more than enough acquaintance with it. In Hong Kong, right after I was married, I moved my wife and myself into a building which had a streetside vendor of stinky soybean curd out front. Most people would have realized living among the malodorous fumes of stinky beancurd is not a great idea for newlyweds and is not something a wife will soon forget, especially during the divorce, but as my Fort Dix basic training sergeant used to say whenever I fell out for inspection in the wrong uniform, "there is always that two per cent that don't git the word." So no offence to Mrs. Pockmark, but if it hadn't been for beancurd I might still be married and I've had it with beancurd and if she tries to push her dish on me, she will quickly find out what she can do with it.

Liu was not at all happy and grumbled: "Why did we depart in such a rush?" "An overly zealous man cannot eat hot beancurd," was the reply.
The Scholar and the Maid – famous Ch'ing Dynasty court case

With great caution, I dig into my pepper-laden fish and, out of the corner of my eye, cast furtive glances at the waitress. I decide to keep my eye on her. For one thing she is whistling. It is just barely audible, but, still, there is no doubt that she is whistling. The relevant Chinese saying is, "A whistling woman and a crowing hen; neither is good for gods nor men." For another thing, she has told me that she is originally from Ningpo. The relevant Chinese saying is, "Better to have an argument with a person from Soochow (Suzhou), than to chat with a person from Ningpo."

Although her whistling and place of origin raise my suspicions, I have to admit the waitress is attractive, despite a kind of Monica Lewinsky-fleshiness; but not particularly friendly. I assume either the heat has got to her or else somewhere down the line some western man done her (or her mother) wrong. Of course, if I were a sexist I might conclude that it was her time of month. During the Ch'ing period, that phenomenon would have been expressed euphemistically, of course, something like, "Little red sister has come," or "The red general has grasped the door." I don't know the modern phrase but I suppose modern Chinese society is less euphemistically inclined.

In fact, though, the waitress displays such a haughty attitude and bitchy outlook I suddenly realize she has missed her calling: she would have made a perfect dominatrix in one of America's rapidly expanding houses of domination. Mistress Hunan, maybe. Or Goddess Peach Blossom. Or Empress Dowager of the Mountains. It is easy to envision her wearing a shiny black corset, garter belt, stockings, lace-up leather boots with mile-high stiletto heels. And of course standing in front of some kind of torture contraption holding some kind of instrument of punishment. "Mistress Chili Pepper – Role Play Specialist."

> Morgana the goddess
> Therefore is her name
> However men resist they
> Surrender just the same
>
> *Sir Gawain and the Green Knight*

Although China experts in the West never mention it publicly, and will no doubt vehemently deny what I am about to tell you, privately they admit that this is one of China's most pressing problems: with the possible exception of Hong Kong, there are no houses of domination anywhere in the country. When people in a society have basic shelter and enough to eat, the more enlightened eventually wish to experiment with the roles they were assigned by that society. This naturally leads to experimental role playing in places like houses of domination, and the more houses of domination a nation has, the more advanced it is. I suppose in a China where millions of people are scrambling for enough to eat, it will be difficult to persuade the leaders to implement a five-year plan to build such places; but until China closes the house-of-domination gap, it is clear no major power will take China very seriously.

(There is, at least, a bit of hope in Hong Kong, as can be seen in this snippet in a local Hong Kong paper regarding the closing of the ex-colony's Fetish Fashion Sex Shop: "A barrister representing five gay rights activists accused of obstructing a police officer during a protest said yesterday they were only expressing their opinions about bondage and sadomasochism when they tied one of the group to the gates of Central police station.")

But this waitress with an attitude does remind me of a caution expressed by the writer Nelson Algren. Algren is given credit for saying: "Never play cards with a man named Doc, never eat at a restaurant called Mom's, and never go to bed with a woman with more troubles than you have." Based on my experiences in China over the years, I have created my own version of Nelson's caveat: "Never play mahjong with a man named Old Lau, never eat at any restaurant called Golden Dragon, and never go to bed with a Chinese woman with more attitude than you have."

When the waitress presents the bill, I realize I don't know how much to tip but I do have a pile of small bills and coins I need to get rid of. So I pay the bill by employing what I believe was Balzac's method of tipping. I take a coin and place it in her hand, then a note, then a coin, and continue in this manner until the waitress's face lights up in a smile. Then I reach over and take back the last coin I gave her and, according to Balzac's theory, the tip should now be exactly right. Maybe so, but the waitress is staring at me and at the coins in her hand and especially at the one I took back. She has begun glaring at me and mumbling under her breath so I make a hasty exit.

Back at the hotel, I am too tired to go out and explore the town and so I stay in my room and jot down a few thoughts for my long-planned "relationship" book: *Women are from Hunan; Men are from Szech'uan.* (If you can't beat them, join them.) But eventually I am too bored to stay in my room, so I get on the elevator and get off at the floor with the nightclub. The woman who escorts me to a seat is almost as lovely as the woman who isn't going to be my guide but she quickly disappears.

The decor is a series of neon lights lit up as a palm tree and the acts are amateurish and a bit bawdy but, perhaps unintentionally, reminiscent of vaudeville, which makes them fun. A Chinese woman, somewhere between young and middle-aged, does a kind of belly dance in which her navel contracts and expands in such a way that it makes me think of the narrow passage the fisherman had to squeeze through to find Peach Blossom Spring. Watching this woman's belly button alter its shape like the pupil of a cat's eye under various light conditions reminds me that I probably should say something about what could be called the Freudian interpretation of Peach Blossom Spring. Fortunately, there isn't any. But there is no doubt that some fool critic out there with too much time on his hands will eventually come up with one so I may as well mention it myself. The precise interpretation of the Chinese character "yuan" of *T'ao Hua Yuan Chi* would be "source of the water," not simply "spring" or "springs." So here we have a man in a skiff who is sailing between riverbanks covered with peach trees; a man who, reaching the "source," will have to squeeze through a very tight opening that emits an eerie radiance, and, once inside, a man who then finds the greatest of all rewards.

Obviously, in the fool critic version, the peach trees and their petals lining both sides of the river would be interpreted as a woman's soft pubic hair, the opening would be what the Chinese call the woman's "jade gate," and Peach Blossom Spring would then be what the Chinese call a woman's "grotto of the white tiger." And, in this version, the man would then no doubt insert his "jade stalk" and employ one of Master Li's techniques such as "flailing out to right and left in the way a courageous general disperses the enemy ranks," or "letting the positive peak muck about in the hallowed field and the deep glen, like a farmer in the fall hoeing his field." (Too bad I'm here in July).

The poet, therefore, would be simply dismissed as yet another sexually repressed male erotomaniac who wrote a priapic parable of a man's relations with a woman, a metaphorical tale pregnant with obvious libidinous symbolism. People who believe that might even be shameless enough to continue along the line of march and describe my own search for Peach Blossom Spring in much the same light.

In my opinion, this is all American pop psychology gobbledygook and, regardless of which critic writes it up (the giveaway phrase will be if they use the term "sexual sublimation"), or what newspaper it appears in (the giveaway phrase will be if they use the term "all the news that's fit to print"), I hope you don't believe a word of it.

Furthermore, it is known that T'ao Yuan-ming was married at least once, probably twice, had five sons and at least one daughter. (Traditionally, as girls would eventually be married into another family, they were not counted, so a man who had only daughters, if asked how many children he had, might reply "none." So it is not always possible to determine how many daughters somebody had. And you thought *today's* census takers have it tough.)

But, getting back to this nightclub, what bothers me is the fact that the drummer is enclosed in what appears to be bulletproof glass. Why a drummer in a band should be behind bulletproof glass I don't know, but then I've never been in a band. At one point, the male actor shuts one eye and struts about attempting a ferocious and menacing demeanor, with about as much success as Charlton Heston had playing Long John Silver in *Treasure Island*. As I watch, I can't help thinking how the material could be improved, which only goes to prove what we say in theater, i.e., there are three basic needs of human existence: food, sex and the need to rewrite another person's play. Even in Zhangjiajie.

Several young women are sitting at tables, some with customers, some alone. Eventually, the hostess returns and sits next to me and asks if I would like a companion. Just as I was thinking it was my lucky night, she indicates that she is referring to the other girls.

Having a girl sit at my table would be nonsensical; the music and noise is too loud to allow conversation and in any case the girls look too young and uninteresting. We would no doubt bore one another but the girl would be making money and I would be losing it. But the hostess is a bit older and very beautiful and I make it clear that if she would stay that would be fine. Unfortunately, she cannot and so despite my best efforts and my shameless flattery, she disappears into the darkness. Although I speak with her a bit from time to time as she passes by, it becomes clear that I am destined to share the fate of Tantalus, son of Zeus, sentenced for all eternity to stand beneath luscious fruit which, whenever he reached to touch it, moved out of reach.

The following morning, Slick Willy introduces me to a dark-complexioned, thin, serious young man who will be my guide for three days. Slick Willy tells me the guide speaks no English but I assure him that will be no problem. The guide speaks mandarin to me very slowly and clearly. At first, I assume he is doing that for my sake; later, I will realize mandarin is a kind of second language for him as well and he speaks it haltingly.

It quickly becomes evident that, in any case, the guide speaks so seldom that he would make Calvin Coolidge seem like a chatterbox. He is also a straight arrow, very straightforward and I think very honest. So him I dub "Cheyenne."

Slick Willy leaves and Cheyenne and I board a local vehicle obviously designed to register every bump on the road and head for the mountains of Zhangjiajie. Once we arrive, Cheyenne has me check in my large bag at a booth at the entrance. He carries my shoulder bag for me; I carry a bottle of water. He asks if I would prefer to walk up the mountain or to take the cable car. Not being terribly bright, I opt for walking.

An hour later, drenched in sweat, completely out of breath and with legs aching, I ask how much farther we have to go to reach the top. He says we have gone one-tenth of the way. An hour later I ask again and he says we have gone three-tenths of the way. At that point my heart is pounding wildly, my legs ache and I realize I am not going to make it. I have a choice between retracing my steps and taking the cable car or using the chair bearers as I did at Peach Blossom Spring. Many Chinese in chairs are being carried past me as I ascend so using a chair would not make me feel like a cruel colonial master. In any case, for the oppressed classes of China, as the Great Helmsman would confirm were he around, there was no colonial master worse than the Chinese upper classes. I ask the guide what he thinks. He says it will be no problem for the Tujia bearers to carry me part way up the mountain. He should know: he is also a Tujia.

Once again, I am completely absorbed into the rhythm of the swaying chair as the bearers somehow manage to pass by Chinese tourists heading up the mountain or to squeeze by other bearers heading down the mountain. What I feel is not guilt at using these men to carry me, rather, gratitude. There is no other way to experience what 19th century travelers to China experienced than by being carried in a chair along narrow paths as I am being carried: by coolies. And I use the term coolies with enormous respect. They are not simply workers or employees or assistants: they are the Chinese coolies (*kuli* or "bitter labor") which Lu Hsun and Lao She and John Hersey and Pearl Buck and other writers wrote about. Yet one can't help but ask, in a society in which they have no pension, social security or unemployment benefits, how do these men feed themselves and their families when their strength runs out.

Every so often, the coolies stop to rest. At some of these stops there are Tujia women in colorful costumes who, for a small fee, sing traditional songs. Throughout their history, Tujia and other minority children learned to sing at an early age and the traditions of these people were carried on in song, not in writing. Each fortress or village had a hilly area where the young people would gather – the girls in their finery – and sing to one another with an open flirtatiousness and sexual frankness that shocked the more conservative Chinese.

Through Chinese eyes, the ethnic minorities such as the Tujia and Miao were sexually loose as they did not adhere to Confucius' ideas of sexual morality. Nor for that matter did most of the women bind their feet as did Chinese women nor did the men place such emphasis on virginity before marriage as did Chinese men.

Traditionally the ethnic minorities were not particularly pleased to see Han Chinese civilians and soldiers move into their neighborhoods. For a long time it was a case of NIMBY (Not in My Backyard) and because of this hostility and resentment and sometimes armed conflict, Chinese saw these people as, to use some of the more polite terms, "quarrelsome and superstitious."

While the women sing love songs in mandarin Chinese, Cheyenne tells me the legend of Hou Yu, the Tujia hero who used his arrows to shoot nine of the ten suns from the sky so that human beings would find the world a more suitable place.

At one of the more remote stops, there are a few Chinese tourists and about two dozen chair bearers sitting about having their lunch or simply resting. When the girl finishes her song and after I pay her a few dollars, I sing back to her in mandarin, with faux Chinese opera gestures, about how I know I am only a foreign-devil but I can't possibly live without her. The chair bearers find this hilarious and, encouraged by my having stolen the audience from the legitimate performer, I dramatically recite in mandarin the line Chinese no doubt used over a century ago when first encountering foreigners: "I don't fear Heaven, I don't fear Earth, I only fear foreign-devils speaking Chinese."

The Tujia find this even more hilarious and I realize they apparently haven't heard a lot of my material so I decide to go for broke to see if I can bring the house down. I tell them my mandarin teachers at Monterey, California were originally from Beijing and they used to alter that saying into: "I don't fear Heaven, I don't fear Earth, I only fear Cantonese trying to speak mandarin." This brings howls of delightful laughter from the chair bearers and singers alike and I realize I have missed my calling; I could have been the Lenny Bruce of China's hill tribe circuit. All I have to do is change my name to Jackie Mason and travel from province to province cracking jokes about foreign-devils and "out-of-province people."

Chinese have always enjoyed laughing with or at foreigners. In the 1850's, on Chusan Island, an English officer used to exercise his pony every afternoon from 3 to 4; always taking the same route. So the Chinese proprietor of a restaurant along the route put up a sign announcing that for his patrons' enjoyment he had hired a foreign-devil to ride up and down the street outside the restaurant. Talk about entrepreneurs.

Eventually, we reach stretches of path too steep for the bearers, so I pay them off and we continue walking. The views of the mountains and cloud-covered peaks are spectacular and we pass Golden Whip Stream and stand on a platform amidst the mountains and clouds known as Star-Catching Stage. There are at times heavy showers and the billowy, dramatically colored, clouds descend into the valleys bringing centuries of Chinese paintings to life. On a narrow trail, we are forced to bow low in order to pass under a huge rock on which is painted the Chinese expression, *duibuchi*, "Excuse me." Some clever soul with a bit too much time on his hands must have thought that one up.

Any tourists I pass or sit beside are invariably Chinese travelers from other provinces, and in conversations with them I am always assured that there are still more spectacular mountains in such-and-such province. Chinese tourists always seem to be in better shape than me and to linger less at rest stops. Not to worry: I am too worn out to be embarrassed.

Of course at several points I use my binoculars to see if I can spot any openings in the mountains as described in "Peach Blossom Spring." I decide that later that night I will let Cheyenne in on my real mission but I do ask him if he knows anything about the Lu Mountains where T'ao Yuan-ming lived. He says they are taller and more spectacular than where we are and that some are so high at the top there is no atmosphere. Our conversation is interrupted by his cell phone. It rings again when we're climbing but he can't hear anything because the mountains are between us and the town.

At one point a narrow path meanders out onto a ledge where there is no rail or barrier of any kind. That is when I remember something terribly important: I have a fear of heights. Not if I'm enclosed in a plane or a helicopter or even a cable car; but on the sides of mountains, monuments, temples and assorted high places, my legs have sometimes frozen. The problem is, sometimes it kicks in and sometimes it doesn't.

In Mexico, I had to have two daiquiris at a beach bar before I dared parasail. And at one monument I forced myself to climb it took me twenty minutes to get up the courage to start back down the steep, narrow steps. In India, my legs froze in a fort's battlements for several minutes, as they did at Angkor Wat. And while walking along the heights of a Thai temple in Ayuthya, a young Thai woman had to take my hand and lead me to the stairs before I could continue down. I always forget what fear of heights is called so I just call it fallophobia and hope it doesn't strike. Fortunately, despite my fear, my legs continue functioning and I do not have to embarrass myself by taking Cheyenne's hand.

That night, Cheyenne and I check into a small inn at Zhangjiajie village. There seems to be a better hotel practically beside our own but Cheyenne mumbles something about "Szech'uan people." I am not sure if that means it is only for people from Szech'uan or that it is run by people from Szech'uan, and I fail to understand why we can't stay there even if it is run by people from Szech'uan. But considering that our hotel expenses are now coming out of the portion of the money that Slick Willy gave him, I can see Cheyenne wishes to count pennies. That would be OK with me except that our room's air-conditioning doesn't work and there are no bourgeois niceties such as towels and toilet paper. Also, my rain hat and rain jacket are in the bag I checked in before we entered the mountains, so I got soaked in the rain and, as my change of clothes are in that same bag, I am going to stay soaked for some time. Cheyenne goes out and brings back a horribly thin face cloth and hands it to me as a towel. He means well so, of course, I thank him and tell him that will do very well.

The room has three narrow beds and I sleep near the window. Outside the wooden shutters, the moonlight spills unevenly and mysteriously through copses of trees on a hillside and transforms a bamboo grove into a hauntingly beautiful black-and-silver landscape. Some of the bamboo is a Hunan type "speckled bamboo," made famous by the legend which says that the wives of an ancient emperor cried copious tears over his grave and onto the surrounding bamboo, creating the new variety. And, indeed, with a bit of imagination, the wind rustling the bamboo could be construed as sobbing.

Although one of the wooden shutters doesn't quite close all the way, Cheyenne assures me there are no mosquitoes; a statement I would place more faith in if it weren't for the anti-mosquito gadget on top of the room's only table.

Asian customs are of course different than our own but when I travel I am not crazy about having a guide stay in the room at night. I tell him it is all right if he'd like to go back to stay with his wife. He says it would take five hours to get back to where he lives near the train station. After a bit of desultory, before-lights out, conversation, he sighs and says something about wishing his wife made more money at her job.

Me: Oh, your wife works outside the house?
Taciturn Guide: Yes.
Me: Where does she work?
Taciturn Guide: In a hotel.
Me: Really? Which one?
Taciturn guide: Where you stayed your first night.
Me: The Dragon? Really? What does she do?
Taciturn guide: She is the hostess in the nightclub.

Bop – agghhh! Jesus Christ! I don't believe it! So that's why she looked darker than the ordinary Chinese women: she's a Tujia. Now I've got to get the hell out of Hunan Province before Cheyenne finds out I was after his wife. Anywhere in the mountains he could push me off a cliff and easily claim it was an accident! *Wait! Don't panic, damn it! You didn't really do anything with her.* Yeah, but who knows what the customs are here? Maybe the Tujia are the Sicilians of China. Maybe I'll be sleeping with the (spicy, of course) fishes. Wait, think: what did I actually say to her? *You told her she was gorgeous, remember? You told her her face was more beautiful than Wang Chao-chun's or any of the classic beau-*

ties in Chinese history. And after you finished your fourth bottle of Tsingtao beer, you asked her if she had ever read Master Li Tung-hsuan's erotic classic in which he describes various bedroom positions like "reversed flying ducks" and "donkeys in the third moon of spring" and "wailing monkey embracing a tree" and "phoenix in" – Will you shut up! *Relax! Even if she mentions you to Cheyenne how will they know it's you?* Of course they'll know it's me! Do you see any other foreign-devils jiveassing around these mountains? After he's asleep, I'll just open the shutters real quiet-like, slip out the window, cut through the bamboo grove and shag ass down the mountain. *But Baudelaire said "the real travelers are those who leave for the sake of leaving, so –"* No, the real travelers are those who get the hell out for the sake of living; and that's just what I'm going to do. Besides, I doubt that Baudelaire made a pass at a Tujia guide's wife. *But as long as you're in these mountains he can't get any calls on his cell phone, remember? So you're safe.* Yeah, right, I'll just make sure Cheyenne and I spend the rest of our lives up here so he can't take any calls from his wife. *OK, look, calm down, nobody has to get hurt here. I mean, if in "Oklahoma!" the farmer and the cowboy can be friends then surely in the mountains of Hunan province Tujia guides and American tourists can get along. Why can't you be more like Kuan Yu?* Who? *You know, the guy who became the god of war. In* Romance of the Three Kingdoms, *he stood in the doorway of a barn all night holding a lantern just to prove to those nearby that he wasn't doing anything with the women inside.* That's it! That's what I'll do: tomorrow I'll buy a lantern and – Wait a minute, I'm forgetting to ask the all-important question: what would Paul Theroux do if he were in this situation? *He would take it on the chin and move on, dummy. You can do the same; just be cool and tough it out.*

Cheyenne sits up on his bed and begins drawing lines on a detailed map of the area – where we have been and where we are going tomorrow. The time has come to let him in on my real motive for coming to Zhangjiajie. He listens patiently and attentively to my theory that Peach Blossom Spring could be somewhere in these mountains. But when I'm finished he shakes his head and says he knows every valley in these mountains and he has never seen anything like that. Still, seeing that I'm not about to abandon my search, he makes a few changes on our itinerary so we can check out some of the more remote areas. We can also cover more ground but do less actual climbing. And we will cover some of the ground by hired minibus which, unfortunately, means I have to pay more. The rule seems to be: the less I climb the more I pay.

Needless to say, throughout my trip, Chinese men indulge in spitting. And Cheyenne is no exception. In fact, while listening to someone in the courtyard expertly and raucously clearing his throat in preparation to spitting, I come across this in my *Lonely Planet* guidebook: "Facts for the Visitor: Clearing your throat and discharging the phlegm on the floor or out the window (to the peril of those below) is perfectly acceptable in China. Everyone does it – any time any place."

Every traveler to China – including Paul Theroux – has something to say about the Chinese penchant for loudly clearing their throats and spitting and I suppose I have to add my two *renminbi*'s worth. Personally, having lived in Hong Kong for so many years, I hardly even notice it anymore and just don't care. In fact, during this trip to China I noticed far less spitting than before and I think it has to do with the fact that nearly every Chinese male now spends much of his day talking into a cell phone and they haven't yet mastered the art of spitting and holding a cell phone conversation simultaneously. If it must be a choice between listening to people shout into cell phones or listening to them spit, I much prefer the expectorations to the conversations.

Without question, the most learned comment ever penned on this subject was written by Jacques Marcuse, a correspondent in

Peking in the early 1960's. He had been in China before and in his caustic and perceptive book, *The Peking Papers: Leaves from the Notebook of a China Correspondent,* he had this to say on the subject:

There was something about spitting in those days. It was a national trait – a national bond–like the Chinese script which knew no difference in dialect– only it was more widely used. When it came to the lengthy process of expectorating, you could not tell a dock laborer from a warlord....There were roughly two types of spitters: the slow, careful yet determined, strictly *vertical* spitter and the quick-on-the-draw crack shot who could hit the target from any angle. Careful planning and execution with the former; brilliant improvisation coupled with superb precision with the latter. Two schools, in fact, and within each, tremendous scope left to individual style and stance....

Marcuse was also perceptive enough to wonder if the government's campaign against spitting was being implemented to improve hygiene or to discourage self-expression. Whatever one thinks of spitting, I have found it best not to judge Asian customs by western values. For example, many people traveling through Asia make derogatory comments on the way some Asian males blow their noses into the street by pressing a forefinger to one side of the nose and then to the other. But in his book, *A Single Pebble*, John Hersey's narrator on board a junk on the Yangtze River says that "when (the cook) saw me one day deposit two blasts of nasal phlegm in a square of cloth and treasure these excreta in one of my pockets, he actually went to the owner and complained, requesting that I be put ashore at the next port on the river."

Perhaps propriety, like beauty, is often in the eye of the beholder.

The following day, after an indescribable Chinese breakfast of "pork and century eggs congee," a breakfast which begins with Cheyenne whispering "Be careful, there are rocks in the rice," I lean against a rail on a mountaintop and look down into a mysterious, mist-covered valley below.

Me: Have you been down there?
Cheyenne: No, nobody goes there.
Me: Why not?
Cheyenne: (gesturing with hands held wide apart) Snakes. This big!
Me: So nobody goes there because there are huge snakes?
Cheyenne: Yes.

Aha! So he *hasn't* covered every inch of this territory, after all! And if I were living in a remote, idyllic, Chinese-style Brigadoon, and I wanted to keep people from nosing around, what better way to do it than by floating the rumor that the valley has huge snakes! It's a dead giveaway! I take out my notebook and write:

Possible Peach Blossom Spring Location Number Two:
"Snake Valley," Zhangjiajie

Whatever is or is not hidden here, the mountains of Zhangjiajie are among the most interesting, bizarre and strangely shaped I've ever seen. Kuo Hsi, an 11th century painter who described the "general features of mountains," could have been describing these:

Mountains are massive things. They rise and fall, and, in repose, unveil themselves; they should be expansive and imposing, imperial and dynamic and severe; they should gaze in one direction, should appear to lift their heads and to genuflect; they should have a pinnacle above and be buttressed below, adhere to something before and be supported by something behind; their majestic gaze should encompass the entire valley, and, when descending, they should appear to issue commands to those below.

The journey by a miniature minibus back to where I had checked my bag is long and tiring; the journey back to the town of Zhangjiajie – despite the beauty of the ricefields and distant mountains – even more so. I am hot and tired and sweating and exhausted and I have a headache. Cheyenne is scanning the streets for something, no doubt the cheapest hotel in town. I tell him any hotel will do as long as it has a clean room.

Each Chinese town has small vehicles used to taxi people about. They may differ slightly in size or shape but the main characteristic all such vehicles have in common is that they *never should have been allowed on the road*. The vehicles in Zhangjiajie are known as *man man you* ("slowly traveling") and the slightly larger vans are called *myanbau che* because they resemble a loaf of bread. What they really resemble is a coffin on wheels. The one I am riding in is similar to almost all the rest: it has three wheels and a roof but no door; it is obviously falling apart; and, most fascinating of all, it has no side mirrors or rear view mirror. Cheyenne says these are "fun" vehicles. If one thinks of suicidal transportation as fun, he's right.

At some point we get out. Cheyenne tells me he will be right back and disappears into the darkness of a narrow, eight-story building with vertical strings of colorful flags along the front, suggesting it just opened. I pick up my bags and cross to the other side of the street and wait. I happen to sit in front of a hairdresser's and the young women come outside to talk to the foreigner. We talk for just one or two minutes before they bid me a hasty farewell and return inside their shop. I soon understand the reason for their abrupt departure.

A swarthy, barefoot, disheveled, elderly man sauntering down the street notices me and comes over to sit beside me. His longish hair has been bundled up and fixed on top of his head, somewhat similar to the Ming dynasty style, but it is so matted in the rear it hangs down in a small queue, Ch'ing dynasty style. He is wearing dirty trousers, torn in several places and a filthy black shirt which here and there reveals patches of its original blue. A kind of wave pattern along the sleeves and lower front lends him a slightly nautical air. His black eyes fix hypnotically on mine and, for several panicky seconds, I feel as if I am being confronted by a Chinese version of the Ancient Mariner. Then his face relaxes and he looks me up and down, not in disapproval but in curiosity, taking in my shorts and short-sleeved shirt with the top few buttons open.

Disheveled Man: You are hairy!
Me: That's true!
Disheveled Man: Even your arms and legs have hair!
Me: Yes, that's true!
Disheveled Man: You even have hair on your back?
Me: Yes.
Disheveled Man: All over?
Me: All over.
Disheveled Man: Aiiyaaaah!
Me: I am in fact the Monkey King!
Disheveled Man: Aiiyaaaaaaahhh!

The man says no more but continues to stare – as if he has come face to face with one of the world's wonders – repugnant yet fascinating. Sitting before him is one of the hairy beasts he has no doubt seen on wall paintings of Taoist temples – one-eyed monsters who saw evil eunuchs in half and throw dishonest magistrates into steaming cauldrons of fire.

Cheyenne reappears in a happy mood, tells me he got the room for just over 200 renminbi (about US$22), and grabs my luggage. I wave goodbye to my newfound friend, and follow Cheyenne into the hotel, trying not to stagger from fatigue and heat exhaustion.

Cheyenne: This is a new hotel.
Me: Great.

Cheyenne: They just opened!
Me: Great. What floor am I on?
Cheyenne: Six.
Me: Where's the lift?
Cheyenne: There isn't any.
Me: No lift?
Cheyenne: No, in Zhangjiajie only the four star hotels have lifts.

As we climb the stairs, we pass by a kind of dimly lit Chinese establishment with young women standing near the door to welcome guests; the kind of establishment that might either be a restaurant or a massage parlor. It was six of one and half dozen of the other. The second you walked in the door, the experienced staff made up their minds about what it was you desired and either led you to a table and brought you a menu or else led you to a cubicle and brought you a woman. Either way, you would most likely end up with Hunanese crabs.

In the hallway, the *fuwuyuan*, or, person in charge of our floor, opens the door for us. The room is clean, I will give Cheyenne that. There are, however, a few problems. To begin with, there seems to be no way to turn on the bathroom light and, as seems to be ubiquitous in hotels in this area, if there is any air conditioner at all, it is turned on and off by a remote. Not only does the remote seldom work, but there seems to be no level of warmth or cold in-between on and off.

When this is more or less straightened out, I sit on the bed trying to find the resolve and strength to get up and head for the bathroom. Cheyenne sits down on the other bed but, as always, seems to be immune to fatigue.

Me: "I'm going to take a shower."
Cheyenne: "Why don't you wait."
Me: "Wait for what?"
Cheyenne: "For the hot water."
Me: "You mean, there is no hot water now?"

(Cheyenne shakes his head to indicate that there is no hot water now)
Me: "When will there be hot water?"
Cheyenne: "Between 8 and 9 tonight."

He warns me the water will be very cold now. I explain to him that I don't care how cold it is, I *have* to take a shower. When I enter the bathroom, fastidious foreign-devil that I am, I spot a few things I don't like. I don't like the fact that there is no shower curtain; the fact that the toilet continuously runs but doesn't flush; the fact that there is no clothes hook on the bathroom door; the fact that there is no toilet paper; the fact that there is no hot water handle on the sink; the fact that the toilet tank has been built in such a way that the toilet seat cannot be raised far enough to stay upright and keeps crashing down; the fact that the cold water handle is so loose I can actually take it off; the fact that when I run water in the sink it ends up on the floor. And this is a new hotel. It is at times like this that I understand why Paul Theroux quoted the late poet, Philip Larkin, who said: "I wouldn't mind seeing China if I could come back the same day."

In fact, as one stays in hotel rooms farther and farther from any major center, the scenario becomes very predictable. The first thing to go is the hair dryer and the "good night" chocolate on the pillow; then the little bathroom basket with extra toothbrush, comb, shampoo and shower cap; then the carpet without cigarette burns; then any carpet; then the towels and toilet paper become, in terms of quality and size, almost interchangeable. And, finally, at the very end of the road, the hotel room will have either no soap or, far worse, a sliver of soap enmeshed in the previous occupant's hairs; there will be hot water only at scalding temperature and that only for a few minutes; there will be no shower curtain or else one with bizarre red stains which appear to have been left over from the movie, *Psycho*, and there will be no fully functioning light bulbs except when you want to sleep. I realize Cheyenne has taken me pretty far down the hotel room road and I am just a bit annoyed.

When I reenter the bedroom to convey my discovery to Cheyenne, he is lying on the other bed laughing hysterically at a Chinese soap opera which he has turned up very loud. I ask him to turn it down as I have a pounding headache. He kindly turns it off. I do understand that with his background, he naturally sees this as a very decent hotel. However, with my background, from my viewpoint, the Chinese government should take those involved in the building of this hotel as well as the builders of all other hotels like this one and make an example of them a la Ch'ing Dynasty Penal Codes.

As I need to change money, Cheyenne takes me to a bank. When we arrive, we find it is closed. Cheyenne shakes his head in confusion and says he doesn't understand why the bank is closed. Later, I realize it is Sunday. Sometimes I wonder about Cheyenne. Despite being a square shooter, he sometimes acts as if he isn't playing with all his mahjong tiles on the table.

We visit a museum of Tujia culture, opened and run by Tujia themselves. The beautifully carved beds of the Tujia are known as "water dripping beds," partly because they incorporate the carved eaves of the Tujia houses, but also because newly wedded women were supposed to cry for three days to show how sad they were over leaving home. The museum guides are young Tujia women and I ask one if Tujia brides still cry for three days. She says now they cry for only about half a day. I ask her how long she would cry if she married me. She says, "A long time." Someday I hope to figure out if that was a compliment or a putdown.

I treat Cheyenne to a Chinese lunch at one of the town's best restaurants. The service is good, the air-conditioning is excellent, and we have a view of the Lishui River. It is here that I show what I am made of. It is here that I carry out a deliciously rebellious act; a revolutionary, wicked, defiant gesture for which I shall receive eternal damnation from both travel and food writers alike. There have been acts of protest among writers before but to travel all the way to western Hunan province and to *order sweet-and-sour pork* – the most touristy of all Chinese dishes – that surely takes a certain kind of perverted panache; a kind of Cyrano de Bergerac bravado, a devil-may-care flourish, a gustatory blasphemy, if you will, that will serve as a kind of thumb in the eye of haughty travel/food writers for generations to come. Of course, one who initiates such a desecration of all that is holy in dining never remains completely unscathed: even the sweet-and-sour pork is *incredibly spicy.*

Back at the hotel, it is clear Cheyenne intends to spend the night in my room. I assure him I am an adult and can manage on my own but he reminds me that early tomorrow morning we are going down the Maoyan River rapids and he will take me to the shop/office when it opens and get the tickets. He will go on the bus with me but not on the boat. So while I am searching for Peach Blossom Spring along the Maoyan River I can rest assured that he is watching my luggage.

At some point, Cheyenne must have called Slick Willy (and his own wife?) because there is a knock at the door and Slick Willy enters. He has brought some bottles of very welcome cold water. He also seems to think every foreign male traveler is interested in sleeping with a Chinese woman because he repeats what he first told me way back (it seems like months before) at his office when we first met – that women are available. I assure him I am too old and too tired but would be happy to take both of them to a *western* dinner in the best restaurant in town. My treat.

At dinner Slick Willy opens up a bit about his background. It seems his wife has graduated from college and he hasn't and I get the impression he feels somewhat defensive about his lack of formal education. I assure him that to do well in business a formal education might be more of a hindrance than a help. (I'm a perfect example but I don't mention that.)

He says he first saw his wife when she was working in the post office and it took him three months of effort on his part before she would go out with him. But once they did go out, "there were chemicals between us." Right, I've had explosive relationships in my day, as well. And he speaks of how in the first few weeks and months with her he hated to even get out of bed.

Then, incredibly, he tells me that there is only so much fruit to be picked from one tree and so it is necessary to try other trees as well. And he tells me that he had an affair with a beautiful woman who was in a group he was guiding. And that she cried and cried when she had to leave him and board the train for Beijing. But that he gave her a number to a cellphone his wife doesn't know about and sometimes she calls.

I am not the type to judge anyone for having an affair; that is their business. But something about his cheating on a wife he claims he worked so hard to get bothers me. If I hadn't seen her it might be different, but something about his cheating on a truly handsome woman I can only drool over makes me upset. And his story of a lovely Chinese woman crying her heart out over him as she boards a train to Beijing makes me outright jealous. The story is so, well, Dr. Zhivagoish; Anna Kareninaish.

I have never had a woman cry her heart out over me while boarding a train to Beijing or anywhere else. Although I have had women flee from me on trains. In fact, women have fled from me on just about every means of transport imaginable: train, plane, boat, bus, tram, motorcycle, bicycle, hydrofoil, jetfoil, ferry, water scooter, skateboard, in-line-skates, rickshaw, trishaw, parasail, what-have-you – but here is a man – a Tujia version of Aleksei Vronski, married to an incredibly lovely woman for two years, a woman I would crawl on shards of Ch'ing Dynasty porcelain for, and, to excuse what he does with other women, he is already bullshitting me about single trees not having enough fruit. I'm not sure if it's my masculine side that's upset or my feminine side.

Or is my irritation with Slick Willy simply because at heart I'm a Romanticist and, despite my age, and despite all I have learned about the human condition, I like to cling to the American fiction of couples living "happily ever after?" His experience reminds me of the brilliant breakfast scenes in "Citizen Kane" wherein the newlyweds' relationship "progresses" from extreme passion to eventual boredom. There is a sadness about Slick Willy cheating on his beautiful wife; a sadness that lies beyond questions of fairness to a spouse or equality of the sexes.

I had previously asked Slick Willy what he thought a proper tip would be for Cheyenne. He had said that it was up to me. Later, when Slick Willy was not around, I had given Cheyenne US$100, about 20 dollars for each day he had been with me. He had begged me not to tell Slick Willy that I had tipped him because some percentage would then go to the company. With dinner nearly over, Cheyenne goes to the men's room and Slick Willy looks at me.

Slick Willy: So, what do you think?
Me: (innocent smile)
Slick Willy: About his tip?
Me: (trying not to stumble over words) Oh. Well, he seemed happy with the meals I've been buying him and I said I would send him something from the States.
Slick Willy: (pregnant pause) Sure. Anyway, I only mentioned it because you asked me before about his tip.
Me: Right.

So now Slick Willy no doubt has me pegged as either a liar or a cheapskate but as Cheyenne returns he abruptly changes the subject. He tells me he thinks it would be a good idea for me to open an office in Zhangjiajie. As a writer without a company I find the suggestion somewhat unrealistic. But I have to admit that after a fine dinner and sparkling white wine and after feeling the effects of air-conditioning that actually works I feel a great deal better. And, of course, my Tujia friends again insist that I should spend at least a few hours with a beautiful Chinese woman.

And now we come to a fork in the road or perhaps a pair of chopsticks on the literary highway. How much does a writer impart to his reader? Take Paul, for example. (I hope by now he won't object to a slight bit of informality.) In *The Great Railway Bazaar* he was taken to a brothel near Madras and, he tells us, due mainly to the horrors of the rooms, he shied away from having sex with Kerala maidens from the Malabar Coast. And in *Riding the Iron Rooster*, he tells us that in Moscow, although he went with women to an apartment and sex was suggested, even encouraged, he again declined, this time with a slim woman with "china-blue eyes" and an "expressive Russian mouth" named Natasha. And, again, in *Riding the Iron Rooster*, Paul says he was "repeatedly accosted" by the pretty girls of Xiamen who snatched his arm and pinched him. Now it may be that what he wrote in those scenes is exactly what happened. It may not be. Whatever it was, a travel writer does not have an obligation to divulge anything he does not wish to report.

But, if in his books, Paul Theroux revealed that he had in fact had a tryst with naughty Natasha or had Done the Deed with the Kerala cuties or had agreed to an assignation with the pretty Xiamen maidens, and perhaps even wrote it up in his books, no matter how tastefully, would that change our opinion of him? If we knew for certain that he was one of those who, in the Chinese phrase, "seek out the flowers and amuse himself with the willows," would he be compromised as a writer? Would his writing then in some way be changed, even tainted, in our eyes? And if so is that a reflection on him or on us?

And so the question must be asked: What kind of man would wish to spend the night with a beautiful Chinese woman – a woman who, in the Chinese phrase, "sells her spring," and "sells her glances" – a woman he doesn't even know and will, in all probability, never see again? But a woman with thousands of years of Chinese culture and history flowing through her veins. A woman whose very being is the product of the incredibly rich tapestry of Chinese history – with all its beauty and all its horror. Its brilliant painters, its gifted poets, its omnipotent emperors, its ravishing concubines, its scheming eunuchs, its brave generals, its suffering peasants, its exotic gods, its benevolent goddesses, its curious legends, its vengeful ghosts, its glorious victories, its tragic defeats.

A woman whose heritage if not lineage might be traced to P'an Ku, the great architect who gave his life to create the universe; Emperor Yao of China's golden age who, it is said, was born with eyebrows of eight different colors; a legendary general who surrendered his army because the calligraphy of his opponent showed clearly that he was the superior man; Wang Chao-chun, the great beauty who, to appease the Huns, was sent by her emperor to a distant barbarian kingdom never to return; Yueh Fei, the loyal Sung general who was unjustly denounced and put to death; Ch'iu Chin, the defiant anti-Ch'ing rebel, and the only woman in Chinese history to be beheaded; Sun Yat-sen, the Father of the Country whose tragic early death led to war between Chiang Kai-shek and Mao Tse-tung.

And somewhere within such a woman would one not find innate knowledge of The Three Kingdoms, Dream of the Red Chamber, the Six Idlers of the Bamboo Brook, the Yellow Turbans, the Son of Heaven, the Seven Sages of the Bamboo Grove, the White Lotus, the Golden Lotus, Red Cliff, the Silk Road, the Jade Emperor, the Yellow Emperor, fox fairies, the purple Forbidden City, the Grand Canal, Buddhist sutras, ancestor worship, the Eight Immortals of the Winecup, the Boxers, the Monkey King, Golden Lilies, the nine Celestial Dragons, the Mustard Seed Garden, White Snake, the Pear Garden, the First Sword under Heaven, the Mandate of Heaven, the Great Wall, the Yin and the Yang, the Book of Changes, the Heavenly Kingdom of Great Peace, the wisdom of Lao Tzu, the teachings of Confucius, and, of course, Peach Blossom Spring.

And what if such a woman appeared with beautiful long raven-black hair, cheekbones so high they were seldom free of icicles, and almond eyes right out of a T'ang Dynasty poem. A woman most likely descended from an imperial concubine. Absolutely gorgeous. A goddess.

And what if, later, at her touch, the earth dissolves and we bestride the White Crane of Longevity and, as it stretches its wings and flies, the goddess and I soar upwards until we enter into the Jade Heaven of the Western Paradise. There, within beautiful peach blossom pavilions set among lotus flower-gardens with steps of priceless ivory and precious jade the goddess and I cavort. And as I bathe in the warm beneficence of her smile, as I willingly surrender to the golden glow of her celestial radiance, sweet-scented peach blossoms flutter profusely from above and brilliantly colored phoenixes sing more melodiously than I could have imagined possible, and the goddess and I wander hand in hand, crossing glittering rivers of the purest green-and-blue liquid jade coursing through misty mountains with cloud-covered peaks from which we can gaze upon the legendary Isle of the Blest, the fabulous Land of the Immortals.

And what if at some point such a man came to realize that such a woman was none other than the Indian maiden that he, as a boy, tried so diligently to catch even a fleeting glimpse of? Were such a man to spend the night with such a woman could he possibly recapture the excitement and wonder of the nine-year-old boy?

You betcha.

Enlightenment at Maoyen River

Early the next morning, Cheyenne and I board a minibus and head for the Maoyan River. The bus is soon blocked on a picturesque mountain road by another which is stuck in the mud. After some time, the road is cleared and we continue. Lovely yellow flowers of the "four seasons" bean seem to surround every black-tiled cottage roof. Yellowish green fields of rice stretch out as far as the eye can see. There is a very special beauty in Chinese landscapes, and a new and equally fascinating view appears around each bend. For miles there are no modern buildings, and I realize I am looking at scenes similar to those which must have existed in the time of T'ao Yuan-ming. To be close to nature as beautiful as this would indeed be a gift.

Eventually, we reach the river and Cheyenne decides to join me and ten others on the 12-seat inflatable raft with a boatman positioned beside the ancient American Johnson motor at the rear. Local people are selling bamboo tubes with a crude but effective plunger, tubes that will soon be used by everyone on our raft to shoot water at people on other rafts and vice versa.

As we start out, I ask the young woman sitting in front of me why she is holding a scoop; I had thought maybe it was to be used for food during lunch later. In answer to my question, she scoops water out of the river and drenches me. Aha! As with the bamboo tubes, it will be employed as a weapon in water fights.

✓ *Peach Blossom Spring Note Number Four:* When traveling on a river in China with a woman who has a scoop in her hand, do not ask the woman what the scoop in her hand is for.

Except for the constant water fights between and among boats, which leave everyone completely drenched, the trip is pleasant. Dragonflies flit along beside us like brilliantly colored darts and in places the rolling hills assume dramatic shapes. But there are so many caves, grottoes and openings in hills along the shore, searching for the one the fisherman might have found is like looking for a concubine's hairpin in a ricefield. I begin jotting down the number of caves we pass and in just one stretch of river alone, we pass nine. If I multiply that number by the number of miles of river left to travel, and then by the number of rivers in western Hunan, the task becomes, to say the least, insurmountable.

The dragonflies increase in number which is not a good sign because the Chinese also call them "typhoon-flies" because they gather in large numbers before a storm. The storm does not arrive but the wind increases and at times the rapids sends our raft speeding along faster than I would like; and I recall Deng Xiaoping's parable describing how China should run its economy: "Crossing the river by feeling the stones, one at a time." If this raft tips over, I will be taking his advice literally.

In the late 1800's, when the foreign-devils began to penetrate China's interior, skilled Chinese artists cleverly painted realistic cannon high up on boulders along rivers such as this so as to scare the Western barbarians from proceeding any farther. Unfortunately for the Chinese, the barbarians had something called a "thousand-mile-eye tube" (telescope) and could tell at a glance that the cannon were not real.

As we round a bend, a few young men stand on a ledge staring down at us. I can't help feeling that I have been on this river before – a sense of *deja vu* and a sense of foreboding envelop me at the same time. And then I remember: this stretch of river looks just like the scene in the movie, *Deliverance*, where those local boys did some baaaad things to the city boys from the boat. As I am drenched with still more water, I make a determined effort to relax.

But something about the jarring of the raft by the rapids, the mysterious caves and mountain streams passing by, and a sudden drenching of chilly, cold water in the midst of a water fight, seem to tap my subconscious. I remember something professor Tan had said on the phone, i.e., there is no evidence that T'ao Yuan-ming traveled as far west as what is now called Peach Blossom Spring. And it suddenly hits me: the poet would never have so freely given away the actual location where he found Peach Blossom Spring, and so he wrote as if he had discovered it in what is now the next province over, Hunan. And I remember reading of how T'ao's cottage faced the Lu Mountains and how he loved to walk among those mountains. And I remember Cheyenne saying that the Lu Mountains are even taller and more majestic than those of Zhangjiajie.

And then I remember something else: there are a few lines of T'ao Yuan Ming's poetry which no one has ever understood. According to Professor Tan, "critics and annotators across the ages have despaired of penetrating the poem's hidden meaning."

> You claim to know of what I sing
> Thoughts inspired by wine;
> To know how numerous these can be
> Harken to the fantastic song on Zhangshan

Zhangshan, or Mount Zhang, also known as "Stone Gate," rises majestically in the north of the Lu Mountains. Suddenly, it is so obvious: T'ao Yuan-ming found Peach Blossom Spring close to his home while poking about the Lu Mountains in what is now Jiangsi Province! Probably sometime after his cottage burned down and before he had built a new one. Peach Blossom Spring is hidden somewhere among some of the most beautiful mountains of China: Lu Shan. And what exactly is the fantastic song on Mount Zhang to which we should harken? The most fantastic song of all: Peach Blossom Spring! That is where he found it! On Mount Zhang in Jiangsi! He wrote the clue right into the poem! Jesus Christ! I've been searching for Peach Blossom Spring in the wrong damn province.

BOOK II

Fear and Loathing in Jiangsi Province

"A confusion of the real with the ideal never goes unpunished"
–Goethe

"Cast away illusions, prepare for struggle"
–Chairman Mao Tse-tung

"China is a sleeping giant. Let her sleep, for when she awakes, she will astonish the world."
–Napoleon

"China is a closet Capitalist. Let her sleep, for when she awakes, she will fleece the world."
–Dean Barrett

Return to China

Dear Dean,

As can be expected, I am more than curious to learn about the way fortune favoured your venturesome quest, in the height of summer, for the legendary Peach Blossom Spring. What I am quite certain about is that this bold venture of yours, by the very formidable challenge it posed, has brought you a great deal closer to the poet T'ao Ch'ien (Yuan-ming) and that it has, moreover, filled me with respectful admiration for the passionate pilgrim from overseas....I wish you every success in your laborious undertaking, the second part of your book – *Don Quixote in China: The Search for Peach Blossom Spring* – in the Lu Mountains.

Yours truly,

Peter (Tan Shilin), Zhong Shan, China

I have returned to China. Or, at least, I am back in the former British Crown Colony of Hong Kong. And this time I managed to check into the Kowloon Hotel with no problems. And I have no doubt I will again be issued a visa to China. But my life has changed. Just over one year has passed since I visited Hunan Province. Somehow – no doubt because of the malicious trickery of Freston the Magician – I am no longer living in a brownstone on East 10th Street in Manhattan's East Village. I now live in a room over the Texas Lone Staar Saloon in Washington Square in Bangkok, Thailand.

And the world has changed as well: a matter of days before I left Bangkok for Hong Kong, in New York – the city I had been living in for 14 years – Muslim fanatics murdered nearly three thousand Americans.

I had thought of postponing my trip into Jiangxi Province but I knew that beginning in late October the weather would turn very cold and snow would soon be on the Lu mountains. And, like most Americans, I was spending far too much time watching news of the attack which was leading me into depression. I knew there would be far less opportunity to watch the unfolding events in the "War on Terror" in the mountains of Jiangxi Province. As much as they felt the need to flee from wars and strife, I doubt that even the inhabitants of Peach Blossom Spring could have imagined such horror.

I fold Peter Tan's letter and place it with another he had sent inviting me to stay with him. For whatever reason, Peter has begun writing to me about my quixotic quest and has invited me to spend the night with him while on my way to Peach Blossom Spring. Perhaps after all these years of withdrawal he is taking tentative steps to reach outward again to a world he no doubt found horribly cruel.

For awhile I sit on the hotel bed listening to the wind strike the panes of glass, thinking of the World Trade Center and wondering what happened to the woman who worked at the Hunan Association; the woman I had briefly spoken to just over one year ago.

The wind increases. A typhoon is heading for Hong Kong and is expected to hit Zhong Shan (central mountain), an area up the Pearl River where Professor Tan lives. Exactly where I am going.

On the elevator I had mentioned to a hotel employee that with a bit of luck the typhoon might miss us. She smiled and said, "Actually, the warning signal has just been raised from one to three." And, sure enough, when I returned to the room, there under my door was a hotel notice in Chinese and English:

Tropical Cyclone Warning Signal No. 3

The Hong Kong Observatory has just hoisted the **Tropical Cyclone Warning Signal No. 3**. This indicates that we will experience strong wind. ..It is very likely that a higher typhoon signal will be hoisted during the course of the night. This indicates that the typhoon is expected to increase significantly in strength and the sustained wind speed is expected to increase and come within the range 41-62 km/h during the next few hours....

And on the bed is a "Typhoon Safety Advice" notice informing me that "though the skies may appear friendly, Signal No. 3 indicates that the weather is likely to change quickly for the worse. You are advised not to cross the harbour, nor to venture too far from the Hotel." If I had any doubts that the typhoon was yet another obstacle in my path created by Freston the Magician, the next sentence dispels them: "Please cancel any immediate plans for an extensive tour." Is this the best trick Freston can come up with?

I snatch my cap off the table by the bed and look it over. It is a dark blue cap with a gold NYPD logo and police department insignia. I had been wearing the cap in Thailand for several months before September 11th, but after the death of so many police officers the cap has taken on new meaning and I again debate with myself whether or not I should wear it. Finally, I decide not many people in Asia will recognize a New York Police Department cap anyway and I decide to wear it into China. Besides, Don Quixote entered into various adventures in full armor with barber's bowl helmet and visor; perhaps as I travel through the Middle Kingdom this cap will serve as my helmet and visor. And the truth is the cap's inside tag says "made in China."

I leave the hotel and head for the China Travel Service, a mere five minute walk. Once again I find myself in their office filling out a form and describing myself as a "musical theater lyricist." A middle-aged woman behind the counter looks over the form and asks me if I know all the words to America the Beautiful. She says she likes that song. I have to confess I don't know them all. The visa costs about US$21.

A young woman sitting beside her looks over my form. She has short hair, pixyish eyes, a thin nose and a generous mouth: With a bit of imagination she could pass as a Chinese version of Julia Roberts. She looks up and asks, "Are you from New York?"

When I reply in the affirmative, she asks, "Did you lose any friends?" I tell her not as far as I know, but that I have a writer friend who lived very near the World Trade Center in Battery Park City. I tell her how she was thrown out of bed by the sound of the first plane hitting and happened to look out when the second one hit. How she saw people falling from the building to their deaths. I tell her how her face and arms swelled up because of the tiny shards of glass and steel that pierced her skin when she ran hysterical from the area as the buildings collapsed and day turned into night. Of how she tried to save her dog and of how she thought she was going to die. How she was ferried to New Jersey and lived in a shelter and now cannot sleep or write, how she has constant nightmares, and has problems with her lungs from the ash of the collapsing buildings.

I had not planned to go into such detail but as I speak I find I cannot stop. It is almost as if her question released all the anger; and all the emotions that I have bottled up inside are at last coming out of me. When I have finished, I see that tears have welled up in her eyes. After several seconds of silence, she says, "I'm so sorry for your friend."

I mumble a thank you and follow another woman to have my photos taken. This time the photos dry quickly and are even placed inside a small glassine envelope for me. Much to my surprise, they take no notice of my reason for going to China: "To search for Peach Blossom Spring." One of the women looks at it but does not cross it out. Perhaps they have heard about me and regard me the way Don Quixote's friends regarded him: as more than a bit addled. A trifle tetched. Or, worse, perhaps they remember me from last year and have lost faith that I will ever find the pastoral paradise I am searching for.

I wait in line before the counter selling train tickets. When it is my turn, I explain to a somewhat bored gentleman how the year before on the train to Changsha, Hunan, I had a hard sleeper, that is, a small compartment with four bunks and a closing door, and I ask if on this trip I could have a soft sleeper. The man explains that that *was* a soft sleeper. "Hard sleepers are six bunks and no door."

But as I will take a boat to Zhong Shan, then a bus to Guangchou (Canton), I must buy my train ticket in Guangchou because "they" will not allow him to sell soft sleeper tickets from Hong Kong if the train voyage does not originate here. "They" could of course be Chinese railroad officials. Or just possibly allies of Freston the magician.

While the rest of the world is anxiously awaiting the American military response to terrorism, even before I leave Hong Kong for China I learn an interesting fact. China's 1.3 billion people are also upset but not so much over any American tragedy. Rather they are furious over a scandal that threatens to shake China to its very foundations: a mooncake scandal. Ugly, persistent rumors have been verified in the press as facts: Some of the largest, most trusted, names in makers of mooncakes have been recycling several year-old fillings, in some cases the reused fillings were said to be from uneaten mooncakes.

Mooncake makers create various types such as red bean paste or white lotus paste or mixed walnuts and ham, and add special ingredients for variety, but most will contain coconut milk, the yolk of preserved eggs, butter, flour, sugar, fat, almond, sesame, and custard powder.

Apparently, to save money, stores and restaurants were allowed to return unsold mooncakes to be recycled into the filling of the following year's mooncakes. As many bakers make much of their annual profit from the sale of mooncakes this scandal is quite a disaster for them.

In each society some things are regarded if not actually sacred, as too pure to be tampered with, and certainly Mid-Autumn Festival mooncakes are close to sacred in Chinese society. Of the many legends involving the moon and mooncakes, perhaps the most dear to Chinese is that in which Chinese coordinated a rebellion against their Mongol rulers by baking a message with details of the rebellion into each mooncake. The patriots launched their attack on the night of the moon festival, overthrew the Mongols (Yuan Dynasty) and established the Ming Dynasty. Hence, mooncakes are seen as a kind of patriotic food commemorating Chinese liberation. In America, it would be as if on Thanksgiving, the apple pie, the pumpkin pie, the turkey and the cranberry sauce were all found to be contaminated.

Even while I am in Hong Kong, cautious immigration officials are preventing Chinese from the Mainland being held inside a Reception Center from receiving 15 mooncakes from friends. Correctional Services Department officers say they fear there might be weapons hidden inside the mooncakes. Yes, Chinese have long memories.

Despite the scandal, I decide to buy a box of mooncakes as a gift for Professor Tan and his wife from a special booth set up in the hotel lobby. The boxes on display are the traditional lacquer boxes and the mooncakes themselves are an inviting light golden hue. Although traditionally mooncakes were round to honor the moon, modern Chinese experiment with different shapes including square and oblong. I ask the bright-eyed, eager-to-please, young woman behind the booth about the mooncake scandal. She hastens to assure me the mooncakes she sells are fresh, locally made; I should not be afraid. She reminds me of the mayor in *Jaws* assuring tourists all is well, or the official in *Death in Venice* assuring von Aschenbach there is no Asiatic cholera. "They are made in our city," she says brightly.

"So was my ex-wife," I think dourly.

༄༄༄༄༄༄༄༄

Fortunately, the television sets in the rooms of my hotel transform into computers and I manage to get onto the internet. Once again, as I did with Hunan, I search the archives of the *South China Morning Post* to learn exactly what kind of province I am getting into. For Jiangxi province, I find this:

5 August 2000: People face slow, agonizing deaths in Jiangxi province's Shangshan village due to a silicosis epidemic that has already killed 25 residents.

6 August 2000: Twenty-one killed as fireworks explosives blast flattens building, Pingxiang city, Jiangxi.

30 August 2000: More than 20,000 farmers have clashed with paramilitary police in Jiangxi province, ransacking buildings and destroying schools and homes.

28 September 2000: An unidentified robber blew up a public bus in Jiangxi province, killing three passengers and himself.

20 December 2000: Nine months after former Jiangxi vice-governor Hu Changqing was executed, six business executives have been sentenced for their part in bribing him.

16 January 2001: Police have arrested a gang of six men who killed two customers and a taxi driver when they robbed a bank in Jiangxi's Nanchang city.

20 April 2001: Chinese raid defiant village, killing 2, amid rural unrest.

4 June 2001: President Jiang Zemin yesterday completed a four-day tour of scandal-ridden Jiangxi province, where he reminded cadres to remain honest and loyal to the Communist Party.

22 June 2001: Classes were well under way at Fanglin Village Primary School in

Jiangxi province when an explosion leveled the interior of the two-story brick school building, killing 42 students and teachers.

28 July 2001: Police in Jiangxi have ordered all discos to close by mid-August in a bid to prevent the province's youngsters from going mad from 'speedy dancing' or the 'violent undertones' of some songs.

3 August 2001: The death toll from a quarry collapse in Jiangxi province has reached 24, with four still missing.

4 September 2001: A peasant in Jiangxi province was allegedly beaten to death after he refused to pay six yuan (US$.72) in overdue tax.

I call an English publisher I have not seen for many years with the intention of asking her to dinner. When I mention mutual acquaintances who have now left Hong Kong, in each case, she responds, "Oh, yes, he did very well!" After 14 years as a writer ensconced in the Arts in Manhattan, I had forgotten how, in Hong Kong, the value of a person depends solely on how much money he made while there.

One of the reasons I moved from Hong Kong to Manhattan was because I was tired of overhearing conversations around me in restaurants and hotel lobbies and everywhere else involving "property, stocks, warrants and money." After 17 years I had had enough. So I decided I would move to New York City's East Village, where I would sit in cafes and restaurants and listen to those around me discuss their works-in-progress, film, art, music, novels, theater; conversations which, like their work, would explore the human condition. So I moved to the East Village and every day in cafes and restaurants and everywhere else I overheard intense, impassioned and totally humorless conversations about "relationships, commitment, communication." A mantra as holy for Americans as *om mani padme hum* is for Tibetans. "Re-*la*-tion-ships!" Let us pray. In a way it is almost a pleasure to hear someone talk about money again.

I say nothing to the publisher who continues to tell me how

so-and-so did *very* well, but I can't help wonder how she describes me to others: "Oh, yes, Dean did OK but then went off the deep end and started searching for a mythical utopia in remote areas of China. Probably a Freudian thing." I decide not to invite the publisher to dinner.

I call a Chinese friend who used to work with me in publishing many years before. It is a difficult call because I have heard he is getting divorced. I also knew his wife well and Rumor-control Headquarters has it that his wife committed adultery; or, as the Chinese say it, "the red apricot has left the wall," and my cuckolded friend is left wearing, in the Chinese expression, a *dailumaozi*, a green hat. A woman answers the phone. Not his ex-wife. It seems my friend has been proactive in his "relationships."

In a bookstore I come across a copy of Maxine Hong Kingston's *Woman Warrior*, a discovery which brings back the student riot days of San Francisco State College during the late 1960's. Whenever any of our Chinese teachers were tied up on business deals in Taiwan and couldn't make it back for the start of the semester, another Chinese teacher would cover for him and would fill in the class by relating all kinds of Chinese tales and legends. Anything! Just so long as it got us through the period. It got so I had practically memorized tales of how mythological figures like Pan Ku created the universe and how his hair became trees, and his something became something, and how his lice became men, *ad infinitum, ad nauseam*.

And, while listening to the tales for the hundredth time, we would look at one other in abject boredom and role our eyes and sigh.

And then decades later, I opened the book, *Woman Warrior*, and there were all these tales that had bored us to death being retold to an American audience who was gobbling them up like hot candied apples.

✓ *Peach Blossom Spring Note Number Five:* Learn to Package! Learn to Package! Learn to Package!

I take the Star Ferry and notice once again that there are no longer any fleets of beautiful Chinese junks with butterfly-wing sails as there still were when I first visited Hong Kong in 1967. I always regret the passing of a beautiful and cultural aspect of an Asian community, but I am careful not to regret it too much. I still remember a German photographer who was always fiercely indignant when some tradition was no longer being carried on. He would straighten himself up, narrow his eyes, and say, "I stand with the past!"

But I noticed that, as with most people who "stand with the past," this man surrounded himself with all the luxuries the present could offer him. He lived in a luxurious, air-conditioned apartment on Hong Kong Island with flush, sit-down toilets and expensive modern art on the walls. And yet he resented it because each year that he would venture out and take colorful shots of boat people living on board their boats, there were far fewer of them; and on those that remained, their picturesque sails were rapidly being replaced by diesel engines.

He never seemed to notice that the boat people lived in cramped, sweaty, constantly moving vessels, working in all kinds of weather, eking out a precarious existence in depleted fishing grounds and, when the need arose, had to shit in the water. If traditions disappear because the descendents of those who created them are finding better lives, it seems to me there is little we can do but wish people good luck. And, as for those who wish to "stand with the past," the ricefields are still there. They can work from dawn to dusk and live in a baked-brick house with a thatched roof in the hills. But they won't.

My last day in Hong Kong is sunny and breezy, the typhoon has passed and the harbor's slightly choppy pea green water rocks the Star ferry almost as gently as a cradle. On my way to visit friends on the Hong Kong side, the taxi passes the American consulate. Along the sidewalk are dozens of bouquets of flowers, notes of condolence, expressions of support, and even an American flag made of flowers which Hong Kong Chinese and others have left in sympathy with Americans. I find myself fighting back tears.

Fighting Pearl River Pirates

In a light rain, under grey skies, I head for the hydrofoil which will whisk me into China, by way of the Pearl River to Zhong Shan. My mind is on Bush's speech to Congress which I saw on TV shortly before I left the hotel. The preparations for America's war on terrorists has begun and I find it extremely difficult to take my mind off the international situation. And so I make an effort to do so.

I start a conversation about the mooncake situation with the taxi driver. Discussing the mooncake scandal will become my way of taking my mind off larger events. The driver reacts as a hungry trout after a succulent worm. "Not only did they recycle moldy paste they also used out-of-date oil! It makes me sick to think about it!" His indignation rises as he repeats a newspaper article about workers sleeping on the same slabs of wood on which they prepared the cakes. He adds emphatically, "Whatever you do, don't buy mooncakes on the Mainland!"

The truth is that even without the present scandal over fillings and means of production, mooncakes were already falling out of favor due to changing tastes among the more modern Chinese. They are said to be too fattening, too sugary, and their wrappings too expensive. And in response to the growing disdain for pig fat in the mooncakes, some bakeries are now using peanut oil. But it seems clear that what was once an esteemed present is now sometimes as welcome among China's urban young as a Christmas fruitcake would be to an American teenager.

At the China Ferry Terminal, I pay HK$189 (about US$16)

for a one-way ticket to Zhong Shan. I laboriously fill out an immigration form only to be told by the immigration official at the counter that I already have a form in my passport.

A Chinese woman with exceptionally large, jet black eyes and perfect heart-shaped lips is stationed in an open hallway, checking tickets and assisting travelers in need. She is well groomed, well dressed, and, despite her less than glamorous occupation, looks as if she was born with a silver spoon – or, rather, jade chopstick – in her mouth. In a puerile attempt to impress her I hold up my ticket and with a heavy Beijing accent say, "Zhong Shan." She replies in perfect English with an upper class British accent, "Make a right, please. Thank you. Have a pleasant journey." Touche. The hydrofoil gangplank is bouncing erratically in the choppy waves but I manage to leap on board without mishap. The boat is not full and it is another one of those Chinese situations in which seat numbers are ignored, so rather than chasing someone out of my seat, I sit in an empty one.

Only after the boat is underway do I notice the signs on either side: In Chinese and English they read: "Urgent disperse" with arrows pointing to bow and stern. But as we are surrounded by water, in the event of an emergency, to where do we urgently disperse?

The fact that we are underway does not prevent the Chinese from indulging in the wonders of speaking with friends on their cellphones in several dialects and at ear-splitting volume. And, of course, adding to the noise, their friends ring them back, showering me with various tinny, annoying and maddening versions of saccharine love songs which should never have been composed to begin with.

We pass by lovely green islands, many uninhabited, then our vessel passes through the Kapshuimun Pass north of Lantau Island and enters the main river, a stretch which has little of interest as far as scenery goes, offering glimpses of modern residential buildings interspersed with boring factories.

But I love the period of Chinese history when foreigners first arrived in Hong Kong waters in any numbers, especially the 1850's, so, steeped in such lore, in my mind I see what I want to see: the well-armed pirate ships with their spectacular bat-wing sails bristling with 24-pounders and swivel guns as they secretly gather at Second Bar Creek, making preparations to attack our hydrofoil as it innocently makes its way upriver.

As a history buff I'm aware that this 80-mile stretch of the Pearl River between Hong Kong, Macau and Guangzhou is a goldmine or, rather, jademine of colorful history. Many of the clashes and conflicts between an imperious China and the Western powers who were determined to open the Ch'ing Dynasty (1644-1911) to trade and bestow upon the Middle Kingdom the dubious benefits such enterprise would entail, took place right on this stretch of water.

The titles of the books written by eyewitnesses of the period are intriguing in themselves. C. Toogood Downing sailed up this stretch of river in the 1830s and wrote a book entitled, *Fan-Qui in China,* (Foreign Devils in China). And what history buff could resist trying to see what inspired 19th century authors to write chapters with headings such as these: Monsoons, Destruction of Native Junks, Barbarous Language, Consumption of Opium, Battle of the Bogue, Native Pirates, Second Bar Pagoda, China Girls, Chase and Capture of a Smuggler, The Seaman's Burial Ground, Foreign Ghosts, Dangerous Routes, Men-of-War, Flower Boats, and, not least tantalizing: Calling a Servant – Getting Rid of one. In my mind's eye, the shrill rings of the cellphones transform into the sounds of sailors being piped aboard, and the barges and hydrofoils transform into a forest of masts and rigging and sails of barques, brigs, schooners, sloops-of-war, barkentines and brigantines, their brilliantly colored flags fluttering above them; the Chinese cargo boats and fishing junks with eyes painted on their bows and chop boats and scrambling dragons and mandarin boats and smuggling boats and opium boats and boats laden with tea or teak or salt. Or pirates.

Of course, when Chinese junks armed with cannon went up against even a few men-of-war, the junks almost always got the worst of it. This was partly because of inferior Chinese cannon and ammunition but also because of superior Western training in that kind of warfare. No doubt it was bloody. But I imagine a scene of over 100 junks, with their magnificent butterfly-wing sails, facing off against British and French ships-of-the-line also in full sail. Flags and pennants flying in the breeze, booms and flashes from the cannon and rockets, fire and smoke on the ships which had been hit, holes appearing in billowing white sails and wooden hulls, and bluish-grey smoke enveloping the entire scene.

I can't help thinking that where foreigners and Chinese smugglers once attempted to smuggle opium into China with oars, paddles, sculls and sails, Hong Kong gangs are now using high-powered speedboats to smuggle in new luxury cars.

But I am determined that the events of the present will not impinge on my journey into the past, and as the hydrofoil proceeds upriver, I look past the container ships, oil storage facilities and modern factories in an attempt to locate any of the crumbling forts or ancient pagodas untouched by time, commerce or property development.

I am convinced that at any minute our captain will sight an enemy sail, the marine drummer will beat to quarters and the deck will be cleared for action. Nets will be hung to prevent pirates armed with cutlasses and flintlocks from boarding. The arms chest will be flung open and I will be given my choice of a pistol, boarding axe or pike. The lids to the gunports will be lifted and the cannon loaded with round shot. Chain shot, grape shot and bar shot will be run out, ready for action. Meanwhile, hungry as I am, I realize I will have to survive as best I can on rock-hard, weevil-infested ship's biscuit (hardtack) and grog (diluted rum). I walk to the ship's store for my ration and return with a carton of steaming noodles and a soft drink. (Not unlike Don Quixote, history buffs must learn to rationalise: I decide they must save the hardtack and grog until after the battle.)

Despite their military superiority, until quite recent times the danger to Westerners traveling in these waters was very real. The head of a foreigner was worth taels of silver and could be sold to Chinese government officials known as Mandarins.

For example, in December of 1856, eleven foreigners on the postal steamer *Thistle,* traveling from Guangzhou to Hong Kong, were murdered by Chinese soldiers disguised as passengers. I look around me but the passengers seem genuinely asleep or else yelling into a cellphone about which stock to buy or to sell. They do not resemble soldiers about to attack foreign passengers; but one never knows. And I remember that on the same day Hong Kong newspapers reported that tragedy, they also mentioned an attack on the river steamer *Fiema* by 50 armed Chinese junks off Second Bar Creek and the capture of the cutter, *Excelsior* by two mandarin boats, and her crew held to ransom. I decide to keep an eagle eye on any ship or hydrofoil that comes near.

A Meeting at Zhongshan

Possibly because of my vigilance, we reach Zhongshan safely. Chinese artists have a splendid palette of interesting colors, so I will render an accurate description of the sky using one of their own color descriptions, i.e., "mucus-of-the-nose gray."

Inhabitants of the Zhongshan area, located in the southern part of the Pearl River Delta, have been active in foreign trade for centuries. (As traders or boatmen or smugglers or pirates, whatever.) It was long known as Xiangshan ("Fragrant Mountain") but was renamed in the early 1950's in honor of Sun Yat-sen, whose name in Mandarin is Sun Zhong-shan. Sun was born in Zhongshan and there are various memorial Sun Yat-sen halls, parks, hot springs and statues as well as his former residence. (For those who can't stand the x's and z's of pinyin romanization, the words may be rendered as "Chongshan" and "Heungshan.")

According to a website I find that Zhongshan City was once named one of "The Ten Sanitary Cities in China" and in 1995 finally made its mark as "The National Sanitary City." Exactly what that means, who makes these tough decisions and who dreams up these superb titles, I have no idea.

Once again, simplified Chinese characters are almost my undoing. I have Professor Tan's address in Chinese but I have no doubt that Freston the Magician was at it again because I mixed up one of the characters of the street. I thought it was *yu* for jade but it was the short (simplified) form of *bao* (treasure). They are not exactly alike but quite similar. And so thanks to my mistake, it takes us quite a while to find the professor's apartment.

The concrete building is not new nor is its façade inviting, but it is located in a pleasant area overlooking a park. I buzz his apartment on a rusty intercom and Professor Tan tells me he will be right down. But the metal door is open and so I pick up my small leather suitcase and begin walking up the seven flights of stairs to his apartment.

At last, in dim light near the top of the stairwell, I catch my first glimpse of Peter Tan – the man who spent three years of his life studying and translating the works of T'ao Yuan-ming, and the man whose book inspired my search for Peach Blossom Spring.

He is dressed in olive green T-shirt, faded khaki shorts and slippers, revealing thin legs and bony knees. His hair is an unruly yin-yang blend of white and black and the scrubby growth of white hair on his chin is not long enough to serve as a goatee nor short enough to pass as stubble overlooked while shaving. His smile is sincere and not infrequent but the wearied expression in his eyes often fails to match the smile. Peter proves to be an excellent and gracious host but he has at times a tired, enervated, almost demoralized, air about him and, indeed, not far into our conversations, he will candidly describe himself as a "pessimist." Given the events of his life one cannot blame him.

His apartment is clean but not sterile, dark but not gloomy, the perfect setting for someone whose scholarly inclination as well as horrible personal experience has rendered him wary of the modern age. He introduces me to his lovely Chinese wife, several years younger than him, and escorts me into my spacious bedroom, complete with canopied bed and mosquito net.

Much of what color there is in the residence comes from dozens of resplendent parrots that brighten up the apartment. On the wall is a painting of Peter's late German mother, drawn by his talented artist son. Her features suggest those of a strong, resolute and determined woman, and I suspect her defiant temperament served her well when she faced the vicissitudes of the Mao era.

She met Peter's father in Europe in the 1920's and soon came to China as the foreign wife of a Chinese husband; which at the time was no doubt scandalous in the eyes of friends of both.

We relax in an already dark room which becomes darker as we talk. In the corner, a computer monitor and keyboard look very much out of place. Peter says he uses a computer to type but will not use the Internet. "That would defeat any hope I have of peace and quiet," he says.

I made a decision before I left Hong Kong not to pry into Peter's life, but I pay attention to whatever he wishes to tell me. And it soon becomes clear that my guess was correct. As with T'ao Yuan-ming, Peter was more than willing to become a hermit. Indeed, my guess as to his motives was correct, and Peter confirms that he has "withdrawn from the world." In our conversations, I learn that he underwent 12 years of hard labor during the Cultural Revolution. I ask him if anyone ever showed him any unexpected kindness.

He answers without hesitation. "Oh, yes, and I am still in touch with them. And conversely some of those I had known well showed me no kindness at all."

I ask if anyone ever apologized to him for being wrong about him and for locking him up.

At that he becomes animated and his smile is genuine when he corrects me. "Ah, but you see they were *not* wrong. I was *not* one of them. I *was* an unbeliever. They were right in seeing something in me to be afraid of! Also, I was young and idealistic and very outspoken." He pauses for a moment lost in his memories. "*Very* outspoken."

I learn that Peter has a son in China, an artist; a sister teaching at Moscow University; a brother in Germany; and another sister in Paris. It is obviously a family with talent and brains.

We discuss the destruction of the World Trade Centers in New York and the plight of Wang Wei, the pilot whose daring but dangerous antics cost him his life while forcing an American spy plane to land on Hainan Island. I ask Peter if the characters for Wang Wei's name are the same as those of the famous T'ang poet and he says yes. I ask him if he thinks that would make Chinese even more emotional about his death and again he says yes.

Peter does not know that Wang Wei flew so close to the American plane that the pilot actually held up his e-mail address for the Americans on board to see, or that the American government had complained about such behavior previously, but he does know about some of the racial problems of New York City as reported – indeed emphasized – in the Chinese press.

Some of the expressions Peter uses are courtly and almost archaic and his speech is only slightly less elegant than his writing. I have fun teaching him such modern terms as "healthnazi," "feminazi" and "politically correct." As for "word police" and "thought police" he no doubt would know far more than I would.

He is no longer teaching and prefers to stay at home and study. I learn that he has "moved on" from T'ao Yuan-ming and for three hours every morning, from 5 to 8 a.m., is learning the *Book of Mencius* until he can recite it by rote. I give him a copy of one of my novels and he looks at the picture on the back and then at me and says, "You look older now."

His wife prepares a dinner fit for an emperor but as Peter mentions they are vegetarian I somehow suspect that he will be giving the mooncakes I brought to a friend or relative. A neighbor and his 13-year-old daughter visit from next door and the five of us have an enjoyable evening discussing every subject under the sun. The girl looks at my picture on my novel jacket and then at me and says, "You look fatter now." I make a mental note to dissuade any publisher from placing a photograph of myself on any novel.

When the girl's father mentions matter-of-factly about how "after liberation," China did such-and-such, I simply smile. I have heard the term all over China and it is well drilled into the Chinese.

No one in China, of whatever political persuasion, ever says, "after 1949," or "after the communist victory," but only "after liberation." How thoroughly indoctrination and a clever and repetitious use of language can penetrate the mind.

I ask Peter what the massive white official-looking building is on the other side of the park. He says it is the Academia Sinica, established to carry out scientific research. But he adds that it has now been transformed into a dancehall. "More profit," he says.

Before we go to bed, Peter gives me several color prints to take with me. They are photographs of Peter exercising on the roof. In two of them, he is upside-down balancing himself on his hands; in another, his legs are spread, bent at the knees, and he seems to be reading even while exercising. Peter at 68 may have a world-weary air about him but he is probably more fit than I am.

When he realizes I will be visiting Jiujiang, he offers to research his library to see what he can learn about memorials and such to T'ao Yuan-ming. He says he might be able to come up with something useful.

I climb in through the many-layered folds of the mosquito curtain and turn in for the night. But sleep does not come easily. My mind dwells on the fact that over a billion people are by rote referring to the communist victory as "after liberation." Perhaps because the terrorists who attacked America seemed so thoroughly brainwashed, I am becoming bored and even irritated with the mindless praising of Chairman Mao and his reputed achievements in China. What in Hunan had seemed naïve, humorous and almost charming, in Kuangtung strikes me as ignorant, annoying and contemptuous. In fact, I find myself becoming more cantankerous, more ornery, more cynical, more critical; I feel as if I'm transforming into something or someone else. Not unlike the guy in Kafka's *Metamorphosis* who woke up one morning to find that he had changed into a giant beetle.

Oh, my God! Can it be? Maybe I'm morphing into Paul

Theroux! Perhaps if a person travels in China long enough he can't help but end up like Paul. How do we know what Paul was like *before* he went to China? Maybe he was an Art Linkletter-type Pollyanna; the Lawrence Welk of travel writers. In any case, now I'm reluctant to go to sleep because I have an unshakable notion, a dead certainty, that I am destined to wake up as Paul Theroux.

The following morning, I check myself carefully but, happily, I find that I am pretty much who I was the night before. Inside his study, Peter hands me a sheet of paper covered with carefully written Chinese and neatly typed English, detailing the sites of T'ao's village, ancestral shrine, birthplace and the boulder "where T'ao Yuan-ming the tippler sought rest." While I was spending an inordinate amount of time worrying about waking up as Paul Theroux, Peter was obviously doing a lot of work on my behalf.

I look at the painting of Peter's mother and mention that she looks as if she must have had a very strong character. Peter agrees and mentions that she had a "very artistic character as well." I also ask if, being German, she was able to escape the consequences of the Cultural Revolution. He says that she gave up her German citizenship to marry his father and she was in theory a Chinese citizen. But he adds that the government did not really recognize that and for all intents and purposes she was "stateless." Wondering what horrors she faced during the Cultural Revolution I ask of her final resting place and Peter says, "She is with me. I have her ashes."

His wife calls me into the dining room. I learn that her family was originally from the north of China and she is in fact a Manchu. Before the 1911 revolution, Manchus were sent to various parts of China to ensure the loyalty of the local Chinese population. After the revolution, Manchus often wisely took on Chinese names to avoid repercussions. Her family name of Li is simply a close approximation of her Manchu name. I reflect on how easy it was for 20th century Chinese to fall out of favor with one government or another, especially if they were a bit different or had given loyalty to a previous regime now out of favor. No wonder the Chinese so desperately crave stability.

After a delightful breakfast, Peter and his wife accompany me to the bus station to buy my ticket to Canton. Before I can stop them, I realize they have paid for my ticket and will not allow me to reimburse them.

We visit an old part of Chongshan, Old Street, where some of the older building decorations display foreign influence, all in view of the stately Fufeng Pagoda. Old Street is closed to traffic and our walk is a pleasant one. The decorations on a few of the buildings remind me of some of Macao's Portuguese-style buildings or early Hong Kong British architecture.

We stroll and chat until we reach a statue of Sun Yat-sen, the "Father of Modern China" who died of cancer in 1925. He is standing near a statue of a rickshaw puller. Peter says Sun's face has been sculpted to show his disapproval of the exploitation of the poor. It simply looks to me as if Sun is bargaining with the rickshaw puller for a ride but I keep that observation to myself.

Peter and his wife make sure that the bus driver knows where I want to get off in Canton, as I will be taking the bus to a taxi station and a taxi will then take me to the train station. Then I shake Peter's hand and thank him profusely. He and his wife sit outside on a bench until the bus leaves – he in T-shirt and shorts and she in a simple blue-and-white dress – and I wave goodbye.

The bus is quickly outside the city and green ricefields are passing by but I find it difficult to dispel an ineffable sadness. I have no illusions that I somehow managed overnight to get inside the true feelings of my host, but I cannot escape a sense of suffering and heartache beyond words. All in the name of the New China.

(On the bus I am handed a bottle of "Eagle Bus" drinking water. In Canton I buy "C'est bon" water, on the train it will be "Sunray Cave" water, in a Jiujiang shop it will be "Wahaha" water. I somehow doubt bottled water in China is much better than that from the tap and my suspicion is confirmed later in a newspaper article about how more than 30 percent of 114 varieties of purified, mineral and spring water flunked a Bureau of Quality and Technical Supervision test.)

When I arrive at Canton's (huge) East Station, I search for the proper place to buy a soft sleeper to Nanchang. Eventually, I enter a capacious hall with long lines of travelers, some irritated, some bored, some patient. Not a good sign. I queue up at a window which most likely has nothing to do with trains to Nanchang, but which has the attraction of having only a few people in line. When I ask the hard-working woman behind the counter where I can buy a one-way soft sleeper to Nanchang, she says, "Here!" I quickly pay the lady 361 yuan (US$43.62) and take my ticket. It is as easy as that.

The train won't leave for a few hours and I have plenty of time, so I hire a taxi to take me to a hotel – any hotel – to kill time and to get a sandwich because I know what the food is like on the train. I hope for a busy coffee shop so that I can be alone with my thoughts. No such luck. I am the only customer and the waitresses – Headwaitress Sherry and her friends, all gussied out in cute blue-and-white hotel version of sailor outfits – are in rapture at this golden opportunity to learn English.

Sherry is the boldest or, more accurately, least shy of the waitresses. Her shoulder-length hair surrounds her oval face and hangs down on either side of her pointed chin like quotation marks. Her lovely apricot eyes perch above cheekbones so prominent that aircraft probably have to be warned away when Sherry is in the area.

We exchange the usual pleasantries, and, at their request, I make a half-hearted effort to correct their English while biting into what may be the soggiest tuna fish sandwich in Kwangtung Province. If it was tuna fish.

As I am about to leave, Sherry hurriedly snatches up a receipt pad and on the back of a receipt writes down her address for me in

Chinese. She hands it to me and asks that I write to her. Amidst the giggles of her friends, she says she hopes to travel someday and when she does she will definitely stop in to see me. I assure her that she would be very welcome and I fumble inside my wallet until I find a namecard. It is one with my New York East Village address. Inasmuch as I have moved to Bangkok I very much doubt there is any danger of Sherry showing up at my door. But perhaps the new tenant in my former New York apartment will welcome her. I bid the lovely young ladies in sailor suits anchors away and walk to the main road in search of a taxi.

Back at the train station, I spot a large room containing a Chinese restaurant and a row of computers. The middle-aged woman behind the counter asks where I am from and when I say New York I once again receive sincere expressions of sympathy.

While waiting for China's maddeningly slow internet to respond, I have lots of time to peruse the local newspapers. One article is on a devastated grandmother who burned her daughter's considerable savings of new bank notes thinking they were only hell notes (ghost money). In a cynical mood, I wonder if she will have to burn more hell notes in order to dispel the evils spirits that caused this calamity.

In another province, a man returned from the dead after his wife collected the insurance. It seems he hadn't drowned after all but merely been swept far away and laid up for awhile. But here she was resigned to his death and already in possession of the insurance money. I wonder if she harbored mixed emotions at seeing him.

One headline reads, "Giant Mouse Attacks Man in Hotel," and yet another article warns that certain restaurants in Shanghai are using dead crabs to cut costs.

Another tells of a businessman spending his money on his stunning new mistress while refusing to pay for his daughter's education. Yet another discusses the fact that Capitalists and entrepreneurs can now enter the communist party. Egads, is nothing sacred?

The last one I peruse describes the "anger release bars" which have opened in various cities; bars in which patrons can "beat, kick and smash furniture and models of people and animals in a private room." Some customers affix photographs of people they despise onto the models and smash them while listening to recordings of voices begging for mercy. I'm only pleased that T'ao Yuan-ming is not around to see this.

I finally log onto the Internet and ask one of the hotels in Nanchang to reserve a single room for me. All Internet service providers in China are subject to government control but the various ministries assigned to the task of policing the rambunctious internet seem to relax or tighten their policies from day to day and, sure enough, I discover I can get into the *New York Times* and CNN websites. I spend longer than I should reading about the devastation in lower Manhattan and at the Pentagon.

I leave the computer room with a heavy heart and head for the train which will leave at precisely 16:47. I have no problem finding my car and my compartment. Inside, three of the bunks are occupied by Chinese men. I nod and say hello to the men and place my bag on an empty lower bunk. There is the smell of stale tobacco but no one is smoking. One of the men is lying on his side sleeping, another is lying on his back staring into space and the third and youngest is reading what appears to be a science fiction comic book through what appear to be incredibly thick lenses. I will later learn that the sleeping man is a salesman from a small town farther up the line, the meditative man is an engineer in Nanchang, and the comic book reader is a student at a college in Canton.

I offer cookies to anyone awake but there are no takers. For nearly an hour into the trip, there is at best desultory, polite conversation. Throughout my journey into China, whenever I discuss the basics, such as origin, age, family, etc., I strive to use the old-fashioned Chinese way of referring to them. If I learn, for example, that I am speaking with a newly married couple, I will say something like, "May your children be as numerous as grasshoppers." And if I am invited to follow someone, I will say something like, "I dare not walk in your jade footsteps."

Hence, whenever I ask questions of others, I use the traditionally polite terms: "Where is your splendid mansion?" "What is your honorable age?" "Is your noble son doing well at school?" They are supposed to reply by referring to their house as a "lowly hovel," their age as a "worthless number" and their son as "my contemptible little bug." Alas, whether it be because of the Cultural Revolution or simply due to the pressures of the modern age, nobody (except perhaps Peter Tan) plays the game anymore. Or, worse, seems to know that for thousands of years there *was* such a game.

It is the engineer who finally asks me where I am going. I tell him I will be stopping at Nanchang for a few days but that I am on my way to the Lu Shan mountains. (*Shan* means "mountain" just as *yama* in Fujiyama means "mountain," so by saying Mount Fujiyama or Lu Shan mountains we are making the kind of tautological mistake purists love to correct.)

The engineer nods, no doubt thinking I am a tourist. Luckily for him he does not ask *why* I am going to Lushan or else he would have to hear about my (thus far spectacularly unsuccessful) search for Peach Blossom Spring. The salesman says something about President Bush I do not catch but repeats himself and I realize he is asking if Bush will take vengeance on those who attacked America. I assure him that Bush will. I have seen enough Chinese sword-fighting movies and kung-fu movies to know that, perhaps more than anyone, Chinese appreciate the value of vengeance.

The student ventures an opinion that it was a wrong thing for Bin Laden to do and says to tell Americans that Chinese do not do things like that. I assure him I will tell them although I cannot help but reflect that during the Cultural Revolution the Chinese penchant for cruelty was demonstrated not by how they treated foreigners but by how horribly they treated one another.

The student is originally from Chong Shan and I ask him if he has ever heard of the bakers from Chong Shan who in 1857 placed ten pounds of arsenic in the bread of all the foreign-devils in Hong Kong, including that of the British Governor and his wife. He stares at me, obviously doubting that what I say is true, and shakes his head.

It was the only mass poisoning of a settled community in world history and it failed only because the bakers used too *much* arsenic. A smaller amount would have ensured that the poison would have been absorbed into the body systems; but such a large amount caused massive vomiting, saving all but one or two. One of the things that attracted me to the tale is that the bakers can be seen as patriotic heroes or heinous criminals, depending on one's point of view. But it is clear from diaries and newspaper accounts of the period that the shock, outrage and anger felt in Hong Kong on January 15, 1857 was not unlike that felt in New York on September 11th, 144 years later.

I head for the dining car, order a beer, and look over my notes about how the various guidebook writers describe Jiangxi province: "A bit of a backwater," "of little interest" and its capital of Nanchang as "somewhat disheveled," "nondescript," "the poor man's Beijing," and "a very miserable place on a cold, rainy day." One of them does mention that the city's aircraft manufacturing plant makes the Silkworm missile. If men were transformed into eunuchs inside the euphemistically named Silkworm Chamber, I dare not speculate on what something called a Silkworm missile has been programmed to do.

One of the guidebooks, *The Rough Guide*, gives me hope that I am indeed on the right track in my search for the elusive Chinese utopia. The writer mentions that "the first major influx of settlers came as late as the Han dynasty, when its (Jiangxi province) interior offered sanctuary for those dislodged by warfare." Exactly. And that description as well as the timeframe fits perfectly with what T'ao Yuan-ming wrote of the origin of Peach Blossom Spring.

Something jars my memory and I belatedly remember that I had meant to buy a Chinese almanac in Hong Kong to help me decide precisely which day and what time would be best to enter Jiangsi province. The exact time for beginning a journey is even today believed by many Chinese to have much to do in determining the success of the trip. Too late now. But, at least if I fail, I will know why.

I begin reading my latest purchase while in Hong Kong: a book entitled *The Chinese Femme Fatale: Stories from the Ming Period.* When I open to the section, "Wicked Women in Chinese Literature," photocopies of Peter Tan's letters as well as four prints of Peter Tan exercising fall onto the table. I love to reread Peter's letters as they are written as if by someone living in a former, more cultured, time:

I received your letter a couple of days ago and was tremendously surprised to learn that you have all this time been active in the South East, while I was labouring under the misapprehension of your still being beyond the waters of the Pacific. Again I must ascribe your unbelievable proximity to the magnetism of the Orient, which keeps drawing you back, whatever the distance, to places that have become part of you, and have, moreover, found a permanent home in your writings, where they proudly defy the ravages of time.

I had forgotten where I had stashed the photographs but now I have the time to take a closer look at them. It is the last of the four that interests me.

Peter is on the spacious rooftop surrounded by plants and, in the distance is a massive, official looking, Soviet-inspired, building, the Academia Sinica, perhaps. He is wearing a grey T-shirt, blue-and-grey shorts which reach almost to his bony knees, and brown lace-up shoes with no laces and no socks. He is in profile, his black-and-white hair slightly blown back in the wind, his shoulders and back hunched, his knees bent. His arms are stretched out before him in a palms up position but his hands are clenched into tight fists. He is staring straight ahead. His face seems a bit pink and bloated, and his expression suggests that he is under enormous strain, as if he is holding his breath or involved in great concentration.

I drink my beer, listen to the click-clack of the train wheels and stare at the picture of Peter, especially at the clenched fists and the determined look in his eyes. I can't help wondering if his exercising is not far more than something physical, perhaps an insight into his indomitable spirit: A gesture of defiance, a demonstration of survival, a sign of triumph, a celebration of life.

Nanchang

At 8:44 the following morning, the train arrives at Nanchang ("Splendor of the South" or "Southern Prosperity"), the capital of Jiangxi Province and a city of almost four million. An early 20th century writer described Nanchang as "unusual among Chinese cities in that it has not been taken and looted for hundreds of years."

This time I did not have to leave the train in the middle of the night and had little fear of missing my destination as I did when traveling to Ch'angsha, and so, after a sound sleep, I feel rested and alert. When emerging from the station the sun's morning glare hardly fazes me. (Nor does what one writer refers to as the city's "grime and gray sprawl.")

Based on my internet research into the city's hotels, I decide to take a taxi to one which seems to be the best located as well as one of the newest – the 328-room, 20-story Gloria Plaza Hotel. Alas, behind the hotel counter, a sympathetic Miss Wong furrows her lovely brow and informs me the hotel is quite full and there is no cheap single room available; nor did they get the e-mail that I sent from Canton requesting one. It is obvious Freston the Magician has done his work well.

The prices of available rooms are not cheap for Jiangxi(about US$80) and I hesitate about staying here, thinking to try another hotel, but then I notice the two wall plaques informing me that the Gloria Plaza Hotel has been awarded "The Model Unit of Fire Protection" and "The appointed foreign affairs concerning tourist unit." How could I not stay at a hotel that has managed to scoop up two such prestigious awards as those?

(A traveler to Nanchang nearly 80 years before wrote that "Nanchang's fires are roaring and picturesque affairs. Men scared half out of their wits were fleeing through the narrow streets carrying their chests and their babies – at least their precious boys; women hobbled past on their crippled feet; children waked out of sleep were whining or weeping as they were dragged along; coolies leisurely jogged away under the loads of excited merchants noisily urging them on." So perhaps this Model Unit of Fire Protection hotel is indeed the right place to stay.)

Miss Wong seems delighted with my decision. She hands me a glossy hotel brochure and requests my passport. I notice her fingernails are long and well manicured, reminding me that scholars in traditional China often kept at least one fingernail long to show that they did no manual labor. I suspect that, other than commiserating with tourists who have to pay top dollar, Miss Wong does no manual labor either.

From the window of my not-so-inexpensive room, I can see the Ba Yi Bridge crossing the Gan River and the nearby tower, the famous Teng Wang Pavilion first built in A.D. 653 and now rebuilt in Sung Dynasty style. With a modicum of imagination, the view offers a glimpse of the city as it once was with traditional Chinese houses and its city walls which measured six miles in circuit. (Chinese history has it that the glance from an especially beautiful Han Dynasty consort could topple a city wall, so for all I know the missing wall is a case of *cheche la femme*.)

The heat is intense but the red-and-green, nine-story tower with its traditionally curved and glazed tile roofs, gilded double eaves, carved screens and vermilion columns is a major attraction and so I venture over.

Despite its interesting architecture, there is not much to see inside the tower other than a teahouse, a few small exhibits and the usual souvenir shops, but the balconies of the tower do offer excellent views of the river and of Hupei province beyond. The tower faces the Western Hills and is usually described as one of the "three famous towers south of the Yangtze River." It was put on the map by the T'ang Dynasty poet, Wang Po, who wrote of its beauty and many other poets have since left their own tributes behind.

The grounds surrounding the tower include pavilions and terraces which also offer some respite from the heat. I wander around the lovely lotus pond and the swaying willow trees and feel as if I had indeed traveled back in time. In my mind's eye I try to conjure up the many scholars and poets who gathered here over the centuries to recite their poems and drink their wine.

As I walk through the courtyards and rock gardens, I make note of the many signs: "Cherish Public Property – Be A Civic Virtues Visitor," "How carefree and leisurely the grass is! And have you the heart to step on it?" "Love the well-known building to the south of the Yangtze," "Uphold civic virtues tendencies," "Noted building and scenic spot – new people with new tendencies."

A large notice board informs me that the Teng Wang Pavilion has been destroyed and rebuilt no fewer than 28 times. The writer of the notice was obviously in a philosophical mood even if the translator was anxious to get home: "The nature varies continuously and this world often in tremendous changes."

Nearby is a row of antique and curio shops with traditionally tiled roofs fashioned in similar style to that of the pagoda, and a Chinese restaurant mislabeled as a hotel. I hail a taxi and head for a huge open area known as Renmin (the people's) Square but although it turns out to be as spacious as the guide books promise, it has little character, and the main attraction seems to be several bored families walking or lounging about. I give the nearby Monument to the (Communist) Martyrs and the Exhibition Hall a miss and head instead into the shopping districts. (Chairman Mao's face once decorated the Exhibition Hall but in the mid-80's it was "removed for cleaning" and hasn't been seen since.)

It was in Nanchang on August 1, 1927 that a revolt broke out which ended in the communists taking over the city. It wasn't long before Kuomintang troops regained control, but the date (8/11 *bayi*) is considered to be the founding of the People's Liberation Army, and many roads and squares in Nanchang are named Ba Yi. the date is also on the war flag of the People's Liberation Army.

I set off in search of *Ha Ma* (frog) street to check out the frog legs and *Li Hao*, the local delicacy consisting of grass grown in Poyang Lake. I also wanted to see if the streets still retained their colorful names, such as, Silversmith, Chopstick, and Wash-horse. But, after walking in the heat for an hour or so, I lose all interest in frog legs and Poyang Lake grass and instead venture into a small restaurant.

During the years I lived in Hong Kong I attained a certain expertise on judging small Chinese restaurants by their façades and often by the girls in cheongsams standing out front beckoning passersby to enter. (The shorter or more glitzy the *cheongsam* the worse the food.) This one has no young women standing outside and I am quite certain that this is one of those offering a bizarre but unique combination of mediocre Western and indifferent Chinese cuisine.

I used to avoid such restaurants but now I actually seek them out for their creative if somewhat whimsical menus and for the amazing clash of cultures one can spot in their decoration. For example, on this menu I find "French toast Hong Kong style." This comes as a shock as I lived in Hong Kong for 17 years and never even knew that we had our own style of French toast.

I pass by several poorly done paintings of Chinese scenic spots, a gaudy red-and-green lantern and ads for soft drinks and look over the not-too-tempting offerings of the small Chinese food buffet. I stand for several seconds trying to make out what one of the dishes is and then I realize I am looking at fried sea slugs. Except the slugs have a strange appearance; as if someone took several small pocket combs, broke off a few teeth on each, expertly scorched each comb in a fire, and then partly covered them in mud. I have no doubt Chinese find them both delicious and healthful but I decide to give the fried sea slugs a miss (as I would have given the Poyang Lake grass a miss had I found it). In fact, in yet another act of culinary defiance, I give the buffet itself a miss and order that most exotic of Asian cuisine, a tuna fish sandwich on white bread.

Exactly as in Hong Kong, restaurants such as this seem to be a refuge for young lovers. I am not certain how these young couples sustain love and romance among the sea slugs and fake flowers and cliched paintings but such restaurants no doubt offer far more privacy for intimate conversations and meaningful glances than do their own crowded homes.

As I scan the booths, I notice that the young men are thin and earnest and serious and bespectacled. The young women are somewhere between plain and pretty and, while listening to their boyfriends' sweet talk and simultaneously using their chopsticks to lug sea slugs to their pretty lips, all have their gazes demurely lowered. I finish my sandwich amidst the soft, cliched sounds of Chinese Muzak love songs, pay my bill, and head back out into the unforgiving sunlight.

I have heard that a company in China has created a computer-generated starlet – its answer to Laura Croft – Tomb Raider – known as *Qing Na* or "Chyna." The licensing deals for this voluptuous, young Asian goddess are said to include dolls, photobooks, clothes and video games and so I brave a visit to a Chinese department store in search of a China doll, so to speak. A very crowded Chinese department store. Not only do I not find Chyna but, within minutes, I realize I have bit off more than I can chew: I get lost and have to ask for the exit.

As I head out, a little girl with bright yellow beribboned braids and a dress the color of the Yangtze river walks beside me. She touches the hair on my arm as one would stroke a passive but potentially dangerous beast and says "hello." When I give her a hello in return, she finds this too funny for words and takes off running and laughing, staring at her now debased little hand that came into contact with the shaggy beast.

I decide to follow my usual plan for seeing a Chinese city. I take taxis to hotels at a distance and walk to hotels that (according to the map which is often wrong) seem to be within walking distance. I waste money at two hotel business centers as their internet connections are too slow and nothing happens.

In the evening, I buy local Jinsheng cigarettes, translated as "Golden Sound," locally made with an attractive red, white and gold package, and head for the Qingshan Hu Hotel. I sit in a bluish haze of cigarette smoke (my own and others), and talk with Miss Lin, the female bartender, about Mao (whom she says she respects) and about Chiang Kai-shek (whom she says she knows little about). She talks about her husband and her job. She in fact works two jobs to make ends meet. On the train the beer was warm. The beer here is warm too but Miss Lin puts ice in it for me.

Before long, I have a few too many beers and I begin mistakenly calling Miss Lin Miss Hu but she doesn't seem to mind. Then I begin mispronouncing the name of her Qingshan Hu Hotel as Cheongsam Hu Hotel, but she takes it all in good spirits. When I finally get around to informing her that I am the First Sword under Heaven, she says something to the effect that, if that is my only skill, it must be hard to make a living. I quickly conclude that Miss Lin is the pragmatic type and decide not to say anything about my search for Peach Blossom Spring.

She prattles a bit more about why Chairman Mao was good for China and I nearly decide to refute her arguments one by one but then I remember the saying "arguments out of a beautiful mouth are unanswerable," and I do my best to translate the phrase. It comes out something like, "I don't agree with you but if what is said is being said by a woman as beautiful as you, then it must indeed be correct."

She narrows her lovely eyes and gives me one of those half-flirtatious/half-indignant Chinese smiles and an adorable tilt of the head. She is one of those women who are attractive not because she is particularly good looking but because she is playful and vivacious. She wags a finger at me as if I have been a bad boy. She says she thinks I like to flirt.

That may be true but I have leaned to be cautious. Chinese is, of course, a tonal language and, sooner or later, making a mistake in speaking which will horrify those around you is almost a given. When I was a young man living on Taiwan, I would tell lovely Chinese women that "I am a very romantic man," (*Wo shih hen yen shih de ren*), *yen shih* being one of the terms for 'romance" or "romantic." Without fail, they gave me strange looks. It was only much later when working on a novel set in 19th century Hong Kong that I learned of an older expression, *yen shih*, spoken with different tones – exactly as I had been pronouncing them – which meant "opium diarrhea." So instead of saying "I am a very romantic man" I had in fact been saying "I am a man with a great deal of opium diarrhea."

When I tell Miss Lin I am off to the Lakeview Hotel, she mentions that they have a bowling alley. As she seems certain that that bit of information will impress me, I assure her I won't fail to try it out. I am just drunk enough to wonder if they have a bowling alley in Peach Blossom Spring.

But when I reach the Lakeview Hotel, I pass up the dubious delights of the bowling alley in favor of a cup of coffee in the Camillia coffee shop. Throughout my travels in China, one thing never changes: the coffee shop of each hotel in China has at least one foreign couple with a cherished, recently adopted, fat-cheeked Chinese baby being held or bounced or adored or cuddled or stroked or caressed or petted or patted or googled over.

China has permitted adoptions by foreigners for some time now and most of the babies are adopted by Americans. Each year now sees well over five thousand Chinese babies leaving the Land of Simplified Characters and heading for the Land of Political Correctness. The average figure bandied about as the cost of an adoption is US$3,000 which adds up to US$15 million per year just for those going to America.

I seem to be the only foreigner in China with no baby. Am I imagining it or are foreigners with babies looking at me with suspicion? Even animosity. I am not one of them. For all they know, I may not even like babies. What am I doing here without a baby? Why come to China if I'm not going to adopt? Why am I not struggling with reams of incomprehensible adoption paperwork or trying to find out if cribs and strollers and formula and diapers are available? No wife, no Chinese baby, no cellphone – talk about a loser. I suddenly feel like Donald Sutherland in *Invasion of the Body Snatchers* (before they snatched him too). Of course, it doesn't help that I am more than a bit drunk.

I finish up my coffee quickly and call for the bill, inadvertently causing a Chinese drama to unfold. I cannot pay for my meal in the Hong Kong dollars I find in my pocket and I forgot to bring enough *renminbi* from my own hotel room safe, so I have to change money. However, at the front counter I soon learn that as I am not a guest in *their* hotel I cannot change money. There are many Catch 22's in China and this is one of them: you must change money to pay your bill but you are not a guest so you cannot change money.

Within minutes, coffee shop managers, waitresses, a cashier and assorted front office personnel are engaged in a somewhat heated conference. God only knows who would have got involved had I said I had no money at all. At last, they reach agreement on the correct course of action. I am allowed to change some money and pay my bill.

When I return to my room at the Gloria Plaza, I decide to forgo the many temptations of the "Hurricane Karaoke Lounge" and fall asleep watching the only news program I can find on TV – in German. Throughout my trip, I will of course be torn between the need to get away from the news about the attacks on America and the need to learn every scrap of information I can. Again and again I will force myself to limit the amount of time I spend watching (or searching for) TV news or news on the internet.

What news I can get from Chinese newspapers is decidedly limited and usually irrelevant. For example, an article almost proudly announced that road rage has come to China. (Must be part of some "Catch up with the West" campaign.) "Du Shugui, who shot and killed a young man in a rush of road rage, and shouted arrogantly that no one could compare to him, will be submitted to the death penalty."

A longer article says the China Tourism industry is marked by two contrary trends: rising numbers of visitors and dropping prices. Mainland china has become the world's fifth most popular tourist destination, drawing 27 million overseas visitors last year. But visitors were spending less and making shorter trips. In response, hotel and restaurant prices have dropped dramatically. In Beijing the average hotel rate fell by 30 per cent between 1997 and last year. I lay back on the bed with pen and paper and work with the figures. Trying to project into the future is not easy but, after a while, I come to the astounding conclusion that if these trends continue, by the year 2011, China will have 68 million visitors but will be receiving no money from them at all.

෴෴෴෴෴෴෴෴

The following morning, I have breakfast behind a tree trunk in the hotel lobby which does not surprise me as, according to Miss Wong's brochure, the lobby has been decorated with "a tropical forest theme." I look over a page I copied from a traveler's colorful report on Nanchang written not long after the fall of the Ch'ing Dynasty (1911), entitled, "Roving through Southern China:"

It was hot in Nanchang in mid-September, and men of the better class held fans over their shiningly shaven heads whenever they emerged from the sunless narrow streets....Their women, less mobile in bound feet but with hirsute protection against the cloudless sunshine, sat placidly in the wheelbarrows in which they sometimes followed their masters. There are stone pillars along the sides of a stone bridge which, it is said, will infallibly bring male offspring to any woman who will come there alone in the dead of night with nothing on but an easily opened gown, and embrace one of them.

Alas, the fans are gone, the wheelbarrows are gone, and, according to the coffee shop's perplexed, increasingly nervous and mildly upset waitresses, Nanchang women no longer reveal their charms to stone pillars in the dead of night in order to conceive a male child.

I leave a nice tip for the flummoxed waitresses and head out to one of Nanchang's main temples. Officially the name is *Youmin Si*, Protecting the People Monastery, but, due to the nature of the signs I come across, I refer to it as the Temple of the Strictly Prohibited: "Strictly prohibit defloration; strictly prohibit photo; strictly prohibit everywhere expectorate."

The entrance building to the temple has been painted a bright yellow and the horseshoe-shaped doorway is guarded by huge stone lions. There is a wonderful smell of "civilization burning incense," the excited voices of children in a nearby school, sonorous chanting of monks at prayer.

The area behind the temple reminds me of the Hong Kong I knew in the early 70's: the faded potted plants at the windows, crumbling brick sections cheek b / jowl with newer concrete blocks, bamboo poles with clothes draped like flags of various nations, faded plastic awnings, glimpses of women working in kitchens with cleavers, and the kitchen sounds of cleavers on chopping boards, haphazardly projecting balconies, some enclosed, some open, old-fashioned windows formed by a dozen small panes of glass, pots of incense, ordinary kitchen utensils beside exotic Taoist symbols of protection, Chinese style bamboo brooms and wicker baskets, wooden buckets hanging outside narrow windows. In a strange way, I find the mundane living quarters behind the temple at least as exotic as the temple itself.

I eventually return to the monastery, and as I pass through the various courtyards, I come across incense burners with gold inscriptions below and coils of red incense hanging from above. Curls of blue smoke rise from huge crimson candles, as if an invisible artist is painting Chinese characters in mid-air. The strong smell of garlic wafts out from the kitchen area. There are stone lions large and small, fierce temple guardians, dragon-decorated pots containing young fir trees, round marble tables and round marble seats, orange-tiled roofs with figurines of exotic animals on their eaves, round Buddhist windows, their panes divided by delicate woodwork in the shape of swastikas. There are baskets of pinkish yellow fruit, bouquets of bright red flowers, and dark green mold on trees.

Believers kneel on cushions and ask various gods and goddesses for favors. Several elderly women are supplicating themselves before a statue of Kuan Yin, the Goddess of Mercy. This lovely goddess was said to have postponed indefinitely her ascendance into heaven because she heard the cries of the world, and in her compassion, returned to aid those in need. I wonder if the women are aware that, centuries before, Kuan Yin began her existence as Avalokitasvara, a male Hindu god, and in her many generations of migration from India, somehow changed sex along the way.

The temple is preparing to welcome the 82-year-old high priest visiting from Hunan and the afternoon quiet is soon broken. I sit on a stone bench in the shade of cinnamon trees to observe the activity at the bell and drum towers. The bell is rung once, after which the drum is beaten four times: boom…boom…boom – boom! Monks by the dozens appear, some clanging cymbals and chanting, others engaged in eliciting a peculiar Chinese sense of rhythm from small drums and gongs and wooden clappers. Their yellow and red robes float past doorways festooned with huge red lanterns, conjuring up the lost splendors of China's many dynasties.

The Chinese characters on the towers are in gold relief against a black background. Very beautiful, but I notice that the drum tower has a simplified character for *lou* (tower), although the bell tower has the traditional character. What does that mean? Does that indicate the drum tower plaque was destroyed during the Cultural Revolution and it was redone? Or am I simply a paranoid foreign devil reading too much into it?

A late middle-aged man in a suit-and-tie stands next to me intently watching the ceremony. I tell him in Chinese that his carved wooden walking stick is beautiful. He studies me over his glasses, as if looking deep within me, then thanks me in English.

After we chat a bit he hands me his namecard. The card is in English and Chinese and has a photograph of him in robes the color of which I associate with Tibetan monks. He is wearing a magnificent tiara. The card says that he is the abbot of "Buddhist Tara's Temple, Nying Ma Pa Chinese North America Mission." There is a Canadian address and a Hong Kong address.

He invites me to stop in and see him when I am in Hong Kong. I assure him I will but when I notice his Hong Kong address is in the ex-British colony's New Territories, I know I will not have time to venture out that far.

Along the sleeping quarters for the monks, yellow air conditioners have logos, cartoon figures of two young boys in underpants hugging one another. The boys are smiling and giving the thumbs up symbol and each holds an ice cream cone. One of the boys is Caucasian with red hair, the other brown with black hair. The cartoonish, the sacred, the temporal, the spiritual, the mundane, the bizarre, the old, the new – all mixed and mashed into an unfathomable, ever-changing stew – welcome to modern China.

Local legend has it that the Flood Dragons in the well of the Governor were fighting and causing terrific storms and unrelenting floods so the tall Buddhist statue that still forms the core of this temple was built. That would have been about 503 A.D. It is said the storms and floods ceased. And then, in no time at all (By Chinese standards that could mean a few centuries), the temple had expanded to such an extent that it was said "One has to ride a horse to close the temple gate." And it was officially named Protecting the People Monastery, but, unfortunately, during the Cultural Revolution the temple needed protection *from* the people, especially the iconoclastic, temple-hating Red Guards who destroyed whatever of China's culture they could find.

The temple was known for a huge copper column weighing 36,000 *jin*. The column was destroyed by the Red Guards but has been restored.

I speak with a few of the monks about the history of the temple. They are more interested in chatting with me about what I am doing in Nanchang. After about ten minutes, I leave the temple and make my way to the street. After a bit of a walk I spot an inviting sign across a congested road which reads, "Biche fried and joyful ice cream room." I brave the traffic to cross the street but find where the biche fried and joyful ice cream room once stood there is a shop selling leather goods.

I hail a cab and, while waiting at a light, I notice the large boards with digital numbers at many intersections counting down the seconds until the light changes. I had not realized I was so close to my hotel and when we pull up the driver refuses to take any payment.

I take a brief respite in the lobby coffee shop (beside a different tree trunk). The waitresses are not the same as those on the morning shift but they seem to keep me under observation so perhaps word has been passed of my morning monologue involving the old Nanchang method of giving birth to sons.

I decide to head for the Provincial Museum. It is near my hotel and I decide to walk. In fact the building actually has three museums within. The guard with the military style haircut at the gate is also the ticket taker and he seems not too disappointed that I pass over the Communist revolution museum and the natural history museum and instead choose the Chinese history museum.

The large building has three floors. The lighting is poor as is what little English is in evidence but still the displays are (as the British might say) not without merit. Bronzes and such are on the first floor, antiques and farm implements of the Hakka lifestyle are on the second floor and *jingdezhen* ceramics are displayed on the top floor. The only other patrons of the museum are elderly Japanese men in a tour group who stare as if they have never seen anyone with green eyes and a long nose before. Perhaps they haven't.

Back in my hotel room surrounded with maps, I decide to travel first to Jiujiang (90 miles north of Nanchang) and then south to Lushan. Jiujiang is bounded on the east by Lake Poyang, the largest freshwater lake in China. The lake forms right at the junction of the Gan river and the Yangtze river. Its Migrant Birds Reserve is probably the world's largest and the lake is home to egrets, white cranes, white swans, storks, widgeons and geese. The fecundity of the lake's plain has earned it the title of "Land of Fish and Rice."

An early 19th century traveler to China described the shape of the lake as resembling an angry cat but as I study the map (perhaps because of reclamation) I cannot see any kind of cat. In fact, its contours look a bit like the port wine stain on Mikhail Gorbachev's forehead.

The traveler also mentioned that during droughts, the lake turned into a series of mud flats giving rise to the saying, "Crossing the Poyang? Carry 180 pounds of rice" (to avoid starving to death during the prolonged journey). But I have no reason to believe

Peach Blossom Spring is anywhere near Lake Poyang and I have no intention of carrying 180 pounds of rice anywhere so I give the lake a miss.

I had thought of taking a bus and visiting nearby Jingdezhen, so famous throughout the world for its fine porcelain; porcelain often shipped through Jiujiang. (Whichever advertising copywriter wrote that "Jingdezhen put the china in China" should be taken out and given 30 strokes of the bamboo.)

Jingdezhen, Lushan and Nanchang are said to be part of the Golden Triangle of tourism in Jiangxi province but I guess I shall be content with seeing only two. In any case, Jingdezhen has nothing to do with my search for Peach Blossom Spring. Which reminds me that Nanchang also has little to do with my search for Peach Blossom Spring. And, to be honest, as Nanchang is one of the "revolutionary" and "heroic" cities of China, I find its atmosphere a bit sterile, its chemical and steel factories a bit boring, and its Soviet-inspired architecture a bit depressing.

True, there are pandas in the zoo but, truth-to-tell, for anyone with an IQ above that of a dying breadfruit tree, pandas chewing bamboo leaves or bamboo shoots or bamboo whatever can get boring quite quickly. And early in the morning one can observe the t'ai chi classes in People's Park but, if you've seen one t'ai chi class in a Chinese park you've, well, you know.

I suppose I could visit the art gallery in the southern suburb which was once a Taoist temple. The famous Bada Shanren did his painting and calligraphy there. (A website mentions that Bada Shanren had great influence on those painters known as the "eight devils of Yangzhou" but, alas, fails to say what nefarious activities on their part caused them to be known as "devils.") But I feel I have spent enough time getting my bearings in Nanchang and so I decide to leave for Jiujiang early in the morning. Peach Blossom Spring beckons and I have not forgotten that Freston the Magician will do anything to ensure that my quest ends in failure.

The following morning, I ask Miss Wong if she knows which hotel in Peach Blossom Spring is the best, then quickly correct myself and ask which hotel in Jiujiang is the best. She writes down a hotel name in Chinese (Qi Shi hotel) and assures me that it is the newest and most comfortable. After assuring her that I did indeed enjoy my stay at her hotel, I hail a taxi to take me to the long distance bus terminal.

My driver is one of the few people who begins a conversation about the attack on New York's World Trade Centers. (The Chinese for WTC is the same as in English, *Shih jye Mao Yi Chung Hsin* – World Trade Center.) He says the attacks were *tai bu limao*! – uncivilized and without a sense of propriety. He mentions that he saw only glimpses on TV but read about it in many newspapers. He also spoke to a relative in New York by phone.

(Later, in Hong Kong, I will learn that it was the Chinese government's policy to place restrictions on news of the attack on television, but that some newspapers and especially websites carried more of the event. Ironically, by banning or downplaying important news on TV, the Chinese government is motivating its people to explore unsupervised and even restricted areas of the World Wide Web.)

I had wondered how crowded the long distance bus would be and wondered if it was one of those which had as many nervous chickens and huge fruit baskets as passengers, but when we pull up outside the long distance bus stop there is no crowd; no chickens; no bus.

My driver claims not to know when the next bus arrives and suggests it may not be air-conditioned, but says for 400 *renminbi* he will drive me the 90 miles to Jiujiang. I know the bus is only 50 *renminbi* but I have no idea when a bus will arrive and how long it will linger before leaving for Jiujiang. Not to mention how crowded it will be. Traveling on rickety boats and busses crammed with chickens and pigs and food baskets is great adventure for those under thirty. Needless to say, that does not include me.

I show the driver the name of the hotel Miss Wong wrote down and he nods enthusiastically. He assures me he knows exactly where the hotel is and agrees that that hotel is the best in Jiujiang. I am swayed. We set out for Jiujiang.

The driver is rotund, chubby, earthy and talkative. His mandarin is even earthier. After discussing the World Trade Center attack and the mooncake scandal, the conversation turns to the policy of having children in China. The driver has no hesitation in admitting that he gave money to certain government officials for the right to have a second child. He is pleased it was a boy.

As we drive, the scenery becomes more interesting and once again I am surrounded by the loveliness of China's unspoiled countryside, red brick farm houses set among rolling green hills beneath a canopy of blue. I begin humming the music to Sun Yat-sen's Three Principles of the People, *San Min Chu I*. The driver seems to like the tune so I begin singing the words and am almost through when the thought hits me that this song is also a kind of anthem for Taiwan as well. Fortunately, the driver has never heard the song before; but I decide to keep my mouth shut for awhile.

Jiujiang

T he southern outskirts of Jiujiang are heavily industrialized and, to say the least, the scene is not as I had imagined it would be. As one guidebook writer put it, "Jiujiang is most definitely not a place to linger." But I console myself with the thought that the charm of the area must lie somewhere beyond the industrial sprawl up in the mountain region.

The driver drives along Bin Jiang Road and eventually stops at the Qi Shi, a modern hotel facing the Yangtze River. I bid him goodbye, enter the hotel and approach the front desk. The clerk's nametag says, "Coco Huang." The hotel looks clean enough but I lament the fact that other than a "Please keep the air fresh" sign, there are no wall plaques in praise of the hotel.

Coco assures me they have a single available and quotes me a good price (about US$35). As I pass by the coffee shop I hear snatches of an instrumental version of Hotel California; but, then, one would expect no less from a coffee shop named "Le Café."

The window of my room overlooks the roofs of some of the older buildings of Jiujiang and, while the scene is not exactly charming, I am pleased that at least one section of the city has yet to be modernized. The mighty Yangtze (Ch'angjiang) flows to the right, a few small boats tied up at the long narrow docks stretching from shore. A four-lane road with little traffic runs parallel to the river and passes by the entrance of my hotel.

The buildings of the newer part of town are close by. They are neat, clean, white, symmetrical and boring. But as I look down I see several untidy blocks of two- and three-story red brick buildings, most with gable, hip or flat roofs. One is large and rectangular and, in the midst of the four inward-sloping roofs, is a traditional skywell providing air and light to the inhabitants below. Beneath a pearl gray sky, a few straggly, pollution-covered green trees sprout between brick buildings ranging in shade from tawny to fawn. Here the area is unruly, cluttered, defiant, jumbled, almost daring an observer to enter into its chaotic community.

In his book, *A Chinese Childhood*, the writer Chiang Yee wrote of his childhood in Jiujiang early in the 20th century, and of walking along the city wall: "…I spent many a joyful hour walking along the top of it, looking down into the courtyards of houses and at their exteriors, with the vast view of the illimitable river and the great mountain ranges on the other side." Alas, the wall was pulled down in the early 1920's, and the beautiful courtyards have disappeared, but at least the river and a small stretch of older buildings remain.

I unpack my bag, speculate about the "no gambling in room" sign on the desk, check the news on television and force myself to stop thinking about the Muslim attacks on America. Within an hour, I am outside the hotel, asking to be taken to the Tung Lin Tzu, a temple which A. R. Davis, a scholar on the poet's life and the author of *Tao Yuan-ming: His Works and their Meaning*, suggested was most likely about where T'ao had his old home.

A sleepy taxi driver waking from his siesta in a battered Citroen ZX says he knows the area well. The driver stretches and yawns and spends several minutes searching for his misplaced keys (which does not give me confidence) but eventually he locates them under his seat and we begin our journey.

My driver has a gaunt face, high cheekbones over sunken cheeks, dark complexion, slight mustache, and when he looks serious – which is most of the time – he conveys an expression of malevolence, malignity and malice. I do not say he is that kind of person; simply that his features convey that image to me.

In fact, his dusky complexion and dark brown eyes remind me of deep-fried bean curd left in the frying pan a bit too long. His shirt is exactly the beige hue of Chinese ginger and he is wearing bottle-gourd-green trousers.

I try to remember why his face is so familiar and finally it hits me. The driver, soon to be my guide, is, if not the spitting image, certainly a Chinese version of the actor Jack Palance, especially as Jack Wilson, the evil-doer in the movie, *Shane*. So, of course, in my mind, my guide now becomes known as Wilson.

As I will learn, Wilson has a personality which shifts back and forth from quarrelsome to, when needed, ingratiating. His face is not as cleanly sculpted as that of Jack Palance (Whose is?) but the occasional baleful stare which pours forth from those dark eyes beneath heavy black brows might cause an unbiased observer to feel he had come face to face with an adventurous rogue, a parlous picaroon, a wily louche.

We decide to visit the T'ao Yuan-ming Memorial Temple first and follow Peter Tan's directions but find that the temple has been moved to another district just outside Jiujiang. Several times Wilson stops the car to ask directions and each time upon his return to the car reminds me that it is fortunate he speaks the local dialect.

The memorial has three main attractions: The museum, the temple and the poet's tomb. Wilson and I walk slowly through the many halls, past red wooden pillars and along winding corridors. The museum houses paintings of the poet as imagined by different artists, calligraphy in praise of his life and work, maps of places connected with his life, and historical relics found in the area. The paintings and calligraphy are interesting as many are from past dynasties.

I linger for a bit beside a fishpond, chrysanthemum gardens and a memorial archway, then head for the Tao Jinjie Temple. This temple was first built in the T'ang Dynasty and then, in

1982, upturned eaves and all, was moved from its original site. Inside the temple is a large statue of T'ao Yuan-ming, traditional Chinese couplets, and stone inscriptions. The lovely "Coming Back Pavilion" was named after his poem.

Wilson takes my picture beside the poet's granite and brick tomb. A stone wall runs behind the tomb over which is an area of profuse weeds, some wildflowers and bamboo. It is almost as if whoever is taking care of the tomb understands that a natural, almost wild, setting best conjures up the personality of the poet.

We drive through a lovely countryside and soon arrive at Tung Lin-tzu, which scholars believe to be very close to the spot where T'ao Yuan-ming was born. Scholars as well as local legends say this temple was probably first built about the 4th century and then repaired and renovated over the centuries. This temple is said to be the birthplace of the "Pure Earth" Buddhist sect, over 1500 years ago. Chiang Yee also writes of having visited this temple in his youth:

…it gave the impression of being very old and of having preserved its original character, the fallen masonry being covered with herbs and creeping plants and the big peach tree seeming as if rooted there for centuries. A small stream, coming down the mountainside, ran in front of the temple. We crossed a dilapidated little wooden bridge, and the young monk from the temple offered us tea.

The setting of the temple has changed but it is still rustic and unspoiled and monks are much in evidence. In a light breeze, bells ring from the upturned eaves of a pavilion's roofs. I hear monks but they seem to be humming, not chanting. The small pond in front of the temple boasts a large Goddess of Mercy statue, a rock garden and imposing water lilies. On a bamboo-covered hill behind the temple a tall pagoda juts upward into a blue sky.

The wind picks up and I watch orange-and-black butterflies ride vividly colored flowers like cowboys hanging onto bucking Brahma bulls at a rodeo. Behind the temple is a sign which would translate as

"Intelligent Spring," said to bring luck to those who drink from it. I decide it would be more intelligent not to drink from its stagnant water despite the bamboo ladle thoughtfully provided.

A path of several hundred steps ascends straight up the hillside behind the temple and leads a traveler to the pagoda. It is a beautiful walk, surrounded by towering bamboo on each side but as I walk I notice that some of the nearest bamboo are covered with graffiti.

At the pagoda is a tranquil scene with monks in saffron robes working among patches of red and yellow flowers and between rows of tiny green vegetables in a lovely garden. Although this is not a Zen temple, there is some kind of perfection in the manner in which the monks have left their sandals, bamboo vegetable baskets, bamboo rakes and brooms upon a sun-dappled brick wall. There is something incredibly peaceful, almost mystical, in the aesthetic arrangements found in China's countryside, be they natural or manmade, accidental or intended. It might be the perfect pattern and texture of brick and bamboo and earth found inside a Chinese temple garden or the placement of paper door gods on the poorest village hut or the way bright yellow flowers interweave themselves among a cluster of black roof tiles. The beauty and harmony in such simplicity brings centuries of Taoist painters and poets to life.

Yet another bamboo grove surrounds a small wooden house nearby. Jiangxi is one of the most important provinces for many items including rice, tea, timber and bamboo, and as I travel in the province, bamboo groves like those surrounding Tung Lin Tze bring such dry facts to life.

While I stand there I reflect on the legend of how T'ao Yuan-ming agreed to join a Buddhist group which met in this very temple only if he was allowed to drink wine. Although this was against the regulations, he was permitted to do so. It is said that as soon as the wine was finished, the eccentric and unconventional T'ao would immediately get up and leave.

I linger in this relaxing atmosphere for quite a while and then Wilson and I walk back to the car. The sun is setting and the green hills transform into imposing silhouettes slowly being consumed in a blue twilight.

Wilson says there is one more place we can visit today and after a short drive we wander about a temple complex known as the Iron Buddha Temple. Wilson says only nuns live here and, sure enough, except for a young man acting as a kind of custodian cum guard, only women are out and about. During a conversation, they point to an area of devastation and inform me that one of the old buildings recently collapsed.

I think of all the dynastic tales and legends of what nefarious activities occur inside the walls of Taoist and Buddhist temples ("Ten Buddhist nuns, nine are bad; the odd one out is doubtless mad") but, looking at these good ladies, one gets the impression of peace and tranquillity.

I leave Wilson at the hotel after promising to meet him early the next morning. A walk about the streets near the hotel reveals a moderately prosperous town with friendly people. I stop in front of one of the fashion shops which for whatever reason displays a pair of bound feet shoes. What kind of statement the owner thinks he or she is making by displaying a pair of "golden lilies" is lost on me, but it does bring back memories of Hong Kong in the late 1960's and early 1970's when I would pause to watch young or middle-aged people escort very old ladies tottering on their bound feet.

The binding of women's feet began in China about the 10th century. These tiny, deformed feet greatly turned men on and, for some, the odor of their putrefaction was the greatest aphrodisiac known. Although, over time, the lower part of a woman's leg lost muscle elasticity, the upper thighs tightened, and Chinese men believed that a woman with bound feet had a much tighter "jade gate" than a woman without bound feet.

Modern Western scholars say this is not true, i.e., binding a woman's feet did not really make the vagina tighter, but, unless they've been to bed with a boundfoot woman, how would these academic know-it-all's know?

I venture down a dark, dimly lit street which finally narrows into a dead end. As I turn about, I notice several young men staring at me without smiling. I think of warning them that if they mess with me they will be sleeping with the fishes. But that expression wouldn't mean anything here. However, Chinese legends always depict a stork carrying people off to the other world and I debate saying: "Don't mess with me or you'll be riding the stork." Nope, doesn't have quite the same power of intimidation. I walk past them and nothing happens.

Back in my hotel room, I catch up on the latest papers from Beijing. This exciting article catches my eye:

WHAT COLOR IS YOUR HARD-EARNED MONEY?
Can you pick out a fake 100 yuan note at a glance? You can use a new fifth-edition 100-yuan note (red with a portrait of the late Chairman Mao Zedong on one side and the Great Hall of the People on the other). Check the green "100" figure on the left corner of the side featuring Chairman Mao. If you look at the numerical figure from different angles and the figure's color changes from light green to darker green or nearly black, you have a real one. If not, you have been duped.

I check my bills and am relieved to see they pass the test. I turn off the light and am soon fast asleep.

Guling

Lu Shan in winter is usually described in such terms as "wet, rainy, damp, soggy, foggy, and miserable." But as the Citroen ZX steadily makes its way up the mountain road, the morning sun is shining and the views of the mountains and valleys are splendid. It is only about 30 kilometers from Jiujiang to Lushan but it is uphill all the way. About half way up Wilson gives me some gum to chew, explaining that ascending the mountain will be something like being up in a plane.

Not unlike Cheyenne, Wilson tells me that I should give him some money so that he can buy anything I want along the way, from snacks to bottled water. He lowers his voice and suggests that because I am a foreigner local Chinese might overcharge me. I go along with this suggestion, knowing full well that, as with Cheyenne, I won't be getting any change, and most likely would have come out ahead by being slightly overcharged by locals.

Some of the twists and turns of the two-lane road are a bit dicey and it is then that I check to see what kind of protection Wilson has for such dangerous moments: Buddhist symbols, Taoist diagrams, a miniature Torah, a small statue of Jesus, anything will do. But Wilson has none of that nor does he have any laminated Mao gobbledygook; simply a traditional good luck charm in traditionally lucky red color hanging from his taxi mirror – which I decide can probably do the job of keeping us safe.

When eventually we exit a small tunnel and enter the town of Guling, Wilson hardly slows down, quickly spiriting me to what he claims is one of the town's best hotels; the one where many tourists stay. To me it looks like a cross between a fortress-like morgue and an eerily deserted Thomas Mann-type sanatorium. An architectural amalgam of pseudo-Gothic and Soviet Revisionism left over from the set of a Boris Karlof vampire movie. (Indeed, some of the once splendid, privately owned villas have in fact been converted to hotels and sanatoriums.) I don't even bother getting out of the car.

Wilson assures me that he has taken many tourists to this very hotel, but I tell him it won't do. He seems genuinely surprised as well as a bit annoyed that I don't want to stay there. It may simply be that he cannot understand my preference for a hotel with a bit of color, life, activity and atmosphere; it may be that he missed out on a kickback from the hotel.

We drive for five or ten minutes in frosty silence and soon end up at another hotel, a bit mysterious as it is only partly visible behind pine trees and mist, but at which someone has at least gone to the trouble of hanging a few red lanterns about its balconies. At the hotel counter, a familiar pattern emerges: I learn that prices are much higher than I had thought they would be. An unsmiling, non-English-speaking, late middle-aged woman stands behind the counter of the small deserted lobby with her arms crossed, ready for battle.

Me: Aiiiyaaahhh! Your prices are high!
Woman: (no response)
Me: This is the off season!
Woman: Yes.
Me: So your prices should be much lower.
Woman: They were last week.
Me: Oh?
Woman: And they will be next week.
Me: What is so special about this week?
Woman: Everyone has booked to come here.
Me: But it is the off-season!
Woman: Yes.
Me: So why has everyone booked to come here now?
Woman: Mid-Autumn Festival.

Uh,oh. That's right. I have been paying lots of attention to mooncakes but somehow it slipped my mind that mooncakes appear during one of the biggest, most important holidays in China: the Mid-Autumn Festival. A time when millions of Chinese travel all over the country; a time when swarming hordes crowd airports, train stations, bus terminals, hotels, restaurants, and, especially, attractive tourist spots such as Guling. And soon it will be the Mid-Autumn Festival. Duuuh. In any case, the prices are clearly posted on the wall behind the dragon lady's counter so this is not an attempt to charge more for goofy foreigners who don't bother planning their trips around China's major festivals.

Then I notice what appears to be a room for the bargain price of 208 yuan. I ask her if I can take that one. She turns to look at the rate-board, then turns back to me with a smug expression that suggests she is about to put me in my place. (It is the type of well-pleased-with-oneself expression that Chinese refer to as "sucking a sugared olive.") That, she says, is not a room; it is for a bed. I look again and then, sure enough, I notice the two (simplified) Chinese characters, *jya ch'iang* (additional bed). And so, defeated but unbowed, I check in.

As I fill out my form, Wilson does what I fear he will do even though I know what he does is inevitable. He asks if he can share the room with me. The room is small but it has two separate beds, so I can hardly say no. I will wish I had.

We unpack quickly and begin our drive around the tiny town of Guling. Behind hedgerows and neatly trimmed shrubbery, Western-style villas with red-tiled roofs and stone bungalows and Germanic cottages and French churches and Victorian chateaux and Swiss chalets are snuggled among pine, cypress, larch, maple and fir trees, conjuring up a misplaced European village.

In the late 1800's Guling was settled by Europeans and Americans who, not unlike the British in their Indian hill stations, were especially pleased to escape the oppressive heat of the lowlands. Christian missionaries, affluent Chinese and assorted foreign-devils rode their horses up the bridal path or were carried up in sedan chairs and before you could say "foreigners building here are in violation of signed treaties" five times without stopping for breath, Lushan had become a fashionable summer refuge and popular resort.

Writing in 1925, Harry Franck gave an excellent and often acerbic description of the development of Guling. He speaks of the difficult negotiations with "Manchus, local officials, priests and monks" before "the outside barbarians were ceded a strip of land along a rock-tumbling stream from which grassy wooded slopes rise swiftly on either side." He mentions "Caucasians being carried aloft by prosperity-spoiled coolies up the great stone stairway framed in jungle."

But it wasn't long before he would write that "foreign-subsidized automobiles drop thousands of our race (at Lushan) between June and September." He mentions the large bungalows of the business houses frequented by various nationalities, including Russian, Norwegian, Spaniards, Italians and French. But always the missionaries predominated and the town hosted "numberless 'conferences' of all the Protestant sects that are afflicting China with their minor differences."

His descriptions of town life are always colorful: "The local council, in its commendable eagerness for income, has issued licenses to every brand and species of peddler who is to be found in that part of China, or who can by hook or crook get there, to prey upon every foreigner in the place and make his porch a sample-room and a daily shrieking emporium." And it seems that the local council lacked the power to enforce the payment of taxes or to enforce laws "…even if I had succumbed to a frequent impulse and gone out and killed a persistent peddler, or even shot a neighbor of my own race for overworking a phonograph that should have long ago been consigned to Chinese rag-pickers."

Then came Chiang Kai-shek and his wife and after their hasty departure came the communists who, fully appreciating the many charms of the area, made Lushan their "summer capital."

Today's Guling has a few not-too-exciting side-streets, a few quaint cobblestone streets, and one not-too-exciting main street selling basic food provisions for hikers, cheap knickknacks for tourists, and one-room shops offering clothing that might have been fashionable at the height of the Cultural Revolution. A few restaurants. A bank. A post office. A long-distance bus station. And, of course, mooncakes. All you can eat. And tea. All you can drink.

I decide not to let Wilson in on my true reason for coming here until the following day. I decide it might be advantageous if he got to know me a bit better before springing my search plans on him. One never knows how a Chinese guide will react to a foreign-devil's desire to discover the Middle Kingdom's Shangri-La.

And so we head out into the mountains to see a few of the usual attractions that "normal" tourists come to see; that is, tourists not searching for a Chinese Arcadia as described by a 4th century poet whose depiction may have been more than a bit enhanced by numerous gourds of rice wine. Checking out standard tourist spots is not, after all, a waste of time: it is always possible that Peach Blossom Spring is hidden within a different mountain valley than I thought, or that because of a river changing its course or the outcome of battles, or the influx of tourists, the utopians have moved their paradise to a different but nearby location.

As we walk up the mountain trails, the scenery unfolds as in a Chinese tapestry. I can already see a few of the 90-odd lofty peaks said to comprise Lushan. It is interesting enough and there are rocky crags and wizened trees immersed in swirls of mist but, despite the raves of most guidebooks and many travelers, it seems to me to lack the dramatically bizarre bluffs and freakish craggy cliffs and spectacular precipices of Zhangjiajie.

As with many such natural wonders in China, each peak or stream or cliff has been described by a famous poet in verse or talented storyteller in fable. And so for travelers who thrill to place names such as "Dragon Head Rock" and "Incense Burner Peak," and "White Deer Grotto" and "Great Moon Hill," or who adore legends involving the Eight Immortals this is the place to be. The famous Sung poet, Po Chu-yi, wrote that it was impossible to discern Mt. Lushan's beauty because when there a traveler becomes an intrinsic part of it.

At various times, Chinese tour groups pass us on the trails and, invariably, the guide is busily engaged in shouting facts, figures, or instructions through a megaphone; an annoying racket which probably prevents anyone in Peach Blossom Spring from taking an afternoon nap.

We walk onto an outcrop of rock and stand in the shade of a large pavilion overlooking the valley below. I have seen the pavilion and surrounding scenery before on tourist brochures. (In July of 2002, lightning will strike the pavilion, killing three tourists and injuring 40.)

During a rest stop somewhere on top of one of the area's many peaks, while I am still gasping for breath, Wilson suggests we might do as the tourists do and get up the next morning extremely early so that we can watch the fantastic sunrise at Hanbokou. I tell Wilson in very clear mandarin that that is a great idea but that on all early morning adventures such as that one he should start without me.

Among the tourist spots we visit are the Three Sacred Trees(*sanbaoshu*)between Yellow Dragon Temple and Yellow Dragon Pool. Two of the trees are gingko bilboa like those in front of my New York apartment, except that these are said to be fifteen hundred years old (give or take a thousand years), and are incredibly thick. As it is getting chilly, I lend my jacket to Wilson, relying on my long-sleeved shirt to keep me warm. It doesn't.

At almost every attraction we visit there are incessant bird calls. Not from birds but from carved bird whistles sold by vendors. The real birds probably got fed up with the racket long ago and fled south.

Wilson takes me to a pleasant area where people sit beneath the shade of trees drinking the famous local cloud-and-mist tea. In his book, Chiang Yee recalls how in his youth the young tea leaves were "picked by monks and dried in the sun, then brewed to entertain visitors." This local tea is now assiduously promoted well beyond Lushan. The tea is not bad, certainly several notches above the murky brew I drank at Ch'angde's Peach Blossom Spring, but I'm fairly exhausted, so at the risk of sounding like a colonial relic, what I would really like is a swaying punkah overhead, a jug of iced tea and a fragrant Manila cheroot.

A spry but very elderly lady collecting bottles approaches us, leans on her gnarled brown walking stick, and asks for our water bottles when we finish. Her brown cheeks are edged with great patches of deep wrinkles but her eyes sparkle brightly. She wears bulky clothes and a brimless "hello Kitty" cap with a cartoonish drawing of a smiling cat. She says she is 97-years-old and has to work because her son cannot find work in Nanchang.

She overhears Wilson giving me a quick rundown on the area's history and is indignant when he tells me that no Japanese were in this region during World War II. She says they were all over the place and in fact her husband beat one to death. We quickly give her our empty bottles.

For whatever reason, I decide to bring up the death of Wang Wei and the forcing down of the American spy plane. Wilson waves that away and says, "That is a small thing." He drinks his tea and looks about unconcernedly.

I am astounded. Also a bit annoyed. I boned up on my mandarin in the areas of aviation and forced captivity precisely so I could defend the American position and here he is dismissing the incident as a small thing.

Undeterred, I continue on: "Well, he did have a wife and child, though, right?" I can't believe it. Now I'm arguing the Chinese position. But I have heard and read that Hainan Island (where the American plane was forced to land) is a wide-open, bacchanalian southern paradise where promiscuous women known locally as "chickens" practically pull men in off the streets. In other words, the type of place that flourishes in China whenever "the mountains are high and the emperor is far away."

Wilson agrees it is that type of place. I suggest to him that the reason the Americans stayed so many days in Hainan was because they were having so much fun. He thinks that is very funny then suddenly becomes quiet and nods. "Yes, that is possible," he says, thoughtfully.

We continue on to tourist destinations such as Small Heavenly Pool and Five-old-men Peak. It is said the water level at the pool never changes even during flood or drought and that the founder of the Ming Dynasty watered his horses here. On a hill behind the pool is an ancient tower of Indian architecture, a tomb for a lama from Tibet.

The steps up the Five-old-men Peak seem endless. I reach the first of the five viewing stations after which my legs refuse to go any farther. It is the first time in my search for Peach Blossom Spring that I have ever refused to climb to the end of a trail and I am not happy about it. But my legs are simply too weary.

Wilson says I am the first tourist he has taken up this particular path and swears the view is fantastic. When I have enough breath to speak, I ask him, "If I die, what good is the view?" I tell him this mountain has no peak; it goes on forever. He laughs and assures me there is a peak "somewhere up the road." And, no doubt, somewhere over the rainbow. It may be true, as the guidebooks say, that the views of the plains and the Yangtze from Lushan are "breathtaking," but for an out-of-shape writer so is the climb itself "breathtaking."

Later when reading about Chiang Yee's 1975 trip in *China Revisited*, I will be comforted by the fact that he too felt much the same as I did:

Next morning I suggested going up to see the famous Five-old-men Peak on the south side of the mountain. My companions thought I wanted to climb it, but in fact I did not.

On one of our drives, we end up at a wind-swept cable car station. Wilson does not understand why I am not interested in taking a ride. While fighting gusts of wind for possession of my cap and camera, I tell him it is incredibly windy (which it is) and the freely swinging cable cars don't look that safe to me. The real reason, of course, is because if Peach Blossom Spring could have been spotted from a cable car it already would have been. My mama didn't raise no fool either.

As if it isn't enough that our small room in the hotel is greatly overpriced, that night Wilson takes me to an expensive restaurant in which, Chinese style, the two of us are ushered into one of several small rooms. Hence, throughout my meal, in a cell-like chamber, I see no one but my famished driver and a taciturn waitress serving (to me) inedible food.

Wilson suggests a few local dishes and I agree to allow him to order. As I am not into exotic Chinese cuisine, I have difficulty understanding what it is we are eating. I do understand that one of the dishes is a local favorite consisting of some small snail-like creatures the color of mud that, according to Wilson, "cling to rocks." And another dish is one of vegetables, bamboo shoots and some kind of "fungus."

I know nothing useful about vegetables, but these range in color from light to dark green and prove to be delicious. As for bamboo shoots, I do know that in traditional China they were given to suckling mothers to increase the flow of milk. Whether it worked or not and whether anyone still believes in that method I have no idea.

The only kind of fungus I know of is that which I came upon while researching China in the 1850's, and it was a medicine rather than food, although, whether something in China should be classified as food or medicine I notice is always six of one and half dozen of the other. Anyway, ailing Chinese in the late Ch'ing period greatly prized getting hold of "the fungus that grows on the inner wood of a coffin, opposite the nose and mouth of a corpse." I take a few bites and silently pray that it isn't *that* fungus, although it certainly tastes like it could be.

When the bill is presented it is over US$40, quite expensive for a small town repast for two in the Chinese mountains. Wilson had mentioned that he had been here several times so he must have ordered whatever exotic dishes he liked, knowing full well I would be stuck with the bill. I make my displeasure known to him. I also try to convey that it would be nice to dine in a restaurant with a bit of atmosphere.

With little else to do in Guling, we turn in for the night. And I quickly learn that Wilson has a snoring problem. All night long he snores and, worse yet, each time the snoring begins to die down it segues into a series of horrific rat-like, teeth-gnashing, cacophonies; a kind of low-key death rattle. But, as the hours pass, the rattles increase but Wilson doesn't die.

Worse yet, at certain unpredictable intervals, he wakes up suddenly, as if from a horrible nightmare, and glares at me while shouting something in some local dialect. He scowls as if *I* have just woken *him* up, then quickly gets back to sleep! I realize he is shouting at something or someone in his dreams, but the effect of his behavior is to keep me wide awake throughout most of the night. Not since Ishmael encountered Queequeg at the Spouter-Inn has there been quite such a ludicrous bedroom scene.

Eventually, I try softly clapping my hands to stir him in his sleep, loud enough to stop the snoring, but not loud enough to wake him. It works but within a few minutes he is at it again. I clap again and again, louder each time. I hit the bedboard with the palm of my hand. I slam the palm of my hand on the table. By morning, my hands will be sore from trying to achieve silence in the room. I cannot understand how his wife can possibly endure noises like this each night.

Traditionally, Chinese cured nightmares by writing the character for "evil spirit" or "devil" on a paper charm, set fire to the charm, and then mixed the ashes with water. The concoction was them poured into the mouth of the person having nightmares. Ahhh, if only I could.

Just as I am drifting off, I hear music from somewhere in the hotel. The clock reads 7:30. In the hallway, the sounds of maids' voices grow louder. I give up and get up and get dressed. Wilson remains in bed, snoring contentedly.

Downstairs, in a depressing basement room, I am the only one at breakfast. Much to my regret, there is a Mao video playing on the TV screen. Watching Mao in a karaoke setting with a lovely Chinese woman plying me with watermelon seeds is one thing, and hearing Mao at an early hour before breakfast after little sleep is a very different thing.

I ask for a "Western" breakfast and get a slightly modified Chinese breakfast of indifferent congee, soggy dumplings, horrid coffee and what, with much leeway and kindness, might be described as eggs. There is no salt and pepper, and I learn the feast will cost me ten yuan extra as breakfast is not included in the price of the room.

I basically sneak out of the hotel to avoid Wilson and head downtown. I had had a glimpse of a small Internet café somewhere on the main road and I fully intend to find it. I manage to stop a minibus in the mist and convey my destination. (As I forgot to remember the name of my hotel, I will have trouble returning.)

The room at night was full of young people completely absorbed in whatever sites they had reached. Now there are only a few customers in the room. One of the young men turns to me and smiles. His T-shirt reads: "They Can't Kill Rock and Roll." I speculate for a few moments as to who in China would want to kill Rock and Roll. The communist party? The classical musicians union? The United Eunuchs-for-rap-music Association? Maybe the same police who are closing discos in a bid to prevent the province's youngsters from going mad from 'speedy dancing' or the 'violent undertones' of some songs?

I check my mail. The only interesting e-mail is that from the Gloria Plaza hotel in Nanchang confirming receipt of my e-mail from Kwangchow and offering a much lower price than I had paid. Of course, too little, too late.

By the time I manage to find our hotel, Wilson is having breakfast and feeling fine. It is as if the disaster of last night never happened. We have a friendly chat about the state of China today and how the gap between the rich and poor seems to be growing. It seems nothing has changed: "He who rears the silkworms seldom wears the silk." We talk about marriage: "If you marry a chicken, you follow a chicken; if you marry a duck, you follow a duck." We talk about the value of travel: "A frog at the bottom of a well sees only the sky." We talk about catching those behind the World Trade Center attacks: *Shwei luo, shih ch'u* ("When the water recedes, the rocks will be visible.")

He finally finishes his hearty Chinese breakfast and says today he will take me to a lovely lake. He is as good as his word. At the lake I walk among the trees and for quite a while sit beside a beautiful "violin-like" gurgling brook. The setting is beautiful and the brook does in fact sound a bit like a violin. And my thoughts turn again to T'ao Yuan-ming. I have said that his poetry is concerned with wine and nature and friendship and can be compared with Frost and (in my opinion) with Bohemians such as Ferlingetti, but among his poetry there is one poem – and only one – which deals directly with love.

And that is the last and perhaps most mysterious part of the

T'ao Yuan-ming puzzle. For, there, amidst all the beautiful nature and wine poems, the poems of family and friends, the poems of farming and home, among all the poet's writing, there is one and only one love poem. And neither Chinese critics nor Western connoisseurs have ever known quite what to make of it.

T'ao wrote the poem according to a kind of formula suggested by poets who had come before him. That is, he allows his romantic fancies to soar freely before bringing them back to earth. In other words, he shrugs the unusual poem off as a kind of didactic lesson to explain why passions must be kept under control; why serenity of mind must always remain the goal. And, indeed, in Peter Tan's translation, the poem's title is rendered as "Passion Checked."

It is a kind of poetic genre which allows the poet nearly free expressions of love while being able to claim that it is written as a lesson in restraining arousing passions. By employing this technique, Chinese poets could have their congee and eat it too.

The poem describes a beautiful and elegant young zither player whom the poet desperately wishes he could approach. As the poet looks upon the lovely maiden, his spirit leaves him to join with hers:

> On her blouse I'd love to be the neckpiece
> To breathe in the fragrance flowing down her lovely hair.
>
> On her jet black hair the pomade I'd love to be
> To glitter from her temples down her slender shoulders.
>
> As silk I'd love to be her shoes
> To ramble about with her ivory feet in my fond embrace.

But in each example, after the expression of desire (*yuan*) there is always an "Alas" (*bei*) to each of his plans as to why it would not work out. For example:

As wood I'd love to be the zither,
Snugly resting on her lap.
Alas, when joy gives way to sorrow,
Would she not leave off playing?

At the end, the poet realizes that to be with this lovely woman is not possible and he casts aside any notion of passionate assignations and recalls the necessity for discipline.

This poem also shows clearly the difficulty (or freedom one has) in translating Chinese poetry. The lines above are Peter Tan's translations. These below are those of A. R. Gurney:

I wish to be the collar on her robe
And receive the lingering fragrance of her elegant head

I wish to be the sheen upon her hair
When she brushes the black tresses on her sloping shoulders

I wish to be the silk of her shoe
And on her white foot go to and fro

Needless to say, Confucian scholars were not pleased with this poem and one critic went so far as to say of T'ao's work that this poem is the only "flaw in the jadestone." And in a society in which arranged marriages through matchmakers ("ten matchmakers, eleven liars") were the rule, this poem could also be read as a defiance of the system.

It must be said that not all Chinese commentators disliked this poem. The great Sung Dynasty poet, Su Shih (Su Tung-po), praised the poem as being fond of feminine pulchritude without being lascivious.

But in a body of work with almost predictable subject matter, and in the face of the many comparisons with Robert Frost and Taoist nature poets, suddenly, T'ao Yuan-ming begins to sound more like Andrew Marvel in *To his Coy Mistress*. I can only speculate as to why he felt compelled to write this beautiful love poem but one thing is for certain – it is certainly not a flaw in the jadestone.

卍卍卍卍卍卍卍卍

I have explained to Wilson about my need for a soft sleeper train ticket from Jiujiang back to Shen Zhen (the now prosperous border town to Hong Kong where wives from Hong Kong shop and where husbands from Hong Kong hide their mistresses from their wives). He has discussed it with the hotel manager who couldn't seem to get through to anyone on a phone and now Wilson is trying his best on his cell phone to call his wife in Jiujiang so that she can buy the ticket for me. This leads to a confusing series of phonecalls between him and his wife throughout the day.

Later in the afternoon, we stop in at the austere stone-and-concrete building known as the Lushan Conference Site. The setting is picturesque and peaceful, but it was here during the 1959 Lushan Party Plenum that Chairman Mao refused to face the disaster of his Great Leap Forward program and, rather than listening to criticism, severely denounced and canned anyone who dared tell the truth, including his outspoken defense minister, Peng De-huai. Ten years later, in this same conference hall, Mao pushed ahead with his plans to name Lin Piao as his head of state, with disastrous results.

I spot someone who looks like an Eastern European and I realize I have not seen another Caucasian face since I arrived in Jiujiang and Lushan. I glance at some of the photographs of Mao and his friends, sit for awhile watching a video of Mao and his comrades, then exit the hall. The videos remind me of how in 1971, in what was then British-run Hong Kong, I used to enjoy watching movies from the mainland of Chinese revolutionary operas. I was always the only *gweilo* (foreign-devil) in the audience.

The themes were always those of intrepid and determined Chinese Communists defeating the Japanese or the Nationalists or the Americans but I watched them simply because the fighting (stylized acrobatics) were incredible. And, well, yes, because the comely young actresses in their blue tunics and blue shorts and blue caps and red neck ribbons were adorable, made even more so by the fierce, self-righteous expressions smoldering in their dark apricot eyes.

Wilson drives me to China's only sub-alpine botanical gardens, and I walk among the flowers and trees, the well laid-out rhododendrons and rows of pines, and chat with a worker in a remarkable hothouse. I sit beside a brook and listen to the gurgle of the water and to the whispering sound of the wind in the bamboo and try not to think what has befallen an area of Manhattan I knew well. But I soon find that solitude allows far too much scope for imagination.

Our last stop for the day is Meilu Villa and we arrive shortly before it closes. The villa was built about 1900 by a British Lord and eventually sold to Chiang Kai-shek's wife, Song Mei-ling. Both Chiang and his wife stayed there as did, eventually, Mao Tse-tung and his various retinues. No doubt in these hallowed rooms Mao came up with still more addlebrained nostrums for curing China's ills.

The bathroom sink and bathtub and pipes and faucets are rather quaint and something about the interior of the villa reminds me of a set for a Noel Coward play or a scene in an F. Scott Fitzgerald novel. But I am not so interested in the period dining hall, bedroom, bathrooms, etc., as I am in the historical photographs of Chiang and his wife, and especially the books under glass that his wife was said to be reading. One is an omnibus of crime edited by the late mystery writer, Dorothy L. Sayers, and another is a book about Islam by the Christian missionary Samuel M.

Zwemer. The title of his book ends with the words "and their Martyrdom."

The title, of course, brings vividly to mind the destruction of the World Trade Centers and (as I am learning) several surrounding buildings in downtown Manhattan as well. I also wonder about the mindset of Song Mei-ling and try to imagine her ensconced in the small but comfortable villa reading stories of mystery and murder or studying Christian tracts while the communist armies were getting ever closer.

That night Wilson takes me to a second floor restaurant right on the main street of Guling. It is a very spacious restaurant with lots of large round Chinese tables and chairs, only one of which has customers. Bored waitresses stand about in what might be called the ultimate or perhaps the nadir of fashion: wearing cheongsams while standing on platform shoes.

Wilson has brought me to an incredibly unexciting restaurant but, for all I know, this is the Four Seasons or Union Square Café of Jiujiang so I accept his choice with resignation. He orders the food and then midway through the meal he begins complaining to the proprietor about the quality of the chicken dish. What is apparently not obvious to Wilson is that he is a terrible actor and everyone can tell that he is complaining only in hopes that we (I) will not have to pay for a perfectly good chicken dish. It is no doubt Wilson's way of trying to save me money, because of my complaint on the previous evening, therefore making this embarrassing scene partly my fault.

Finally, the thick-necked, barrel-chested, gruff looking proprietor tells one of the serving staff to take the dish off my check. Wilson is pleased. I am mortified. As we leave, I hear the proprietor say some nasty sounding sentences to his staff, I think for Wilson's benefit, but Wilson simply continues on out the door, unaware or unconcerned.

That night the snoring continues but at a lower level and far less aggressive. I wet toilet paper with water and shove the wet balls of paper into my ears. It seems to help and eventually I fall asleep.

On my second morning in Lushan, there are still no people at breakfast besides myself and Wilson but at least there is no video and today in the shape of a sesame covered slice of pie is some kind of red bean treat.

Wilson sits at the table speaking with the waitress. The waitress is facing away from him while she responds, busily observing herself in a mirror as she covers her mouth with one hand while expertly employing a toothpick with the other. This is not the first time I have noticed Chinese abruptness in their relations with one another; but the casually curt behavior seems even more pronounced in Jiangxi than elsewhere in China. S. Wells Williams traveled through Jiangxi province in the 1840's. In his book, *The Middle Kingdom,* he wrote that "the surface of the country is rugged, and the character of the inhabitants partakes in some respects of the roughness of their native hills." He got that right.

Although I am grateful that there is no Mao video playing, there is something almost as disagreeable: a Chinese soap opera. The kind of tear-jerking, maudlin, saccharine type that Chinese seem to love. I mention to Wilson that Chinese women on TV programs always seem to be sobbing. Wilson asks what American women on TV programs do. I tell him they talk to one another about relationships and how men just don't get it.

We talk for a few minutes about Chinese history and its present-day situation. Wilson grows thoughtful then nods and says, "This century will be better." Wilson is certainly not without his good points but, before the breakfast is over, I decide not to apprise him of the true nature of my visit. He is a very practical man for whom the idea of a utopia existing in the mountains might make him see me as a bit deranged.

On our last morning in Lushan the weather finally performs as the guidebooks describe it: grey and drizzling; and although I don't know it yet by the time I return to Bangkok I will come down with a serious case of bronchiolitis.

We have not gotten very far down the mountain when we pass a large sign too quickly for me to read. I urge Wilson to stop the car and back up. I am stunned by what I read:

He who does not reach the Stone Gate Gully,
does not know the real feature of Mount Lushan – Xinglong Ropeway.

I am uncertain how to take this. And I don't know what the hell the Xinglong Ropeway is but it is almost as if someone is giving away the fact that Peach Blossom Spring is in Stone Gate Gully. And that is exactly where I am heading. This could be a very good sign indeed. An auspicious omen.

Stone Door Valley

And soon we arrive at the base of the Lu Mountains and, after a bit of a drive, arrive at *the* mountain; the one which overlooked the home and garden of T'ao Yuan Ming. It is the *Shih Men Chien*, the "Stone Door Valley." If my calculations are correct, this is the very Stone Mountain T'ao described in his poem and if it is anywhere Peach Blossom Spring should be here.

As we approach, it is clear I am the only tourist. I get the impression I have been the only tourist for quite some time. Wilson leaves me at the ticket booth and chats with the obviously bored ticket taker, a stout, middle-aged woman with a toothy smile. They are very friendly to one another but it is not quite clear to me if they have met before or not. They give me what appear to be waves of dismissal, turn to chat with each other, and I am off. Little do they seem to know (or care) that Peach Blossom Spring may be just around the corner.

I follow a narrow path and very soon the path becomes steep, bordering (at least in my mind) on precipitous, and there is little in the way of a guard rail. It is now late afternoon. The wind picks up and from far below I hear the sound of rushing water. As I turn a bend in the trail persistent gusts of wind vie with one another to jostle me off the cliff. No doubt the work of evil magicians aware that I am getting closer to my goal.

To my right is a very steep drop and to my left is undergrowth which brushes against me. I do not like heights to begin with and am not thrilled to come upon a sign asking that I "Please protect wild animals." In my overworked imagination, this of course conjures up the sight of a wild boar high on psychedelic Timothy Leary-type mushrooms and Alice-in-Wonderland toadstools rushing out and knocking me off the path to my death.

I continue on glancing occasionally at a small map with certain spots marked with tiny, impossible-to-read, Chinese characters. I begin to realize how enormous this mountain area really is and how readily one can get lost amidst reddish cliffs, bamboo groves, forested glens and ever-changing mist. Every so often I pass by large boulders, each with a beautifully carved Chinese ("cursive script") character filled in with red paint.

Eventually, I come upon a rivulet and follow it as I ascend a mountain. Guidebooks spoke of "thunderous cataracts" but the stream shows no signs of changing into anything so ambitious and continues on as an indolent stream.

Finally, I come upon a dozen or so workers laboriously carrying small boulders across a dry riverbed by placing them in a leather container on a long pole. Each of two men has an end of the pole resting on his shoulder and they struggle with their load. It is a scene one could have found in China a thousand years ago.

Everyone I meet keeps telling me there is a waterfall up ahead. The workers assure me this is true. I tell them I have been walking a long time and I do not believe there is a waterfall.

One of them looks up ahead and then back to me. "If there is no waterfall, where is this water coming from?"

Well, OK, score one for the locals. And eventually I do indeed come to a spot with a sluggish waterfall. And from there I can ascend no farther. But there is something about the sheer, rocky wall of the cliff that intrigues me.

I can readily imagine that what is now merely a rivulet was once a stream; a stream that would have ended exactly where I am standing. I cannot escape the feeling that this is it: I am at the exact spot where the opening in the rock wall allowed the fisherman, or, rather, T'ao Yuan-ming, to squeeze and wiggle his way into Peach Blossom Spring. Somehow, everything seems precisely in place; exactly as the poet described. I can almost *feel* Peach Blossom Spring on the other side of this mountain.

I walk back and forth for awhile, occasionally running my hand over the wall. There is no way I can climb the sheer rock and I cannot see any way around the mountain. I make a few half-hearted attempts at climbing which end in painful failures. I explore still farther to the left and then to the right with no result.

I am about to give in to despair when I suddenly remember something important. I remember how in H. Rider Haggard's *King Solomon's Mines* there was some kind of cleverly hidden lever which raised an enormous stone to reveal an opening. There too it seemed as if it was a solid wall impossible to penetrate, but hidden counter-weights responded to the slightest pressure on a secret spot, raising the massive stone door of the escarpment into a cavity above.

That could be the answer. After the poet found Peach Blossom Spring the people living there must have decided to plug up the crevice that allowed him to enter. But, in case of emergency, they may well have created their own ingenious method of allowing entrance.

I begin pressing the palm of my hand against any irregular rock or unusual boulder or suspicious outcrop of stone or against any spot that I suspect should have had a rock or boulder or outcrop of stone. I am determined that neither crag nor crevice shall escape my touch. I shall, so to speak, leave no stone untouched.

Unfortunately, as with the myriad rivers of Hunan, in this immense mountain face, there are *countless numbers* of rocks and boulders and outcrops of stone. And, as time passes, despite my best efforts, none of them shows the slightest inclination of responding to my touch. And if the river bed has gone down over the centuries, it may be that the secret spot is several yards above my head, far too high for me to reach.

My taps, raps and knocks do, however, cause several of the

local stone-carriers to halt their work and draw near to observe my activity. Dark-faced men in well-worn, practical shirts and shorts or rolled-up trousers, their broad hats protecting them from the sun. Their weathered faces are incredibly lined, the backs of their hands are as brown as the earth and their legs are thin, wiry and muscular. Each could pass as a Chinese version of "The Man with the Hoe."

As I could use their help, I turn to them and say, *yehsu jeige difang you men!* ("There might be a door here!") Without moving a muscle, they continue to stare, mouths agape, looking for all the world like the crowds of silent, staring, uncomprehending Chinese peasants in old black-and-white photos taken by foreign travelers over a hundred years ago.

For a moment, I wonder if I pronounced the word "perhaps" (*yehsu*) correctly. Maybe they thought I said "Jesus" (*yesu*) and they think I'm some kind of demented missionary babbling about how Christ came out of the cave. But then I get it. They know where the door is all right but they've been well paid to keep their mouths shut. Or, rather, agape. Paid by the same magicians who flummoxed Don Quixote or by inhabitants of Peach Blossom Spring – one or the other. And the realization sinks in that I have no hope of getting to the other side of this mountain. Holding my now aching hand (which had already been aching from trying to keep Wilson awake), I decide to give up the ghost. As I pass among them, the crowd of workers slowly parts but the men continue to stare.

I begin my descent. Immediately, persuasive and persistent bearers encourage me to let them take me down the mountain. I explain to them that as I walked up the mountain, I should be able to walk down without a problem. Although in truth my legs are a bit rubbery and eventually I do give in. The sure-footed bearers move quickly down the mountain and in no time at all I am back with Wilson and his friend. Wilson waves and heads for the car.

I bargain with the bearers and then get into the car. Wilson asks me how much I paid the bearers. I tell him 400 yuan (US$48.33). Without a word, he throws open the car door and - - in the manner of Jack Palance – strides over to confront the bearers. There is shouting. Almost all the shouting is from Wilson. Within two or three minutes I see one of the bearers reach into his shorts pocket and hand some bills to Wilson. Wilson marches back to the car and gives me 200 yuan. I cannot understand his swearing but it is clear he feels the bearers were trying to cheat me. A sense of confusion mixed with a tinge of shame comes over me. I have been regarding the driver as a Jack Palance type yet here he is acting more like Shane.

I do want to be fair to Wilson. He has in fact always had his good side. For example, for many Chinese, the birth of a male baby is still a *da hsi* ("great happiness") and the birth of a female baby is still regarded as a *hsiao hsi* ("minor happiness") but Wilson thinks daughters are just as good as sons. He is also thrilled when he sees that I have a copy of the works of Shen Tsong-jen. So he is not uneducated, and is not some kind of ultra-conservative. And he has told me that when the taxi business is slow he works in the same factory as his wife. So he is not lazy. It is just that he has a few flaws in his personality (and his sleeping habits) which to my way of thinking may render him less than the ideal choice for a tourist guide.

Once back in Jiujiang, we head for the Gantang Lake. I stroll around a small museum on a tiny island connected to the shore by a short bridge. Many famous *Romance of the Three Kingdom* battles were fought here and some are commemorated in the museum with statues, maps and drawings. But my heart is not in it. My journey has ended in failure and so I sit on a stone wall and look out at the lake, or rather what are two interconnected lakes.

In his book, *A Chinese Childhood*, Chiang Yee has a wonderful chapter entitled, "Boating by Moonlight." He writes of an arched stone bridge and of how the artificial bank is "covered with green grasses and the edges lined with huge old rugged willows." He writes of the women washing clothes along the bank and of how the "coloured dresses of the women as they bent in a row to their work was a picture in itself and the rhythm of their beaters on the washing possessed a poetry of its own." He writes of the girls collecting the water caltrops and of the melancholy beauty of their songs drifting across the lake. He speaks of a fisherman silhouetted against the bright moon and the soft, poignant sound of an invisible lute.

All of which makes me feel worse because what I see now is a lake which seems to have lost much of its charm just as the Chinese living here no doubt have little time for such poetic sensitivity.

We stop at the Nengren Temple, because I want to explore the temple grounds and to see a pagoda dating back to the Yuan Dynasty. Pagodas have always been pretty big deals for Chinese the saying being, "A pagoda is known by the length of its shadow; a virtuous man by the number of his enemies." (So what is the shadow known by? Never mind.)

What amazes me is that the monk who gives us the tickets actually takes the money and makes change. Of course, Chinese Buddhism is *Mahayana* but I am used to Southeast Asian *Theravada* Buddhism, where a monk deigning to touch money would be severely reprimanded by his abbot. What shocks me the most is how shocked I am.

Wilson doesn't fail to notice my astonishment and asks what is wrong. After I explain, he turns to the monk and laughingly repeats what I said. The monk finds this less than amusing, however, and seems to grow suspicious of me. Now and again I notice him staring at me as I walk about the temple grounds which reminds me of the Chinese Four Cautions: "Beware of a woman before, beware of a horse behind, beware of a cart sideways, beware of a priest every day."

Later, while we are pulled up at a gas pump, a truckload of pigs pulls up nearby. They may actually be large enough to be hogs but whatever they are they are unhappily fenced in with wire. I watch as a boy quickly grabs a hose, walks to the truck and, with much enthusiasm, hoses them down. In off-the-beaten-path Chinese towns, it seems gas stations are for filling up and hosing down.

Wilson and I sit for awhile along the Yangtze River beside the ancient Xunyang Tower. Xunyang is the old name for Jiujiang and the first tower here was built at least 1300 years ago. As with so many Chinese monuments, this one was destroyed and rebuilt many times but over the centuries famous poets wrote about the tower, and their descriptions are well known. One of the characters in the novel, The Water Margin (AKA All Men are Brothers) becomes inebriated and inscribes an insurrectionary poem on an inner wall of the tower.

After a desultory conversation, Wilson looks at his watch and says it is time to meet his wife and pick up my train ticket. We park the car outside her factory and she approaches the car. She gets in the back and hands me the ticket. I quickly make certain it is a soft sleeper ticket, then hand Wilson the money.

His wife is in her early forties and although she has lost her girlish figure, her face is open, intelligent and honest. It is quite a contrast with Wilson's face, which is dark, possessed of a high forehead, and a bit simian. His wife bids me a good journey and heads back to the factory. I suggest we return to my hotel and kill time in the coffee shop until it is time to leave for the station.

In the coffee shop, I order Western and Wilson orders Chinese. I am desperate for coffee but there is some kind of impromptu meeting in the coffee shop involving all employees and I have to wait. The meeting drags on and I mention it to Wilson hoping to goad him into some kind of action but, apparently imbued with a newfound patience, he merely nods.

He begins to speak of his girlfriend, a woman ten years younger than his wife and a woman who has a six-year-old daughter. He has been going with her for six months and she wants him to divorce but he says no way. He met her at a dance hall when a friend introduced them. I begin to wonder if finding a man in China who is not cheating on his wife might not be more difficult than finding Peach Blossom Spring.

As I am still disappointed with my inability to find T'ao Yuanming's utopia, I am preoccupied; and I make polite noises to Wilson about how I bet his girlfriend is attractive and he assures me she is. It is then that I make a very serious mistake. I ask Wilson if he has a picture of the girl and when he says not on him just to be pleasant I say it is too bad I won't have a chance to see her.

I change the subject and talk to him about Jiujiang and its history, but I can see that, from that point on, his mind is no longer focused on our conversation. He glances at his watch and calls for the bill. Or more accurately suggests I call for the bill.

I pick up the check and my luggage and we get into his car. At some point I sense we are not going in the direction of the train station. When I ask, he says he is going to stop at his place first and give me a photograph of his girlfriend. Keeping my voice calm, I remark that we have no time to do that and still make the train on time. He says not to worry, we have time.

He pulls up in front of a series of apartment buildings with what appears to be an unarmed guard in front. He jumps out and disappears. I wait. I wait some more. I am, to say the least, not relaxed. Every few minutes, someone exits – a wizened, elderly man with a limp, a middle-aged woman in a bright red dress, a boy pushing a wobbly blue bike, two young women engaged in a spirited conversation – but never Wilson. It is one of those times I am especially pleased that I do not wear a watch as glancing at it every minute would make me more nervous.

Just when I am wondering as to the best way to commit suicide in China, Wilson reappears. He approaches in a loping, half hearted jog, a relaxed gait which suggests that we have all the time in the world, and jumps into the car.

He hands me a color print of himself standing beside two young women. The picture was taken inside the courtyard of a temple with traditional red pillars, yellow walls, moon door and painted ceiling borders. One of the women has a cute face and her curvaceous young body is enhanced by a tight blue sweater and tight blue jeans. She is apparently a bit bored and is leaning against a pillar. The other, smiling brightly but not quite so attractive, is dressed more conservatively in sleeveless yellow top and black slacks. Wilson is standing next to them, white shirt over grey trousers in need of ironing, holding what appears to be a bottle of Wahaha water.

Wilson points to the photograph, indicating that his girlfriend is the more conservative of the two. She is not unattractive although I find her less impressive than his wife but admittedly I know nothing about his tastes and needs.

Then I understand what took him so long: On the back he has written in Chinese about how he is giving a souvenir to his friend, Mr. Ding Bai Lei (Dean Barrett), to remember him by. After which he has written "China, Jiangxi, Jiujiang" his name and the date. I smile appreciatively and look at the photograph for an appropriate amount of time before putting it away and thanking him for his thoughtful present; all the while contemplating which of China's dynastic tortures I would most like him to undergo.

At last, once again, we are on the road. An observation you will not find in *Lonely Planet*: There is very little traffic in Jiujiang until drivers there are aware that a foreigner is attempting to make a train; then they all get behind the wheel and crowd the streets. No, no, what am I saying – I'm just nervous, that's all.

As we approach the train station, I can see a large station clock. Four o'clock. The train leaves at 4:18. At this point there is no question in my mind that I am going to miss my train because I stupidly opened my big mouth.

But all is not yet lost. Wilson ignores a station official's gestures and angry shouts, zooms up to the entrance and parks where he is not supposed to. I grab my bag and we rush into the station. I hurriedly buy a bottle of water and, in the confusion, cannot find the ticket. But after several horror-filled seconds I do find it and we rush into the waiting room.

Everyone else who is boarding my train has left the room. Two young women in uniform stand at the doorway. As we rush up to them they cease chatting and assume a more official air. As I hand my ticket to one of them, Wilson shakes my hand, calls me a true friend, and wishes me a happy journey.

One of the young women studies the ticket, then looks up and smiles at me. In my mind it appears to be a too-bad-you-aren't-staying-overnight-we-could-have-had-some-fun smile. Nope. That notion is completely dispelled when she says in mandarin: *Jeige shih mingtian de pyau.* "This is tomorrow's ticket." So in fact her smile is a hey-pal-you've-got-the-wrong-ticket-and-aren't-going-anywhere-today smile.

The panic is instantaneous. Wilson snatches the ticket from her hand, glares at it with more fury than Jack Palance ever mustered, and immediately pushes buttons on his cellphone. I smile sheepishly at the two women. They smile back. Within seconds Wilson is shouting at his wife. *Screaming* at her. While he is doing this, it is getting later and later. And I don't quite see how his shouting at his wife in a cell phone is going to aid me in boarding the train.

✓ *Peach Blossom Spring Note Number Six:* When traveling in China by train, do not just check your ticket to see if you have a soft sleeper; pay just a bit of attention to the date of departure as well.

The thought of spending another night in Jiujiang is not a happy one. The thought of spending another night with Wilson in an apologetic mode strikes me as being worse than being with Wilson in his normal Jack Palance mode. He would feel obliged to take me to dinner (or at least to have dinner with me) just when I would most want to be alone with my unhappy thoughts. A very depressing gloom settles over me. Sweat covers my forehead and coats my palms. As I look at his simian features, I suddenly recall the Chinese expression, "kill the monkey to frighten the chickens," and wonder if I strangle Wilson in front of these two women will they be too frightened to prevent me from dashing through the gate.

I expected by this time to be bathing with innocent, young, nubile maidens in some unspoiled, sparkling, bubbling stream inside Peach Blossom Spring, surrounded by frangipani, hibiscus, wild orchids, banana fronds and groves of bamboo rustling gently in the breeze, while in the distance exotic birds flew above emerald green hills reaching into a clear azure sky. Instead I am stranded for yet another night in northern Jiangxi province immersed in a traveler's train station nightmare. This, however, is where Wilson's assertive personality and belligerent manner shine brightly.

I have the wrong ticket and he has none but he pushes me in front of him and rattles off something to the two astonished women. The two of us rush past them before they can stop us. Their loud, excited voices and indignant protests are ignored.

We dash through a tunnel, up what seems to be thousands of steps, still more steps, and eventually I get a glimpse of the train. The only people on the platform are the officials in charge of each car. It is clear that all other passengers have boarded and the train is about to depart. Of course, my train car, number nine, is way off to the right. The eyes of officials follow the progress of the out-of-shape foreign-devil huffing and puffing his way to car number nine. For inspiration, I try to hum the theme music from "Chariots of Fire" but I hate running and I can't quite remember the notes. Wilson, however, proves to be a fast runner.

By the time I reach the car he is already there explaining, annoying, badgering and pleading all at the same time. My heart is pounding dangerously and I am completely out of breath.

He speaks to a young woman in uniform and then to a middle-aged man in uniform. The woman is staring at me as something bizarre if not outright dangerous that might have escaped from a zoo; the man is shaking his head, and I can see that Wilson is not getting anywhere. I step up and in very deferential, out-of-breath, mandarin assure the official that I don't care about getting a hard or soft sleeper or *any* sleeper, but I really need to get on this train.

The man gives me a look of pity then says something to Wilson and gestures toward the train. Wilson shouts for me to wait while he boards to speak to someone. He is not gone thirty or forty seconds before the train lurches forward. I grab my bag and leap on board the train. I stumble, recover and reach out to steady myself. Another man in uniform motions for me to take a seat in the dining car. I throw my bag on the chair beside me and sit in a chair beneath an advertisement for Lu Shan beer. I cannot see Wilson.

Finally, as the train is pulling out, I see him on the platform, running alongside the car and waving to me. I wave back. He points toward another car and I nod as if I know what he is talking about. The truth is I do not know if he saw anyone at all or made any kind of arrangement with train officials but I am at least on the train.

Strange Encounters and Significant Discoveries on Board a Chinese train

I sit quietly, almost motionlessly, attempting to project the image of a foreign devil indifferent as to whether or not he will have to pass the entire night in this seat. A bunch of paper tulips has been set in a vase on each table, red and yellow with green stems and imitation drops of water. The imitation drops remind me once again of the way ricefields were moved close to train tracks so when Chairman Mao passed by he would see fertile fields of green and in turn believe even more strongly in his disastrous economic policies. (It is not only foreigners who have trouble discerning the real from the illusory in China.)

I am at an age when I sometimes see what opthamologists call "floaters," and while taking an unnecessary swing at what is most likely an imagined fly, I accidentally knock over a holder of toothpicks. They spread out across the white table cloth like a poor man's set of pick-up sticks. Across the aisle, an elderly woman in fashionable clothes sits ramrod straight in a straight back, imperial blue chair, framed by blue window curtains and the fading daylight behind her. There is something imperious in her manner and something almost autocratic in her mien. She reminds me of China's Empress Dowager or of the aristocratic Grandmamma in Dostoyevsky's *Gambler*. As I stare back at her I can't help but wonder if she had quite a time during the Cultural Revolution. But, then, what Chinese didn't?

She says nothing but stares at the toothpicks as if she were a sorceress discerning clues to my future, and is surprised and appalled and, perhaps, a bit ashamed at what she sees. I quickly scoop up the toothpicks. Fluorescent ceiling lights slowly, reluctantly, flicker on. For several minutes, there are only the sounds of food utensils and silverware and the constant clicking of the wheels on the tracks. When I dare glance in her direction once again, the grande dame has disappeared.

After about half an hour, a rotund, middle-aged man in a food-spattered white uniform approaches me. He has a large mole on his right cheek, the color of taro, and his lips are an unnatural red, most likely from some exotic dish he has just consumed. He speaks slowly in mandarin as if speaking to someone a bit retarded and informs me that he will try to get me a soft sleeper once we get into Nanchang, but, for now, everything is occupied and I will have to stay where I am. I am uncertain if this is where I should be offering him a bit of "squeeze" to help motivate him in the search for a soft sleeper. Rather than risk insulting him, I smile brightly and tell him that is absolutely wonderful and I thank him profusely. I also apologize for troubling him. His eyes narrow as he smiles, extending a nexus of wrinkles and crinkles down toward his crimson lips and outward toward his protruding ears. He too disappears.

Outside the window the setting sun is hesitantly coloring the clouds, as if awaiting Chairman Mao's approval. And, yet again, an almost magical, unfathomable world appears, as enchanting as it is mysterious: red brick houses with steeply pitched, black-tiled roofs and narrow dirt roads with the occasional bicycle rider. Family dwellings of sun-dried adobe brick walls and baked red-tiled roofs nestle beside homes with tamped earth walls surrounded by large yellow flowers and slender fruit trees; Laughing children lead lumbering water buffaloes silhouetted against small ponds of water. The plodding buffaloes with their hooded eyes and wide nostrils look like mythical beasts from a Chinese fairytale.

The water reflects the primrose streaks and damask ribbons

coloring an azure sky, the yellow and pink rapidly giving way to a rich violescent purple. The banks of most ricefields run straight, but I occasionally spot one that defies the norm, and curves gradually and gracefully inward. The rice in the fields has been harvested and is stacked in conical piles, each tied with a kind of knob at the top, not unlike hats worn by mandarin officials of the Ch'ing period.

As the train speeds past I get glimpses of a wide variety of architectural styles as well as many kinds of building materials. Unlike northern China, dwellings of the south have to deal with the glare of the summer sun and white lime plaster on outer walls aids in deflecting solar heat. Building styles were also developed to increase ventilation, accommodate the local landscape, display status and, of course, as protection against enemies. Some styles developed as northerners moved south and adapted their northern building style to a southern climate.

The train pulls into Nanchang. I notice a woman fanning what at first glance appears to be merely a bare patch of soil, but when I get a better look, I see the clay pot, the fire and the food. But my mistake reminds me of the Chinese legend of the woman whose late husband asked her not to remarry until the soil at his grave was completely dry. The woman had apparently already met someone she was fond of and was spotted by one of the Eight Immortals fanning the recently upturned soil to help the process along.

The train stops for awhile then continues on in jerky starts and sudden stops and finally leaves the city of Nanchang behind, but the officials pass by and say not a word to me about my fate.

Rays of the setting sun splash into the dining car, lighting up a plaque above the door: "Nanjing – Puzhen Railway Rolling Stock Works." Several women who seem to be trainees pass by wearing white blouse, black belt, black trousers and a cap suggesting a vague military air.

One or two glance at me and smile. Their smiles seem to

suggest that they have heard of the lunatic searching for Peach Blossom Spring, and although they have been ordered not to stare, they can't resist glancing at someone so hopeless that he can't even buy the right train ticket. How could such a hapless fool dare hope to find Peach Blossom Spring?

About 9 o'clock the official approaches me again and tells me he has found me a bed but all that is available is a hard sleeper. He sits heavily into a chair opposite me and, if anything, his wrinkles seem deeper and more numerous than before; but his lip coloring is no longer crimson. I offer to buy him a beer, thinking perhaps a beer and a bit of silver crossing his palm might smooth things over and lead to a good night's sleep.

But at the offer of a beer he shakes his head. He does ask me what I am doing in China and I tell him I am a writer. I quickly add that I am not a journalist; I am an (innocuous) writer of novels. He nods and smiles. I tell him that this is not the first time I have been on the wrong train. I once got on the wrong train in Thailand and ended up sleeping overnight on a board in the baggage car so a hard sleeper is fine with me.

He laughs, then pulls out my ticket. He says again, perhaps to make certain I understand, that my soft sleeper ticket is for tomorrow's train. I nod. He says as it is for tomorrow, it has no value today. I nod. So as the ticket for tomorrow's soft sleeper has no value now they therefore have to charge me for today's hard sleeper. Great, I get to pay again. I must remember to send the photograph of Mr. Wilson and his girlfriend to Mrs. Wilson.

The fact that this official is quite helpful does not surprise me. Officials I have dealt with in China have often proved surprisingly friendly; especially when they realize I have made the effort to learn mandarin. When leaving Hunan, returning on the train back from Ch'angde to Ch'angsha, I had a chat with a communist party official who spent most of the journey reading slick magazines on sensational crimes accompanied by titillating pictures. When

I mentioned that I had seen souvenir plates for sale with Mao and his arch-enemy, Lin Biao, he just smiled and said China is changing. I mentioned that in 1971 I could have bought postage stamps with Mao and Lin for pennies apiece but didn't. Then when Lin attempted his assassination of Mao and fled, the stamps were pulled and became priceless. I asked him if he thought I should invest in stamps with Ziang Tze-min and Li Peng together, but he just laughed and said it will not happen again. At Changsha, he walked me out to a taxi and impressed upon the driver that I was a guest in this country. In other words, no cheating. Then he shook my hand and wished me luck.

The official leads me to my hard sleeper which turns out to be the bottom bunk of three vertical narrow bunks. Facing me about two feet away is an elderly lady with mottled brown skin and short white hair sleeping on the bottom bunk of three more vertical bunks. She is making sounds between a soft snore and a repetitious hum. I have no idea what she does for a living, but she is dressed as an amah from the earlier days of treaty port society, traditional *samfu* of black tunic and trousers and tiny green jade earrings.

There are no doors to the corridor and my very being provides entertainment for passing children and more than a few adults. My every movement seems cause for comment and discussion. People in the bunks above and beside me gobble chicken and noodles and various fruits and throw the bones of the chicken and remains of the fruit into an open black plastic garbage bag inside a small trash basket. The basket is between my bunk and the bunk of the elderly woman, so close I could reach out and touch it if I dared. I stretch out on the bunk as best I can and close my eyes.

Students flirting and laughing, babies crying and shrieking, conductors shouting and cajoling, the occasional passerby clearing his throat and spitting – the romance of travel on a Chinese train.

In 1935, C.W.H. Young wrote a book entitled, *New Life for*

Kiangsi and wrote on China's New Life Movement: "In Kiangsi, one noticed a point in striking contrast with Shanghai. In this port (Shanghai), we hear people clearing their throats almost everywhere and spitting at every possible point. In the interior, few such cases were heard or seen." Obviously Mr. Young wasn't stuck on a hard sleeper barreling its way across Jiangxi province.

As I doze off into snatches of a fitful sleep, voices in my head begin to drown out the sounds of the train and its travelers. Anxious voices.

Jesus Christ, Don Quixote gets to travel with Sancho Panza and all I get to travel with is an obnoxious voice in my head.

It could be worse.

How could it be worse?

You could have more than one voice in your head; Stephen King has several – he calls them "the boys in the basement;" anyway, this is all your own fault.

Why *my* fault?

Because instead of searching for Peach Blossom Spring, you should have planned a more conventional journey, something more commercial.

Like what?

You could have done what that Woodstock poet did and tagged along with some eccentric, noodle-eating monk looking for his master's bones. Or, better yet, tried something kinky like that guy who packed Einstein's brain in his car and took off with it across America. Now *that's* class!

You're saying I should steal somebody's brain and travel with it?

Why not?

Whose?

Somebody even more intellectual than Einstein; somebody like, say, Cynthia Ozick.

Never heard of her.

Of course you haven't; nobody has, because she's an intellectual and she writes essays and fiction – a combination that practically guarantees obscurity; but that's the beauty of it.

What is?

It will give us one up on the Einstein caper because she's famous in an obscure way.

Ok, where can we find Ozark's brain?

O*zick*.

OK, whatever, where do we find it?

Well, there's a problem.

What?

She's not dead.

Not *dead*?

No, but that's even better!

How?

We can just put her in the car and take her with us.

That's kidnapping, you idiot!

Hey, you want a bestseller or not?

I am not going to kidnap anybody!

OK, calm down, look, here's a better idea. Somebody has shlepped the brain of a real person across America, right?

Right.

And somebody has searched for his master's bones in China, right?"

Right.

OK, so we up the ante: we schlep the brain of a *fictional* character across *China*. And we search for the bones of the *fictional* character's *fictional* master!

What? Are you insane!

Don't you see? It's sure to make reviewers sit up and take notice. First of all, Americans don't *know* any Chinese fictional characters! Of course they do.

Who?

Charlie Chan for one, and that guy with the mustache and fangs.

I am *not* looking for Charlie Chan's brain and I will not have it in my car!

You don't have a car.

You don't have a brain!

Well, then, maybe we can find Confucius' brain. He was from the state of Lu which I just happen to know is now Shantung Province and his tomb is near Chufu. We could take a train to Shantung, rent a car, drive to Chufu, locate the tomb, borrow the brain, and drive to Inner Mongolia. We could call it, *Driving Mr. Kung Tzu.*

No! No! *No!*

I awake with a start because the old woman humming, snoring and sleeping in the bunk just a few feet from me awakes; probably because an unhappy baby one compartment over is making lots and lots of noise. The woman stretches her head to look toward the other compartment and sees that the woman and baby have been assigned a middle bunk. She gets up and walks over to them. A sense of dread comes over me. I know what is happening and I am powerless to stop it. The kindly old woman thinks the mother should have a lower bunk and will offer to change places with her – thereby placing the mother and her screaming baby two feet from my bunk.

It is done. The old woman picks up her few belongings and departs. I smile at the young mother and in a brief conversation learn that she is from Henan province and her baby girl is one year old.

Over the next several hours, when all (except foreign-devils) are asleep, this obviously fatigued, exhausted mother will be forced to get up several times and walk about with her baby to keep it quiet. The unheralded sacrifice of mothers never ceases to amaze me. But just as I am thinking wonderful thoughts about mothers and children everywhere, just as I am developing a great empathy for the human condition, what I had feared the most happens.

From the corner of my eye, I see the mother holding her baby from behind and positioning him over the black bag. Facing me.

So to the leftover chicken and rice, cold noodles, cigarette butts, fruit rinds and cookie crumbs is now added – you guessed it – baby urine.

✓ *Peach Blossom Spring Note Number Seven:* When traveling in China by train, should you have the misfortune to be traveling on a hard sleeper, do whatever you can to avoid a lower bunk.

I roll over, face the wall, and try not to think about it. I try *very hard* not to think about it. And of course the more I try not to the more I think about it. As I drift off to sleep, the clacking of the wheels seems to mock me: "Peach Blossom Spring, Peach Blossom Spring, Peach Blossom Spring."

And at first my dreams reflect my failure to find the Chinese utopia I was seeking. I seem to be falling – or rather floating gently downward – from the side of a forested mountain and in my dream I recognize much of the scenery I have seen before: the bizarre formations of Zhangjiajie, the rolling green hills of Ch'angde's Peach Blossom Spring, the hillside temples and pagodas, the mist-shrouded bamboo groves of Lu Shan. And then I see the faces of those I have met: Peter Tan, Cheyenne, Slick Willy, Wilson. Wilson is on a cliff waving to me but as I drift near him he transforms into Miss Pong. She is using the same gestures Wilson used when pointing to the next train car but she is pointing toward a temple. But when I attempt to land at the temple gate I miss the temple and have to walk up a series of steps. Inside, instead of the buddhas and incense I expected to find, I see the bedroom of Mr. Lau, the young man who let me use his computer in Changde. The young man who found his freedom on the internet.

And in the corner I see the computer and then I seem to be entering it. And then I have the revelation. In the poet's version, people grew weary of the real world and entered the

Shangri-La of Peach Blossom Spring. In today's China, millions of Chinese are doing the same thing, withdrawing from the world to enter a portal to a parallel universe – the world inside the computer.

According to T'ao Yuan-ming, twenty-two hundred years ago, non-conformists tried to escape the control of China's central government as well as avoid endless wars and almost certain starvation by creating their own utopia in a mountain hideaway. And who in China is doing that today? Of course! Today it is those logging onto forbidden internet sites and participating in chatrooms who are escaping authority; nonconformists escaping the confines of government control. Could it be that the modern Peach Blossom Spring is located in the ungovernable cyberspace which tens of millions of Chinese are entering?

I know it may seem strange to think of someone like Bill Gates as the new T'ao Yuan-ming but men like Gates are also offering a way out of the unpleasantness of reality; an electronic, cybernetic crevice which leads to a world not hidden behind a stone mountain but behind a silicone firewall, in both cases worlds safely removed from the prying eyes of officials. Even for China's zealous officials, it is virtually impossible to control web pages which may have been hosted on a computer server thousands of miles away from Chinese territory or to prevent Internet dissidents from entering them.

Officials sent out at least one expedition attempting to find Peach Blossom Spring. Today's Chinese officials are working equally hard to find forbidden sites in cyberspace and to keep their people behind a new Great Wall of ignorance. And, for millions of Chinese, is not the purpose of these fiber-optic networks with their high-speed-data transmission much the same as the pathways which traversed the dikes of Peach Blossom Spring allowing residents to move about and converse freely? All away from the prying eyes of officials attempting to combat the dark forces, the "cyber-opium," unleashed by China's digital revolution?

But, just as I have myself convinced that the World Wide Web is indeed the new Peach Blossom Spring, as the train nears the Hong Kong border, I finally get around to reading some photocopied pages of A. R. Davis's book on T'ao Yuan-ming. In his book he discusses the period when the poet had left his home and ventured off:

He first comes into view in the fifth month of 400, returning home from Chien-k'ang (Nanjing)after an absence, in my opinion, of six years. What he had been doing in these six years…cannot be known. Probably the most that can be said is that his experiences during this absence from home had reinforced his natural inclination to keep apart from the world.

This reminds me of something and I shuffle quickly through the photocopied pages until I come to the page in which Davis discusses one of the versions of the Peach Blossom Spring story which includes this: "Wu-ling Source lies in Wu-chung….By tradition it was to here in the disorders at the end of Ch'in that the men of Wu-chung fled to escape the trouble…."

And in a footnote, Davis writes: "Wu-chung should indicate the area of modern Soochow so that in this version a transfer of the locality from Hunan to Kiangsu seems somehow to have occurred."

Of course! If the two pieces of information are put together, it all makes sense. During the period the poet served as some kind of government functionary in Nanjing, he would have had ample time to explore the mountains and foothills and plateaus and valleys in the vicinity. And Soochow is just a bit south of Nanjing. Marco Polo went as ga ga over Soochow and he did over Hangchow.

In fact, the distance from Nanjing to Soochow is only about one-fourth the distance between Jiujiang and Nanjing. Even in those days, T'ao Yuan-ming could have reached it easily. And in all those years he was away, it is extremely likely that "Wu-chung" is where he discovered Peach Blossom Spring – in the mountains outside of Soochow. *That* is where he found it! Jesus Christ! I've been searching for Peach Blossom Spring in the wrong damn province.

THE END

Peach Blossom Spring – Translation

At the close of the 4th century, during the T'ai Yuan era of the Tsin Dynasty, a certain fisherman lived in the village of Wu-ling. One day, so engrossed in exploring the stream of a river, he failed to notice how far he had traveled.

Suddenly, the fisherman saw that he had chanced upon a forest of peach trees in full bloom lining both banks of the river for a great distance. Within this peach orchard, there were no other trees.

A myriad of scented petals floated gently downward, lining both sides of the river. The exquisite beauty of the scene as well as the perfumed fragrance of the peach blossoms filled the fisherman with awe. Anxious to see how far this scene of enchantment extended, the fisherman quickly continued onward. He found that the forest of peach trees ended at the source of the river, at the base of a mountain. And within this mountain was a narrow opening illuminated by a shaft of light.

The fisherman tied up his boat and struggled to squeeze through a passage so narrow that a man could only with great effort continue on. But when at last he had crawled out the other side, he found himself looking out upon vast farmland and imposing farmhouses, fertile fields, beautiful lakes, mulberry trees and bamboo groves. The fields were divided by footpaths, cocks crowed, dogs barked, and the dress of the inhabitants at work or at leisure was not unusual. Both young and old seemed cheerful and content.

The people were naturally astounded by the unexpected appearance of the stranger. Once the fisherman had answered their many questions, the people invited him to their home, brought out their wine, prepared a chicken and feasted him. Word of his arrival quickly spread, and soon all within Peach Blossom Spring gathered to welcome the visitor.

The people spoke of how their ancestors lived during the tumultuous upheavals of the Ch'in Dynasty (221 – 208 BC) and how they had gathered their wives and children and neighbors and fled to this hidden world. Since then, no one had left and they had had no contact with anyone from outside.

The people then asked about the world the fisherman lived in now. He gave them a detailed account but soon realized they had not even heard of the Han dynasty, let alone those dynasties which had followed. When the fisherman had finished his description of the world outside Peach Blossom Spring, the people sighed deeply, full of sorrow over the misfortunes of humanity.

Each family in turn invited the fisherman to a feast in their home and treated him with gracious hospitality. After several days, when he decided the time had come to depart, he was told that "there is no need to discuss what you have seen here with outsiders," after which the fisherman returned to his boat.

On his return journey, the fisherman did his best to mark his way. When reaching his home, he immediately reported his discovery to the district magistrate. The magistrate sent men to accompany the fisherman in hopes of discovering this mysterious community. But the fisherman could find no trace of the markings he had left, became disoriented, and the search was abandoned.

An acclaimed scholar and recluse, Liu Tzu-chi of Nanyang, heard of the fisherman's discovery and planned his own expedition, but fell ill and died even before setting out. Henceforth, no further attempts were ever made to find Peach Blossom Spring.

Books referred to in the text:

The Complete Works of Tao Yuan Ming
Translated and annotated by Tan Shilin
Joint Publishing (HK) Co., Ltd.
Published 1992 Hong Kong

A Chinese Childhood
Chiang Yee
The Norton Library
Published by W.W. Norton & Co. Inc.
Published 1963 New York, USA

Real China: From Cannibalism to Karaoke
John Gittings
Simon & Schuster Pocket Books
Published 1997 Australia

Tao Yuan-ming: His Works and their Meaning
A.R. Davis
Cambridge U. Press, 1983

The Peking Papers: Leaves from the Notebook
Of a China Correspondent
Jacques Marcuse
E.P. Dutton & Co. 1967

Daily Life in China on the Eve of the Mongol
Invasion 1250-1276
Jacques Gernet
Stanford University Press, 1970

A Word about the Author

Dean Barrett first arrived in Asia as a Chinese linguist with the Army Security Agency during the Vietnam War. He returned to the United States and received his Masters Degree in Asian Studies from the University of Hawaii. He has lived in Asia for over 20 years. His writing on Asian themes has won several awards including the PATA Grand Prize for Excellence.

Barrett is the author of five novels set in Asia, *Memoirs of a Bangkok Warrior*, *Hangman's Point*, *Kingdom of Make-Believe*, *Skytrain to Murder* and *Mistress of the East*. His mystery novel set in New York City, *Murder in China Red*, stars a Chinese detective from Beijing.

His plays have been performed in eight countries and his musical, *Fragrant Harbour* (music: Ed Linderman), set in 1857 Hong Kong, was selected by the National Alliance for Musical Theater to be staged on 42nd Street. For five years, he wrote a satirical column for the Hong Kong Standard under the name Uncle Yum Cha ("Uncle Drink Tea"). He is a member of Mystery Writers of America, Private Eye Writers of America, Dramatists Guild and the China Round Table.

Praise for *Murder in China Red*

"I was riveted by Dean Barrett's portrayal of the tensions, and excitement, of the East-West interchange. Beautiful writing, and edge-of-the-seat suspense kept me anxious to the finish."
— Sujata Massey, author of *The Bride's Kimono*

"With *Murder in China Red*, Barrett has spun a well-crafted murder mystery filled with characters that leap off the page."
— Stephen Leather, author of *The Tunnel Rats*

"A highly focused plot, classy prose, and a complicated protagonist merit wide readership."
— *Library Journal*

"*Murder in China Red* tells a good story and keeps the reader wanting more....The graphic economy of the writing places the book with films of this genre and could easily become one. This is a superior book. The writing is good, with clever, useful and apt images."
— *Asian Review of Books*

"Dean Barrett has packed everything he knows about Asia as well as the streets of his native New York, into a promising series debut, '*Murder in China Red*'"
— *Chicago Tribune*

"A great serial detective character. A strong character, one who you enjoy reading about....This book is very appealing, especially to anyone who loves an old time mystery. Instead of concentrating on the forensic aspects of the crime, we watch Chinaman do old style gumshoe work following leads and looking for clues and putting together pieces with his own mind, not a computer. I hope to see more adventures with him."
— *MostlyFiction.com*

"Clearly, Chinaman is no stereotyped private investigator. Barrett takes his hero through the Big Apple's underworld. The story is fast-paced, one-liners abound, and the mix of mayhem and humor is nicely balanced. Private-eye enthusiasts will put Chinaman at the top of their list. Even the reader who isn't particularly caught up with the genre will find plenty of entertainment in this novel."
— *Everybody Loves a Mystery Newsletter*

Praise for Memoirs of a Bangkok Warrior

"*Memoirs of a Bangkok Warrior* is a marvelous novel, yes-novel, about the Vietnam era. So marvelous that upon finishing it, I promptly handed it over to my brother, the Nam vet, and told him, read this - you'll love it. So, read it. You'll love it. I promise." Stars 5+
– *Buzz Review News*

"Funny from the first page to the last. A fine and funny book, ribald and occasionally touching. One of the better Asian reads of the past few years."
– *The Bangkok Post*

"Succeeds nicely in the creation of a time and place that transcends mere setting."
– West Coast Review of Books

"This is a funny and human book which can describe sex without descending into sheer nastiness."
– *South China Morning Post*

"This is M*A*S*H, taken from behind the Korean lines, set down in the rear-echelon of steamy Bangkok–titillated with the tinkle of Thai laughter and temple bells. And it is an even funnier triumph of man over military madness."
– Derek Maitland, author, *The only War we've Got*

"An Awesome read! Way out, Far out, Groovy....I can smell the smell and see the green and feel the magic of Thailand!"
– Terry Ryan, TCLB (*Thailand, Laos, Cambodian Brotherhood*)

"*Memoirs of a Bangkok Warrior* is recommended reading for anyone who ever donned a uniform and found themselves far from home."
– Midwest Book Review

"*Memoirs of a Bangkok Warrior* remains one of my favorite books about Thailand. Excellent characters and dialogue. It would make a great movie."
– Dave Walker, author, *Hello My Big, Big Honey*!

Praise for Kingdom of Make-Believe

"*Kingdom of Make-Believe* is an exciting thriller that paints a picture of Thailand much different from that of *The King and I*. The story line is filled with non-stop action, graphic details of the country, and an intriguing allure that will hook readers of exotic thrillers. Very highly recommended."

– BookBrowser.com

"A tantalizing taste of a culture, worlds apart from our own. Dean Barrett paints a sharp, clear picture of the reality of life. An excellent account of one man's struggle to find the truth in his existence. Very highly recommended."

– Under the Covers Book Review

"An absolutely astounding novel. Its depth and layers of perception will have you fascinated from start to finish. Highly entertaining!"

– Buzz Review News

"Barrett spins a tightly packed tale that is part murder mystery, part midlife crisis love story and part travelogue, with vibrant and seductive Thailand in a leading role. This mystery keeps the reader guessing at the next plot twist."

– Today's Librarian

"A gripping mystery documenting Dean Barrett as a writer in full possession of his craft."

– Midwest Book Review

"Sharp, often poetic, and pleasantly twisted, *Kingdom of Make-Believe* is a tautly written fictional tour of Thailand. Author Dean Barrett has woven a compelling and believable tale about a country he knows well. Barrett's prose is spare but his images are rich: a winning combination. His obvious intimate knowledge of Thailand combined with a very considerable writing talent make *Kingdom of Make-Believe* a tough book to put down."

– January Magazine

"A thrilling page turner. Barrett brilliantly evokes the suffocating fumes of Bangkok traffic, the nauseating stench of morning-after alcohol and smoke in its go-go bars, as well as the lurid lies and deception of washed-up lowlife expats in Thailand. God, I miss that place!"

– Stuart Lloyd, author, Hardship Posting

"Barrett has a gift for taking us into cultures worlds apart from our own, displaying a reverence for their exotic and grotesque as well as their beauty and history."
— *Poisoned Pen Reviews*

"Barrett is a powerful storyteller who has a feeling for language that's lacking in many contemporary novels. His dialog is a pleasure to read, and his descriptions from the nightlife in Bangkok to the Thai countryside are vivid."
— *Laughing Bear Newsletter*

Praise for Hangman's Point

"Setting is more than a backdrop in this fast-paced adventure story of mid-nineteenth-century British colonial Hong Kong....A riveting, action-packed narrative....Chinese scholar, linguist, and author of two previous books, Barrett draws on his vast knowledge of southern China during a time of enormous change and conflict, providing richly fascinating detail of the customs, fashions, ships, and weapons of the times."

— *ALA Booklist*

"An expert on Hong Kong and the turbulent time period portrayed, Dean Barrett has fashioned a swashbuckling adventure which will have both history buffs and thriller readers enthralled from the very first page. An outstanding historical novel."

— *Writers Write Reviews*

"If Patrick O'Brian's Aubrey and Maturin ever got as far as Hong Kong in 1857 on their world travels, the aged sea dogs would feel right at home in China expert Dean Barrett's totally convincing novel of high adventure."

— Dick Adler, *Amazon.com Reviews*

"A great epic of a historical mystery."

— *Bookbrowser Reviews*

"The adventures of this latter-day Indiana Jones will leave him fleeing for his life through the town of Victoria (Hong Kong), bring him face to face with the perils of the pirate-infested waters of the Pearl River, and finally fix him a date with death at *Hangman's Point*....The novel is peppered with well-defined characters from all walks of life....It would be just another potboiler a la James Clavell, but Barrett's extensive research sets this novel apart: as well as a ripping adventure story, it is an intimately drawn historical portrait."

— *South China Morning Post*

"There is adventure and mystery in every corner of this well-researched and well-written historical."

— *1BookStreet.com*

"Rich in historical perspective and characters, Barrett's debut is good news for those who love grand scale adventure."

— *The Poisoned Pen Booknews*

"*Hangman's Point* is vastly entertaining, informative and thought-provoking....Dean Barrett weaves an intricate and many-layered tale. Barrett clearly has in-depth knowledge of his field, more so than most Western novelists can command....Barrett offers more than an exciting story. He provides an understanding view of China and the Chinese, guiding readers toward a fuller appreciation of that complex culture."
– *Stuart News*

"*Hangman's Point* is a great historical fiction that, if there is any justice, will enable Dean Barrett to become a household name. Highly Recommended."
– *Under The Covers Book Review*

"Excellently written and steeped in details of the times, all obviously very well researched and accurate."
– *The Midwest Book Review*

"Adams's adventures take him on a thrilling chase, almost an odyssey...*Hangman's Point* is a page-turner that is guaranteed to keep both male and female readers enthralled to the very end. Romance and high adventure."
– *Romantic Times*

About the Book

This book was typeset in Adobe Garamond, a typeface based on the types of the sixteenth-century printer, publisher, and type designer Claude Garamond (1499-1561), whose sixteenth-century types were modeled on those of Venetian printers from the end of the previous century. The Garamond typeface and its variations have been a standard among book designers and printers for four centuries; nearly every manufacturer of type or typesetting equipment has produced at least one version of Garamond in the past eighty years. Adobe designer Robert Slimbach went to the Plantin-Moretus museum in Antwerp, Belgium, to study the original Garamond typefaces. These served as the basis for the design of the Adobe Garamond romans; the italics are based on types by Robert Granjon, a contemporary of Garamond's. This elegant, versatile design, the first Adobe Originals typeface, was released in 1989.

Book design and composition by Robert Stedman Private Limited, Singapore.